Building Your Home Inspection Business

A Guide to Marketing, Sales, Advertising, and Public Relations

Carson Dunlop & Associates

Dearborn™
Home Inspection
Education

This publication is designed to provide accurate and authoritative information in regard to the subject matter covered. It is sold with the understanding that the publisher is not engaged in rendering legal, accounting, or other professional service. If legal advice or other expert assistance is required, the services of a competent professional person should be sought.

President: Roy Lipner
Publisher: Evan Butterfield
Associate Publisher: Louise Benzer
Editorial Project Manager: Laurie McGuire
Managing Editor, Production: Daniel Frey
Typesetter: Todd Bowman
Creative Director: Lucy Jenkins

Published by Dearborn™ Real Estate Education,
a division of Dearborn Financial Publishing, Inc.®
30 South Wacker Drive, Suite 2500
Chicago, IL 60606-7481
(312) 836-4400
http://www.dearbornRE.com

Printed in the United States of America.

0 9   10 9 8 7 6 5

Library of Congress Cataloging-in-Publication Data

Building your home inspection business : a guide to marketing, sales, advertising & public relations.
     p. cm.
  Includes bibliographical references.
  1. Dwellings—Inspection. 2. Dwellings—Valuation. 3. Real estate business. 4. Small business.
I. Title.

  TH4817.5.B84 2005
  643'.12—dc22

                                                      2004025177

CONTENTS

SECTION TWO

ADVERTISING, PUBLIC RELATIONS, AND SALES

INTRODUCTION

Welcome! *Building Your Home Inspection Business* covers a topic that many home inspectors find both fascinating and frustrating: marketing and growing your business. This book is designed to give you the benefit of our extensive experience in marketing a home inspection company. Not only will we share our own secrets, but we also will share what we've learned by working with many other home inspection companies. We will provide you with the knowledge and tools to help you grow your business quickly, while you invest a minimum of time and money.

ORGANIZATION

The book is divided into sections:

- Section I: Marketing Concepts and Practice
- Section II: Advertising, Public Relations, and Sales

Study Sessions

Within each section are several Study Sessions to guide you through the material. The Quick Quizzes at the end of each Study Session will help you check your progress.

Assignments

Three assignments are included to help you turn your knowledge into practice. These assignments are useful exercises. In fact, they are part of an overall business growth strategy for any company.

Final Test

Each section has an associated Final Test (available in a companion volume to this book or from your course instructor) designed to ensure that you have mastered the material in the section, and that you are ready to move on.

STUDY TIPS

If you are using this book as part of a self-study training course, we encourage you to set up a regular time to work on the program. You are the best judge of your attention span, but for most people, working in blocks of one hour to two hours is about right. Find a time of day when you are rested and not likely to be disturbed. A comfortable, well-lit workplace is critical. Make sure you have everything you need.

Make sure you understand what you are reading. Taking notes is helpful, but only if they are brief. Try to use a single word for each major point. The margin notes printed in the book may also help you keep track of significant issues.

The Quick Quizzes and Assignments are important. Do not skip over them. It's not enough to read the material; you want to learn it. Adults learn by doing, and they learn best by thinking about what they are doing.

We have built some repetition into the book because it helps the learning process. You'll find that some key issues are addressed more than once. We have used slightly different approaches when repeating key points to help ensure effective learning. When you read a section and recognize it as a repeated concept, that's a good sign. It means that you are learning what you are studying.

RESOURCES

The compact disk (CD) that accompanies this book contains examples of many of the marketing, sales, public relations, and advertising collateral discussed in the text. Some of the examples are meant to trigger your own creative ideas; others can be modified with just a little effort to suit your needs.

In addition to this book, you may want to investigate resources from the American Society of Home Inspectors (ASHI®) for guidance in building your business. ASHI provides marketing materials for members, including more than ten consumer brochures and an ASHI publicity kit with press releases that you can modify for your company. ASHI also offers three videos suitable for real estate professionals and consumers that help people understand the home inspection profession.

We hope you enjoy this book and develop a solid understanding of the concepts that will bring your business to the next level, whether you are just starting out or operating an established company.

Good luck!

ACKNOWLEDGMENTS

Thanks to all of our clients and the real estate agents who have worked with us for 26 years. Thanks to the pioneers in small business marketing and sales—Michael Gerber, Jay Abraham, Brian Tracy, and many others who have paved the way for our success by sharing their wisdom.

We are grateful for the contributions of the following people:

- Graham Clarke
- Bob Sunstrum
- Charles Gravely
- Andra Woolley
- Shawn Carr
- Laurie McGuire

Special thanks are also extended to the following reviewers, who provided useful feedback on the manuscript for this book:

- Thomas G. Lauhon, Midwest Inspectors Institute
- William (Bill) E. Rice, Construction Analysts and Associates, Inc., and adjunct instructor at Houston Community College System
- Ken Trussell, Continuing Education for Licensing, Inc. (CELI) and Texas A&M University–Commerce
- Samuel A. Wood, P.E., Advantage Home & Environment Inspections, Inc.

SECTION

I

MARKETING CONCEPTS AND PRACTICE

Section I is all about marketing. We will cover the basic concepts of marketing a home inspection service. In addition, we will investigate specific marketing tools and strategies that work.

OBJECTIVES

The goal of *Building Your Home Inspection Business* is to provide you with an understanding of basic marketing and business concepts that you can apply to your home inspection business. At the end of this book you should be able to design your marketing and business growth strategy and implement its elements with skill and confidence.

While there are other texts on marketing and business practices, most do not focus on the home inspection profession. Many traditional methods of business growth and marketing don't apply to the home inspection business. Our goal is to share our experience to help you avoid pitfalls and focus on winning strategies. In short, we want to save you time and money and help you quickly grow your home inspection business into a moneymaking machine, making sure you have fun while you do it.

*Not the
Final Word*
This book is not the final, or only, word on the subject. You should investigate many other resources. Local colleges have courses on marketing, business development, sales, negotiating techniques, and so on. Bookstores and libraries are full of books on these topics. We urge you to investigate these resources.

In this section we will

- review the concepts you need to know to successfully market your home inspection business, and

- discuss examples of strategies that work, and others that don't.

You will learn how to

- make your business grow,

- give exceptional customer service by understanding what your clients and customers want,

- price your services,
- set up a referral network,
- assemble a marketing plan, and
- handle complaints.

INSTRUCTIONS

There are 11 Study Sessions in this section. Each session should take 30 minutes to 90 minutes to complete. The entire section—including Quizzes, Assignments, and the Final Test—should take a total of 10 hours to 20 hours. It's all right if it takes more or less time than we have estimated. Don't rush or try to do more at one time than you can absorb.

1. Read each Study Session.

2. At the end of each Study Session, take the Quick Quiz to review what you have learned.

3. Do the Assignments to turn your learning into practice. The Assignments are important steps in growing your business. In other words, these are things you should do anyway; they are not just a learning exercise. We encourage you to take the time and spend the effort to complete these assignments to the best of your abilities.

4. Take the multiple-choice Final Test (available in a companion volume to this book or from your course instructor).

Here we go!

Donald Cruz
March 22. 2011
Davenport Fl.

S T U D Y   S E S S I O N

1

BASIC MARKETING CONCEPTS

Study Session 1 deals with fundamental concepts you need to know before you can develop a marketing strategy.

LEARNING OBJECTIVES

At the end of Study Session 1 you should be able to

- define, in one sentence each, your customer versus your client, and develop marketing strategies for each;
- describe in one or two sentences your target market;
- identify six different marketing elements of a home inspection business;
- describe at least three features of your service, and the corresponding benefit of each;
- write your own marketing materials from a benefits perspective;
- define your USP (unique selling proposition) in one or two sentences, demonstrate it to a prospective client, and integrate it in your marketing material;
- define in two sentences your value proposition;
- list at least three tangible benefits of your service to the customer; and
- develop well-designed marketing materials.

Study Session 1 may take you roughly 60 minutes to complete.

Before you can develop a marketing strategy for your home inspection business, you should understand some fundamental terms and concepts. In Study Session 1 we will look at the difference between sales and marketing, and describe key marketing concepts, such as features, benefits, unique selling proposition, and value proposition. We will also look at the issue of identifying who your customers are, which isn't always obvious. Finally, we will consider the concept of company image, and how to develop yours.

MARKETING VERSUS SALES

Marketing Makes Phone Ring

Marketing and sales are not the same thing, although many people use the terms interchangeably. *Marketing* is an activity designed to encourage prospective customers to contact your company. Marketing in the home inspection business includes advertising, brochures, business cards, presentations at real estate offices, direct mail pieces, Web sites, trade-show booths, and so on. Marketing is also inherent to the inspections themselves, the inspection reports, and any of the follow-up activities, such as thank you notes to the clients or real estate agents. All contribute to attracting prospects.

Sales Picks Up Phone

Sales, on the other hand, is typically a one-on-one activity with the goal of converting an inquiry into a sale. Sales may be made face-to-face, over the telephone, on the Internet, or by e-mail. Sales usually involves a real-time or virtual conversation. The conclusion to a sales activity is an order for the company.

You might think of the difference between marketing and sales this way: Marketing makes the phone ring. Sales picks it up.

Because marketing is often the precursor to sales, we will look at marketing first.

FEATURES VERSUS BENEFITS

Client's Perspective Is Key

The distinction between a feature and a benefit is a key marketing concept. A **feature** is a quality of your service from your perspective, whereas a **benefit** expresses a quality of your service from your customer's perspective. Put another way, a feature is an element of your service; a benefit is what this element does for the prospect or the customer. For example, "Open 24 hours!" is a feature that the company offers. Convenience is the benefit that the customer enjoys.

The success of any professional service depends to a large extent on its ability to put itself in the customer's position. All the customer cares about is how one service will help them more than another. Everything in marketing, advertising, public relations, and sales should focus on what aspects of the service are going to benefit customers (see Figure 1.1). To successfully market your business, you need to adopt the credo, "It's all about the customer."

Features Describe; Benefits Sell

Features are easier for us to promote because they are the parts of our business *we* think are desirable. It's always easy to speak from our own perspective. Benefits, on the other hand, are a little more difficult to identify. They require us to justify the value of the features to someone else. In other words, a benefit is what your *customer* finds desirable about your features.

For example; you book a flight to Europe for an important business meeting. The airline is advertising business class seating. You are trying to decide if you should fly business class or coach. The advertisement states that business class

FIGURE 1.1   Focus Your Services on Customer Benefits

has larger seats and more legroom. You immediately book the coach tickets. Your rationale: You aren't going to pay twice as much just for a little extra legroom and a larger seat. You will tough it out in coach. The airline failed to sell you the more expensive seats because they only provided you the features of a business class seat, rather than showing the benefits of these features.

A more compelling airline ad would have demonstrated that the larger seats in business class provide ample space for you to set up a workstation. And the extra legroom, which makes it possible for you to comfortably stretch out, means you can sleep during the flight, if you choose. With proper room to work and a comfortable place to sleep, you will arrive for your meeting prepared and refreshed. You will excel at the important meeting; you will get a promotion and a big bonus at the end of the year.

Show Benefits of Your Service

Although benefits are the obvious and logical conclusion of features, it's a mistake to assume your prospective customers will make the connection between the two. Most people don't have the time or inclination to fill in the blanks. Furthermore, it's your job to make the benefits of your services immediately apparent. You can demonstrate benefits without discussing features, but not vice versa. You must focus on selling the benefits.

Let's look at another example. Let's say you are in the market for a new flashlight and you walk into a store and see a display with this headline: "The world's first steel flashlight!" The fact that the flashlight is steel is clearly a physical feature of the product that the manufacturer is very proud of. What is important, however, is what that feature will do for you. The value of that feature lies in describing what that product actually does. The fact that the flashlight is steel will help justify the added cost, but the manufacturer should be telling you that the added weight of the steel means that if you drop it, it won't break. The manufacturer should tell you that you will never have to buy another flashlight again—guaranteed! So the feature is steel construction, but the benefit is durability and reliability. The functional aspect of this particular product (not the physical feature) intensifies your desire for it.

Benefits Are Explanations

If you are giving a presentation to a real estate office, or speaking to a client or agent, you have all the time in the world to describe the benefits of your features in detail. But in written marketing materials you need to be concise or you will lose your reader's attention.

Features are easy to come up with, and to position in a brochure, because they amount to basic descriptions. Benefits are harder to express because they are explanations of the descriptions.

Inexperienced marketers make the mistake of filling a brochure with features, resulting in an unconvincing and weak piece. Have a look at your competitor's brochure. It will likely be filled with a list of features only. Any marketing piece that you put together should list the benefits. Marketing materials that would benefit from this philosophy include a

- brochure,
- business card,
- Yellow Pages ad,
- mailer to agents, and
- Web site.

Good Layout Helps

Here is an example of a successful marketing piece. A Web-site ad for a software company features a simple two-column fact sheet. The left-hand column lists features and the right-hand column lists benefits. Each feature lines up with its associated benefit, clearly demonstrating the added value inherent in the feature. After seeing this ad, we decided to try it out in some marketing pieces for home inspection services. It has been a very successful layout. It's simple yet effective. Try it in your brochure.

Show Features and Benefits

Here is an example of how to think about the benefits associated with the features of your services.

Feature	Benefit
We are available seven days a week.	The benefits to your clients are convenience and accessibility. They can reach you when they need to.
We have been licensed builders for 20 years.	You have the experience to detect problem areas. What is the benefit to the client? You can potentially save them headaches and money down the road.
	What's the benefit to the real estate agent? Because you have years of experience in problem solving, you may be able to suggest a simple solution to a problem. Your suggestion could help the client avoid an expensive fix. This could make the difference between the deal going through and the deal falling apart.

Writing a concise benefit is not as easy as describing a feature. Writing about benefits requires more time and finesse, but if you hope to make an impact, you have to show the benefits of your service. Benefits are an essential part of *all* your marketing material.

A benefit often sounds like a promise. It is frequently followed with a description of the feature that shows how you can make good on the promise.

UNIQUE SELLING PROPOSITION

What's Different
About You

In order to successfully build a marketing or sales campaign, you need to identify what is special or different about you and your inspection service. In the terminology of marketing, this is your **Unique Selling Proposition,** or USP. The concept is that if you can think of something unique to your business, you will have an easier time differentiating yourself from the masses.

Differentiate Yourself

The more distinctive you are, the stronger the message. For example, let's say what makes you special is that you are a building foundation specialist. Maybe you used to work for a company that designed repairs for house foundations. You know more about foundations, and foundation problems, than anyone in town. This area of expertise makes you stand out.

In contrast, if you used to be in the construction business, you won't stand out as much because many home inspectors used to be licensed builders. This is not to say that being a licensed builder does not give you a powerful competitive advantage, it's just not quite as distinctive as the first example.

Remember: The more distinctive, the stronger the sell.

VALUE PROPOSITION

Market Yourself
to Callers

Your **value proposition** is what you offer to a prospect. This is a combination of your USP, your position, and the benefits of hiring you. In short, your value proposition is what you tell a prospect who calls and asks, "What will I get if I hire you?" If your answer is, "You will get a home inspection," you need to do some work on your value proposition.

You need to create a quick, concise statement that explains how the client will benefit from your service and how it is of sufficient value to justify your fee.

It helps to have a few tangible items in your value proposition. Why? It becomes much easier to create a sense of value in your client's mind. At Carson Dunlop, we publish and use the *Home Reference Book* as our main tangible item. It's a 400-page guide to the average home. If you haven't seen it, you should get a copy just to get an idea of the marketing impact it has on clients.

If a client calls and asks what they get from Carson Dunlop for their $400 inspection fee, we answer with the following value proposition:

- You get a professional engineer who inspects the structure, the roof, the exterior envelope, and all of the systems of the home including electrical, plumbing, heating and air conditioning, and so on.

- You receive a customized report and a 400-page guide to your home, the *Home Reference Book.*

- You receive discounts on products and services you will need, such as home and auto insurance and alarm system installation.

- You receive a free one-year subscription to *ManageMyHome.com,* an Internet-based maintenance program customized to your home.

- You get a lifetime of free telephone technical support on anything involving your home.

This list of features becomes even more powerful when accompanied by the corresponding benefits.

CUSTOMERS, CLIENTS, AND TARGET MARKETS

Who is your customer? In the home inspection business, the answer to this question is not always clear. For example, a homebuyer might book an inspection with you, based on a referral from a real estate agent you have been soliciting. You do the inspection for the buyer, but at the end of the inspection the agent pays for it, while the buyer gets the report. Now who is your customer?

It is not our intention to discuss professional practice or professional ethics in this section, just marketing. To clarify the situation, let's define a few terms.

REALTOR® Versus Real Estate Agent

Several different terms can be used interchangeably to describe an individual who works in real estate. A REALTOR®, for example, can be a broker, manager, real estate professional, real estate agent, or any associate who holds active membership in a local real estate board that is affiliated with the National Association of REALTORS®. A *real estate agent* is a person who is licensed to negotiate and process the transaction associated with selling a home but is not necessarily associated with the National Association of REALTORS®. For convenience and simplicity, we will refer to real estate agents or agents unless otherwise specified.

Broker Versus Real Estate Agent

A real estate *broker* is a real estate agent who has taken additional training to enhance their professional skills and has earned a broker's license. A broker may own a real estate office, supervise a group of agents, act as an office manager, and sell real estate. Although many people use the term broker and agent interchangeably because both are licensed to show and sell homes, we will refer to brokers in the context of owning or managing the real estate office. As such, the broker is in charge of supervising other real estate agents and making decisions such as scheduling office meetings.

Your Client Is the Homebuyer

For a standard prepurchase inspection, your **client** is the person, or people, buying the home. Your client is relying on the information you provide from the inspection to help them make a decision about proceeding with the purchase. The homebuyer is your client regardless of who pays for the service, where you target your marketing efforts, or who referred you.

Your Customer Is Anyone to Whom You Market

Your **customer** is anybody who gives or sends you business. If you solicit referrals from real estate agents, they are your customers. Lawyers, bankers, and other businesses are also your customers. Your client, the potential homebuyer, is also your customer because he or she may refer you to other people.

Know Your Target Market

Your **target market** is the group or groups of people toward whom you direct your marketing efforts. The strategies you employ will be drastically different depending on which customers you are targeting. Later in this book, you will learn whom to target and which strategy to apply to particular customers.

The main markets for your business may be real estate agents. Many home inspectors believe this to be the case because targeting agents is much easier than targeting homebuyers. It is easy to know who the real estate agents are. It is difficult to identify people who are about to buy a home. While this market is not your only target, it may be an important one. That said, it's important to understand that your relationship with agents presents a number of complex issues that you should carefully consider as you build your business.

Real Estate Agent: Friend or Foe?

Should you create relationships with real estate agents? The home inspection world is divided on this question. One school suggests that a working relationship with an agent is ethical while another thinks that a close relationship with a real estate agent presents a conflict of interest.

The real estate agent has a lot to lose if the deal does not go through. The agent's livelihood depends on the sale of the house. If you find too many problems with the house, the deal may fall apart. In other words, what you say to your client may directly affect how much money the agent makes that year.

So, it's possible that an agent will recommend a home inspector who makes fewer waves. If you have a reputation for meticulously critical work, you may not get the referral from the agent.

Here's the other side of the conflict. The agent refers business to the home inspector. The home inspector's livelihood depends on these referrals. The home inspector may, therefore, be inclined to work in the agent's best interest rather than in the best interest of the homebuyer client. For instance, although the inspector will not turn a blind eye to a major structural problem, he or she may choose to "soft sell" or to understate certain problems.

For these reasons, some consumer advocates suggest that homebuyers not hire the home inspector that their agent recommends. And some home inspectors themselves suggest that homebuyers not rely on referrals from real estate agents.

Strive for Mutually Beneficial Relationships

On the positive side, the relationship between an agent and a home inspector can be mutually beneficial and can remain ethical at the same time. Good real estate agents are looking out for the best interests of their clients. Good agents are in the business for the long term. They build their business success on referrals from satisfied homebuyers. Most professional real estate agents take an agent-for-life strategy—they know that most people live in their starter home for only a few years. The agent wants to help these folks find their next home. If the deal falls through because the home inspector finds a problem, the agent will simply find another house for the potential buyer. In the meantime, the agent looks good because he or she referred a professional home inspector that helped the home-buyer avoid a costly mistake. Referring a top-notch professional is also in the agent's best long-term interest from a liability standpoint.

Professional home inspectors have integrity and work in the best interest of their clients. If they are not doing a good job for their clients, they will not be in business very long because the complaints and lawsuits will get the better of them. Our firm has decided that the best approach is to consider the home as our client, and we try to represent the condition of the home as accurately as possible, reporting on each situation as we believe it to be.

At the end of the day, there are valid arguments for and against soliciting referrals from real estate agents. You will have to decide which one is the right business decision for you.

Marketing to Agents Is Cost-Effective

What are the advantages of marketing to a real estate agent? First of all, most new home inspectors have a limited marketing budget and limited time to spend on growing the business. So where will you spend your time and money? Let's say you have $50 to spend on marketing. You decide the best use of this money is to take the customer out to lunch and educate him or her on the benefits of your home inspection company. If that customer is the homebuyer, it will have cost you $50 to obtain, say, $400 worth of business (one inspection fee). If the customer is a real estate agent, and he or she refers 15 customers to you (potential home-buyers and other agents) throughout the year, it will have cost you $50 to obtain $6,000 (15 × $400) of business. When you took that agent to lunch, you were 15 times more effective.

Marketing to Others Is Not as Cost-Effective

Other professionals involved in the real estate transaction could refer business to you with much less of a perceived conflict, such as bankers and lawyers. While they are good sources for soliciting new business, they have not been as effective historically as the real estate agent.

The agent is in the right place at the right time. Although a small percentage of the population will research everything they need to know about how to buy a home—interviewing and selecting a home inspection company, banker, mover, and so on—most people don't think about home inspections, or home inspection companies, until they need one. This need usually comes to light after the home-buyer has made an offer on a home, conditional on a satisfactory home inspection within four (or so) business days.

The client will need to call a home inspector right away. Who will they ask for a referral? They will most likely turn to the person sitting next to them. That person is neither the banker nor the lawyer; that person is the real estate agent.

Agents May Be Best Market

Many home inspectors believe that real estate agents are their best target market. Many home inspectors, and just about everybody else involved in the real estate transaction, are looking for referrals from the agent.

Agents Are Easy to Find

As we mentioned earlier, it's much easier to identify a real estate agent than a person who is about to buy a house. This is another reason that many home inspectors market to the real estate community.

Can you build a business without real estate agents? In a word, yes. If you have an ethical objection to soliciting referrals from agents, you can still build a strong home inspection business. But you may take longer to establish a customer base, you may spend more money, and you may work harder for every dollar you make. This will be your business decision. Regardless of your decision, we will show you some strategies to maximize your returns.

YOUR COMPANY IMAGE

Your company image is not what you *say* you are; it's how your clients perceive you.

You may think you are a high-end home inspector because you've targeted a market willing to pay more for your services. But if you show up on the job wearing ripped jeans, a paint-stained t-shirt, and worn-out sneakers, your image no longer says high-end, professional service.

Your clients aren't evaluating you according to *your* set of criteria for good performance. They are evaluating you based on *their* criteria. Why? Because they don't know what your criteria is. They only know what they hope to gain from the inspection.

Here's an analogy. Say you buy a new audio system for your home. You apply a number of criteria to the system to determine its value—not its general value in the world, but its value to you. Sure, the salespeople at the audio store talked up the system's superior subwoofers. But you care more if it will deliver on the high-end of the range, with crystal-clear pitch. You and the sales staff at the store have different criteria for evaluating the same thing. But at least you both have a tangible characteristic on which to base your opinions—sound quality.

A home inspection service has no tangible attributes on which a customer can form an opinion or base a decision. All you have to offer your client is the promise of an expert inspection. The clients have to trust that you are not selling them a bill of goods. Most will have no idea what you do. As a result, the clients latch on to every intangible stimulus they can get their eyes and ears on—your professional manner, your vocabulary, eye contact, anything that will give them a clue about you. In other words, your clients are constantly evaluating you from the moment they see your business card, brochure, or advertisement to the time you hand over your final inspection report. All of these evaluations factor into your company's image as your clients see it.

Clients do this because they are in no position to evaluate your technical expertise. It's like taking a car into the shop for service. It's hard to know whether the mechanic did a good job, but if there is grease on the upholstery, you will have a definite opinion about the service you received.

The following are the points in a transaction during which your clients form an opinion of you. Beside each point, we've suggested the point's relative importance with respect to its marketing value:

- Referral from someone the client knows (15% importance)
- A good business card (5% importance)
- A good brochure (5% importance)
- Telephone conversation with the client (15% importance)
- First five minutes in which the client meets you at the purchase property (20% importance)
- The inspection—the professionalism, approachability, and expertise you demonstrate to the client during the inspection (25% importance)
- The inspection report (15% importance)

The following is a discussion of each of these points of contact and its relative influence on how your company is perceived.

Referrals Indicate Satisfaction

Client referral is worth a lot, much more than a business card or a brochure. The client forms a favorable opinion of you based on someone else's satisfaction with your services. The client will likely put a lot of stock into the referring person's opinion, especially if the person giving the referral is a real estate professional of some kind.

Good Business Cards Essential

A business card is not worth much from a marketing perspective. And we're talking about a good business card here. Sound contradictory? Let us explain. A well-designed business card is simply the standard for any industry. If you have a business, you require a good business card. But in terms of marketing, a good business card is not what will bring you business. Everyone has a business card, and if yours is high quality, it will simply confirm the good opinion a client forms about you from other points of contact. If, on the other hand, you have a low-quality, amateurish card, you have just given yourself a huge marketing disadvantage. A low-quality business card gives the impression of having been made the night before. Particularly obvious are the business cards that come in sheets that you feed through your printer. Even the well-designed cards printed on these sheets don't pass the test. If you look carefully, you can see evidence of the perforations from where the cards tear away from the sheets. For a service that depends on the experience of the practitioner, anything that suggests the inspector started the business yesterday is not comforting to the client.

Brochures Not Best Tools

The brochure has the same effect as the business card. You have an opportunity to make a favorable impression with a well-constructed brochure, but the message is not as powerful as other points of contact with the client. And a low-quality brochure is a detriment. The bottom line is if you can't afford to create a high-end brochure, it's best not to create one at all. There are lots of other ways to get the message out there that require less cash and make a stronger marketing impact.

The telephone conversation is the client's first opportunity to truly evaluate you. Clients listen to how you speak—the clarity and tone of your voice, the vocabulary you use, and so on. It is extremely important to have a professional and approachable telephone manner. You don't have to be slick, but you should always be prepared to answer questions in a friendly and professional manner.

If you sound irritated because you are on the roof of a house while talking to the client on your cell phone, that's the impression you've left with the client—irritable. That's one reason it's preferable to have someone else answering the phone for you while you are inspecting. Another reason is the lack of respect it shows for your client attending the inspection. A spouse, an answering service, or a full-time receptionist are all good options, as long as they have the sales tools to work successfully with prospective clients. If none of these options works for you, however, find one that allows you to *not* answer your phone during an inspection. An answering machine, for example, is acceptable.

See Study Session 9, "Managing Customers and Building Relationships," in Section II of this book, for telephone techniques and scripts.

The first five minutes of contact with the client is more important than the rest of the inspection. We all have a tendency to form opinions based on first impressions. Homebuyers form their opinions immediately because that's all they have to work with. If you show up wearing ripped jeans and a T-shirt, how will your customers perceive you? Your personal image is important because you want to present yourself in a manner that is appropriate to your profession. Remember, we are not salespeople; we are consultants offering a professional service. Our appearance should exude professionalism. Dress like people expect you to dress. Don't jar them by being over-dressed or under-dressed.

If you are feeling a little tired on a Monday morning, don't let it show. It's your job to find the energy to make a good first impression when you meet the client. You need to appear ready, alert, and able to get the job done. Smile when you introduce yourself to your client. Let them know you are very glad to see them and show that you appreciate the opportunity to help them with their buying decision. Your goal is to be accepted right from the beginning so that they form a positive opinion about you.

Scripting your discussion helps, but don't let the script become obvious or sound like you are dragging the client through a scripted process. Here is a good script for meeting the clients:

Introduce yourself and give the client a business card. Ask the client if you can spend a moment explaining what you will be doing. After getting permission, proceed to describe what you do, including how long the inspection will take, the path of the inspection through the home, and, most importantly, that the client is to accompany you, asking questions along the way. Show the client the preinspection contract, if they have not already seen it.

Ask the client if there are any areas of the home that concern them. Assure them that you will be looking at those areas, and that you can discuss them further when you look at them. Ask the client to read over the contract and sign it while you have a look at the roof. After looking at the roof, explain your findings about the roof, then ask if the client has any questions about the contract, the roof, or anything else to do with the rest of the inspection. Make sure your client has signed the contract.

You have now set the stage for a professional, friendly inspection that includes client participation. You have helped build the client's confidence in you.

Inspection Process

If you are like most inspectors, you will ask your clients to attend the inspection. The clients follow you around the home as you inspect. You report findings and answer questions as you go. The benefits for the client are significant. They get a much better understanding of the home. The benefits for the home inspector are also significant because you get a chance to develop a rapport with the client that helps to reduce your liability. Clients who attend the inspection and see how hard you work on their behalf are far more likely to call you if they have problems later than they are to sue you.

While you inspect the home, your clients form an opinion of you. Most will not be in a position to know if you are doing a good job or not. If an actor were trained to act like a home inspector, to walk the walk and talk the talk, most clients would be fooled. So all the client has to go on is trust. That means, *how* you say something is more important than *what* you say. Clients can gage your communication skills but not your technical skills. Of course, from a technical point of view, what you say is much more important, but we are talking about marketing and your company image.

Here are a few dos and don'ts.

Don't Say, "I Think"

New home inspectors often make the mistake of placing "I think" into their analysis of problem areas. "I think the crack in the wall could be caused by this or that." If you want to sound like an experienced professional and to inspire confidence, don't sound uncertain during a home inspection. Remove conditionals from your vocabulary.

This may sound like a tall order. Of course, you can't know everything or see everything. You are conducting a nondestructive inspection. In fact, a specialist is often required to determine the answer to some questions you and the client may have about a problem. So how can you avoid sounding uncertain?

The answer is: You can be unsure, but you have to be definite about it! Suppose you see a vertical crack in a poured-concrete foundation wall. Because the house superstructure is wood siding, you can't see if the crack continues up through the house, indicating a settlement crack. The crack is small and in a location that could indicate a settlement crack or a shrinkage crack. From the size and shape, and based on your experience in house cracks, you suspect it's a shrinkage crack, but you can't be sure because you simply cannot take apart the outside wall or spend time monitoring it.

Instead of saying, "I *think* this is a shrinkage crack in the foundation" better to say one of the following:

1. It is a shrinkage crack.
2. It is not a shrinkage crack.
3. It is not possible to determine, during a single visit, or during a nondestructive inspection, whether this crack is from shrinkage. Further investigation is required to determine the cause of the crack
4. The evidence suggests that this is a shrinkage crack, but we don't have enough evidence to be conclusive.

Uncertainty on your part will diminish your client's confidence in you. If you don't know the answer, it's best to say you don't know, but with confidence. You do not want your client to get the feeling that if they had hired another inspector, that inspector would have known the answer. You need to tell the client that a conclusive assessment will require a destructive investigation, doing calculations, and/or monitoring the situation.

You will be drawing conclusions with certainty in some cases. In other cases you will be drawing conclusions based on deduction and incomplete information. It's not your fault that you don't have all the relevant information. So don't guess about the situation without qualifying your position; give your professional opinion, but make it clear that only with more pieces of the puzzle could you be definitive.

Your Final Report Is Important

The only thing more important than the first impression you make is the last impression. The inspection report is not only the impression that your clients leave with; it's also the only tangible evidence of your inspection.

The report has to knock your client's socks off. It is the tangible proof that they have received a professional assessment. From a marketing perspective, the report is what will get you future referrals.

If your report is unimpressive, your client's image of you and your whole business, will be unimpressive.

No report system or format is perfect or the best. And in most areas of the country there are no industry standards. Opinions abound on what looks best. Whatever you choose, make sure it is your best effort, and that it reflects how you would like your company to be perceived.

KEY TERMS

benefit	customer	unique selling proposition
client	feature	value proposition
company image	target market	

STUDY SESSION 1 QUICK QUIZ

You should finish Study Session 1 before doing this Quiz. Write your answers in the spaces provided. Then check your answers in Appendix A.

1. Put the letter F beside the item that is a feature and a B beside the item that is a benefit of a home inspection service.

    _F_ a. Available on weekends!

    ____ b. Need an inspection before your offer expires on Monday? We can get the job done on Sunday!

    ____ c. With 20 years experience in foundation work, we spot the problems others miss.

    ____ d. Friendly service!

    ____ e. We believe in addressing your concerns and putting your mind at ease.

2. The potential homebuyer is both your client and your customer. Circle one.

    a. True

    b. False

3. If a real estate agent pays for the inspection, does that make them your client? Circle one.

    a. Yes

    b. No

4. The most cost-effective target market for your services, according to a majority of inspectors, is (Circle one.):

    a. homebuyers.

    b. bankers.

    c. lawyers.

    d. real estate agents.

5. Customers form an opinion of you at a number of points of contact. List three points of contact with your customer in the order of their potential marketing importance, with the most important at the top (you don't need to write the percent of importance).

    1. _____

    2. _____

    3. _____

6. You have marketed yourself to agents working in residential areas in which average home sales start at $500,000. Your business name is Wall-to-Street Inspections. (There is nothing like evoking the wealthiest district in the world!) You will be meeting a prospective client and performing the inspection at the same time. What do you wear? Circle one.

    a. Top hat and tails

    b. Three-piece suit

    c. Clean button-down shirt, blazer, and slacks

    d. T-shirt and jeans

7. During an inspection, you notice a gap between the top of the stairs and the wall beside it. The stairs could be pulling away from the wall. But you can't tell for sure unless the drywall beside the stair is removed. Because your inspection is nondestructive, there's no way to give the client a conclusive answer. Choose the best answer to give your client.

   a. "I think the stairs are pulling away from the wall."

   b. "I think the stairs are pulling away from the wall, but it could also just be the trim."

   c. "There's a gap between the stairs and the wall. The drywall beside the stairs will have to be removed to determine the cause and need for correction."

   d. "It's possible your stairs will need replacing in five years, but I'm not absolutely sure."

8. What is a value proposition?

   _____

   _____

   _____

If you had trouble with the Quiz, reread Study Session 1 and try the Quiz again. If you had no trouble with Study Session 1 Quick Quiz, you are ready for Study Session 2!

STUDY SESSION

DEVELOPING YOUR COMPANY IDENTITY AND MARKET FOCUS

Study Session 2 gives you more marketing concepts to help you formulate an effective marketing strategy.

LEARNING OBJECTIVES

At the end of Study Session 2 you should be able to

■ define, in a few sentences, your clients' needs, and identify what they are really buying;

■ design a marketing message to alleviate client fears;

■ generate three good potential company names with branding in mind, and choose the best one for your company;

■ define, in one sentence each, segmentation, targeting, and positioning; and

■ write all marketing material with branding and your target market in mind.

Study Session 2 may take you roughly 60 minutes to complete.

Now that you understand some fundamental marketing concepts, you can begin looking at developing your company identity. This includes creating a company brand and naming your company. We will also look at sharpening your market focus by segmenting the market and targeting your marketing efforts. We begin with a consideration of what your clients are really buying, which is both more specific and less tangible than you might imagine.

WHAT ARE YOUR CLIENTS REALLY BUYING?

Let's step back and look at what the client is buying. It's not always obvious. Here are some examples.

When someone buys a car they are not really buying a car, they are buying

- safe transportation for their family,
- a status symbol,
- a thrill.

When someone buys a pair of jeans they are actually buying

- status,
- an opportunity to think they are as good-looking as the model wearing the jeans in the magazine, and
- sex.

When someone buys a power drill they really want holes.

How about a home inspection? What is your client buying?

In many ways, your client is buying peace of mind. They may also be buying positive reinforcement of their buying decision. They are not buying an audit of the problems in the home; they are not buying a guided tour of the home by an expert; and they are not buying "20 years as a builder." Your client just wants to feel that they are making a good decision.

Once you know what your client is actually buying, you can use this information in your marketing, advertising, and sales materials and campaigns.

Don't Promise What You Can't Deliver

Be careful what you promise. Although your goal is to create marketing, sales, and advertising messages that appeal to your client's need for peace of mind, the home inspection process is inherently imperfect. You can't detect every problem. In fact, there may be a very significant problem that you can't detect. Here is an example.

Consider a house with a fully finished basement. Most, if not all, of the foundation walls are hidden behind drywall, concealing any cracks in the walls. The worst kind of crack in a foundation wall is a horizontal crack below grade level that runs the length of the wall. This crack indicates foundation failure—that the wall is no longer able to hold back the surrounding soil. This crack is not visible from inside because the basement is finished; it is not visible from outside because it's below grade. There may be no associated cracking in the interior or exterior finishes until it is too late.

What are you going to do about this problem? You can't tell every client with a finished basement that they could have a horizontal crack indicating failure of the foundation! But you can explain that your inspection is a visual, nondestructive inspection, and that there are limitations to such an inspection.

So what does this have to do with marketing?

You have to be careful not to promise too much in your marketing pieces. For example, if your promise "complete peace of mind," your client may use this promise against you later. They could say they were counting on you for peace of mind and you agreed to provide it. So the trick is to develop a marketing piece that gives the client "peace of mind" without promising them that they will never have a problem with the home.

People Are Motivated by Emotions

Most purchase decisions are emotional, although we want to believe they are rational. Home inspections are no exception. From a marketing perspective, it is helpful to understand the emotional forces driving your clients, in order to create marketing messages that address those emotions. Let's look at a partial list.

Client's Feelings	Your Solutions
nervous	assurance
at risk	risk reduction
worried about making a mistake	security
worried about losing money	savings, good investment
uncertainty	certainty
apprehension	comfort
isolation	support
bad decision	good decision
money pit	dream house
fear of the unknown	knowledge

It makes sense to incorporate these solutions to clients' problems into your marketing message.

YOUR BRAND

A name **brand** is a powerful thing. The busier we get, the more we rely on brands to help us make a decision. There is an old expression, "Nobody ever got fired for buying IBM." The expression brings to mind an image of an overworked employee given the task of buying a new computer system for the company. Faced with too many options, many of which require time-consuming research, the employee decides there is safety in choosing a name brand.

Make Your Name Known

Branding a product simply means finding a way to make that product, or service, a household word. While a home inspection company will never be the main topic of dinner table conversation for your average North American, you can at least make your company a household word within your sphere of influence—with real estate agents, real estate lawyers, and other professionals associated with your business.

If your name is on everything you and your customers touch, eventually people will recognize your name as the brand name.

Franchises, "branchises," and affiliations can help create branding for you. For instance, if you use a name that is already recognized, you start your business as a brand name, rather than taking years to develop one.

You don't have to be a franchisee, "branchisee," or part of an affiliation to have a brand, but it sure helps. Furthermore, keep in mind that the brand is just a small part of an overall campaign to grow your business. By the same token, being part of an established brand does not guarantee success.

Start Branding Immediately

The way to build your brand is to start right away. It seems obvious, but many home inspection companies take years before they finally have a coherent design for their business card, brochure, letterhead, and advertising. It costs money to have this marketing material designed, and when you start your business you don't have a lot of money to throw around. It is well worth the money, however, to have a professional-looking brand image from the beginning.

NAMING YOUR COMPANY

There are a few rules, and many guidelines, for naming a company. The guidelines are, understandably, contradictory because there are many philosophies about how to choose a company name. But the rules are pretty straightforward, especially if you are registering your company name. Let's start with the rules.

Legal Restrictions

Taken Names

When registering your company name, you have to consider the legal implications of your chosen name, such as taking a name that is already in use by someone else. You will have to investigate the legal requirements for registering your name/company. If the company name you pick is already in use, depending on whom that user is, and where they are located, you may not be able to use that name.

Name Sounding Like Another's

If someone else has protected their name by registering, incorporating, or trade-marking it, not only can you *not* use the same name, but you may not be able to use a similar name because it might confuse the public. For example, if your name is John McDonald and you are opening a hamburger restaurant, you may be tempted to call your restaurant McDonald's Hamburgers. This choice seems reasonable because your name is McDonald, and how can anyone stop you from using your own name? Besides, your restaurant is McDonald's Hamburgers, not McDonald's. Guess again. You can't do it. It's confusing to the public.

Guidelines for Choosing a Name

There are no surefire names that will guarantee success, but here are a few tips that may help you choose a compelling name. Don't go through all of these guidelines with the goal of finding a name that satisfies each one or you will never name your company. Pick out a few guidelines that strike a chord with you and then brainstorm.

Think Domain Name

One of the first things you should do is to check if your name idea is available as a **domain name** on the World Wide Web. Now that most companies have Web sites, the proliferation of domain names, cyber squatters, and businesses on the Web might make it difficult to find a name that is not already taken. If your company name is a single word, you can be sure it's already taken. All combinations of single, double, and triple letters are already taken.

Your domain name does not *have* to be the same name as your company name but it's better if it is. Why? The more you use the same name in all parts of your business, the closer you are to branding your company. Nike is a great example. Nike doesn't have a billboard ad with a logo that says Nike Shoe Company while their Web site address is *www.nikemakesbouncyandcomfortableshoes.com.* Nike puts "Nike" on everything. Wherever possible, you should get your company name front and center on everything you do. Your company may never be a household word, like Nike, but it might become an industry brand name that comes easily to your customers' minds.

If you are going to call your company *Home Sleuth,* you want to have the Web domain *www.homesleuth.com,* not *www.thehomesleuth.com* or *www.homesleuthinspector.com.*

Even if you have no immediate plans to build a Web site, you should register the domain name so that someone else does not get it.

Consider Acronym and Abbreviation Effects

While there are many extremely well-known companies that use three words in the company name, you should understand that the words may be shortened to a three-letter **acronym** whether you want this or not. This is really BAD if your company name is Building Analysts of Detroit (BAD).

Keeping branding in mind, you want to have a consistent name that can be heard over and over. But if your name gets abbreviated in some way, make sure this does not hurt your branding efforts. Let's say you want to call your company *The Greatest Inspection Firm.* You start branding that name, putting it on your brochure, your Web site, *www.thegreatestinspectionfirm.com,* your letterhead, and so on. The next thing you know, agents start referring to you as TGIF. Maybe you should have called it TGIF from the start.

Consider Using Your Own Name

There are lots of reasons to use your own name. Every time you introduce yourself, you increase the awareness of your brand. "I'm John Smith of *Smith Inspections"* sounds good and stimulates the prospect's brain twice with a single introduction.

One possible downside to using your name might arise if you decide to sell your company down the road. You may not want someone else to be carrying on a business with your name on it. This is the classic objection to using your own name, but it's a small downside because the likelihood of someone wanting to buy a business with your name on it is slim.

Another disadvantage is that everyone then wants Mr. Smith to do their inspections. If you want to hire other inspectors, you might have to make sure their name is Smith!

Avoid Clichés

The Sherlock Holmes/private eye image is worn out in the home inspection business. If you collect 100 business cards from home inspection companies, about 30 percent of them have a magnifying glass, or an eye, in the logo and a name like *Super Sleuth, Home Sleuth, Sherlock Homes, Baker Street, Home Detective,* and so on. There is nothing wrong with these names; they are simply no longer distinctive.

Words Should Flow Together

If you are going to have two or more words as your name, the words should flow together, making them easy to say and pleasant to hear. Many company names are difficult to say because the two words in the name were chosen to maximize the information contained in the name, rather than for their flow.

Here are some examples that flow well: Inspect-Tech, HomeTech, Bricks R Us, Brick Kickers, Carson Dunlop. On the other hand, a company name like Urban and Rural does not roll off the tongue easily.

Invent a Word,
Coin a Phrase

Consider attaching two words together to make a single word, such as Inspectionmen. Or, invent a word that sounds like it could be a real word, such as Inspectionarian.

Say It Out Loud

An old trick for naming your dog is called "the park test." Once you have picked a tentative name for your dog, go to the park and call it out as loud as you can, as though you were calling your dog. If you are embarrassed, don't use that name for your company, or your dog.

Similarly, if you are planning to call your company *Cracker Jack Inspections,* imagine introducing yourself at a meeting of real estate agents, or imagine yourself at a party where someone asks you what you do for a living. Are you comfortable telling them your company name?

Maximize Information

One branding philosophy says your name should describe what you do. But this approach often results in boring names. If you are a home inspector, you might be tempted to call yourself *John's Prepurchase Home Inspection Services.* You would certainly be getting the message across about what you do, but the name is not very exciting. Boring is not your only choice.

A great example of a catchy name that also states the company's service comes from the company, *Namelab.* The name rolls off the tongue, it's distinctive and it's memorable. Best of all, it's not hard to guess what the company does. They specialize in coming up with names for companies. Any guesses what their Web address is? *www.namelab.com.* If someone asked you who they could hire to come up with a name for their company, I bet you say this name in a heartbeat.

Following are a few other memorable names that also describe what the company does:

- Toys "R" Us
- Futureshop (sells consumer electronics)
- Staples (sells office supplies)
- fatbrain.com (sells text books and reference books)

No Information

Incredibly, names that say nothing about the company can be successful as long as they are catchy, memorable, and they flow off the tongue. Here are a few companies that have names that provide no information about what the company does at all, but are very successful nonetheless.

- Nike
- Guess
- Xerox
- Kleenex

These names are successful because of smart branding and advertising. Creating a brand with this kind of power, and instant recognition, takes lots of money. For this reason, names like this may not be ideal for a home inspection company with limited resources.

There are no hard and fast rules for naming your company, only opinions. If you are having a hard time coming up with a name, look at each of the suggestions above and brainstorm.

SEGMENTATION, TARGETING, AND POSITIONING

Segmentation, targeting, and positioning are three related concepts. In the end, the three concepts say the same thing—you should narrow the focus of your marketing efforts.

What do we mean? You are a home inspector, but you could specialize in one or more of the following:

- High-end homes
- Old homes
- Structures
- New homes
- First-time buyers

Let's look at the definitions of segmentation, targeting, and positioning. Then we will give you a few ideas about how these concepts can help you.

Segmentation

Narrow Your Focus

Segmentation divides up the "mass market" into smaller, distinct markets, or "micro" markets.

Segmentation is the opposite of mass marketing. Most home inspection firms practice mass marketing rather than segmented marketing. Mass marketing is ineffective for any professional service. Segmented marketing, on the other hand, is effective for professional services.

Why do we break down the market into micro markets? This segmentation process enables us to design a specific marketing strategy for that micro market.

The idea is to tailor your campaign to exactly what people in that segment are looking for. Marketing experts suggest that in a competitive market, you can't compete effectively in more than one segment.

Here are two things to consider as you look for segments to target:

1. The segment must be large enough. For example, it does not make sense to target the segment of the market that includes houses over $10,000,000 if there are only a few such houses in your service area.

2. Based on your market size, on the other hand, you may have to opt for a mass marketing strategy. For example, if there are only 500 real estate transactions per year in your service area, you can't afford to specialize.

Targeting

Design Focused Strategy

Targeting means designing a marketing strategy for a particular market segment. For example, rather than creating a brochure for home inspections, you would create a brochure for new home inspections, inspections for first-time buyers, inspection of old homes, or any other market segment you decide is worth targeting.

Positioning

Your **position** is how your customers see you. For example, let's assume you are very good with first-time buyers. You are trying to create your position by targeting a market segment and by building a specific marketing campaign. Understand that the public decides your position, not you. You may guide the public with your marketing campaign and careful segmentation, but in the end, your customers decide. People who use "position" as an action verb are missing the point. The actions are targeting and segmentation. In this respect, there is no such thing as "positioning."

An Example of Segmentation, Targeting, and Positioning

What do segmentation, targeting, and positioning have to do with the home inspection business?

The typical home inspector sets up shop, picks a name for the business, gets a business card, buys a Yellow Pages ad, and is in business. This home inspector is entirely generic. This home inspector does not stand for anything.

If this same home inspector is a great inspector, who is good with people, who puts things into context and who does all the other things that clients and real estate agents expect, he and she will eventually carve out a market share and have a referral base. The problem is, it typically takes three years to build a self-supporting business using this strategy.

Here's an example of a home inspector that uses the principles of segmentation, targeting, and positioning to create a memorable inspection company that will enjoy success in a much shorter period of time.

Our inspector chooses to be a specialist in first-time buyers. (First-time buyers are the biggest market segment today.) Now, rather than embarking on the daunting task of a global marketing strategy that appeals to all, the inspector designs a strategy that appeals to first-time buyers. The inspector's goal is to create a position in the minds of his or her customers, particularly real estate agents, as the inspector who specializes in first-time buyers.

How does the inspector get the message out? He or she makes a brochure or cover letter designed for the real estate agent. The letter indicates that the inspector specializes in first-time buyers:

■ We are experts at communicating with your first-time buyers. We leave no questions unanswered (feature). At the end of the inspection, your buyer will feel comfortable knowing they are making the right decision (benefit).

■ We know how to explain house conditions in proper context to avoid unnecessarily alarming your client (feature). Deals will not fall through because of unimportant deficiencies. This means more money in your pocket in the long run (benefit).

■ First-time buyers are easily panicked; we know how to hold their hand through the process (feature). At the end of the inspection, you will have a happy confident buyer ready for the next step (benefit).

■ We tell your clients what they need to know to operate the home and maintain its systems (feature). Clients will move more quickly through the transaction, and the cold feet problem (or "buyer's remorse" as it is often called), will be less intense (benefit).

■ We are available free of charge at any time after the inspection to answer your clients' questions and concerns (feature). This saves you time and helps you enhance your reputation as an agent who has happy clients for life (benefit).

The home inspector might have a special first-time buyer package. As part of the inspection fee, the inspector's clients get a free book about maintaining their home or a discount on a follow-up inspection. He and she might provide a digital camera on site that clients can use to take pictures to send to friends and relatives or to use for selecting drapes and paint colors. The inspector e-mails the photographs to clients at the end of the day, posts them on the Web site for clients, or copies them to a CD-ROM at the end of the inspection.

Deliver the Goods

Home inspectors could come up with a number of strategies so that they are not only *saying* they are the specialists in first-time buyers but also *delivering the goods*. Delivering on your promise creates your position in the minds of your customers.

With a segmentation and targeting strategy such as the one just described, you have something interesting to tell a real estate agent. For example, you could call the broker of a real estate office and tell them that you have designed a special process for dealing with first-time buyers. You would like to drop in at their next weekly agent sales meeting to tell them about how this process will help the agents streamline the process and save time and money. Remember, the real message is in the benefits rather than in the features.

Stand for One Thing

The key to a solid marketing position is to stand for one thing. That one thing should be clearly identifiable and presented in a simple, clear message. This position should differentiate you from all of the other home inspectors.

Let people know what you stand for at every opportunity. For example, you can create a tagline for your company like, ABC Inspection Services "The new home specialists." This tagline would appear on your e-mail correspondence, on your letterhead, on everything your company name appears.

Specialize

Why are home inspectors afraid to specialize? They fear that by standing for one thing, they will eliminate much of the market. For example, why would they want to target only first-time buyers when they want *all* of the business? It doesn't make sense to reduce the size of the pool, right? Wrong. You will get more business by reducing the size of the pool. In fact, you are not really reducing the size of the pool at all; you are just saying that you are a specialist in one area.

Let's say an agent has a client who is not a first-time buyer. Do you think the agent won't refer this client to you because you are a specialist in first-time buyers? Don't you think that the agent wants a home inspector to treat every client as a first-time buyer? The agent will most likely think, "If this inspector is an expert at handling first-time buyers, then other clients must be a breeze."

The fear of focus is a common theme in every business. You have to trust the experts. You will broaden your appeal by focusing on and targeting a single market segment.

KEY TERMS

acronym	domain name	segmentation
brand	positioning	targeting

STUDY SESSION QUICK QUIZ 2

You should finish Study Session 2 before doing this Quiz. Write your answers in the spaces provided. Then, check your answers in Appendix A.

1. The last thing you need to do when naming your company is check the World Wide Web to see if you can register your chosen company name as your domain name. Circle one.

    a. True

    b. False

2. Well-worn images, such as Sherlock Holmes and magnifying glasses, are good to choose when naming your company because everyone is familiar with them. Circle one.

    a. True

    b. False

3. What is a domain name?

    _____

    _____

4. Using your own name for your company name is never a good idea. Circle one.

    a. True

    b. False

5. Which type of marketing strategy is better for a home inspection company in a large competitive market? Circle one.

    a. Mass marketing

    b. Marketing to a single market segment

6. The key to a solid positioning strategy is to stand for many different, but clearly identifiable, things. Circle one. Explain.

    a. True

    b. False

    _____

    _____

7. There is no such thing as positioning. Circle one. Explain.

    a. True

    b. False

    _____

    _____

If you had trouble with the Quiz, reread Study Session 2 and try the Quiz again. If you did well, it's time for Study Session 3.

SERVICE PHILOSOPHY —PART I

Study Session 3 deals with the basic concepts of customer service that you need to know before looking at specific strategies.

LEARNING OBJECTIVES

At the end of Study Session 3 you should be able to

- develop a service philosophy;

- create a "blueprint" for your customer service, including identifying all points of contact with the customer;

- describe for each point of contact on your blueprint at least one tactic for providing excellent customer service;

- identify the components of a customer-centric business;

- identify customers' perceptions of their needs and develop at least one strategy to respond to each need;

- create a distinctive service;

- define in one or two sentences the Pareto Principle;

- apply the Pareto Principle to your service philosophy and marketing strategies; and

- design a questionnaire for customer feedback.

Study Session 3 may take you roughly 60 minutes to complete.

Develop Customer Service

A **customer service** philosophy refers to the ways in which you think about, and develop, your business. Your **service philosophy** is the total of all the strategies you employ in order to deliver a high-quality service that "blows your customers away." We've spent some time talking about how to market your services. But you have to have an excellent service to market because no amount of marketing will sell a service that's not good. You may fool people for a while with your dazzling marketing strategies, but word will get out if the service is not up to snuff.

If you offer a professional service, you must deliver good service. You can market your service as "the best in town," but if you perform below standard, you will not sustain your customer base. This section will help you develop ways to approach customer service to create a winning business.

STRATEGIZING EXCELLENT SERVICE

Create Customer-Service Blueprint

The first step in developing a top-notch professional service is to identify every point at which you contact the public, a process called **blueprinting your business process.** Blueprinting is a kind of map that shows you the **points of contact** where you can enhance customer service. Draw a dotted line in the middle of a piece of paper. Label it "line of visibility" or "line of interaction." On one side of this line, write the section or sections of the public with whom you interact. On the other side of the dotted line, draw a flowchart showing the flow of your business. Draw an arrow to connect the points between the public and your business to show each time they interact. Each point of contact is an opportunity to offer exceptional customer service. Most home inspection companies have very simple blueprints for this process. Figure 3.1 shows a typical home inspection company's customer-service blueprint.

You might have a completely different chart for your relationship with real estate professionals. It would include items like office presentations, calling agents, lunch with agents, and so on.

Point of Contact = Service Opportunity

What's the point of blueprinting your business operations? It forces you to think about a strategy for every point at which you interact with the public. Each of these points is an opportunity for you to create exceptional, and memorable, service. Below is an example of the thought process.

Brainstorm Strategies

In our example blueprint chart in Figure 3.1, report delivery is one of the significant points of contact. Let's say that you mail your reports to your client. The client receives the report without any personal contact with you. What can you do to spice up this aspect of your business? Let the brainstorming begin. You can

- send the report by courier,
- deliver the report in person and spend time discussing it with the client,
- e-mail the report, or
- upload the report to a secure Web site and e-mail a link and a password to the client. The report has built-in links to documents that contain more information on the condition described. A floating document box allows the client to type in questions as he or she reads the report. After reading the report, the questions document gets e-mailed to you for a response.

The key to effective brainstorming is writing down your ideas without criticizing them as you go. For example, the last idea above is fairly elaborate and

F I G U R E 3.1   A Customer Service Blueprint

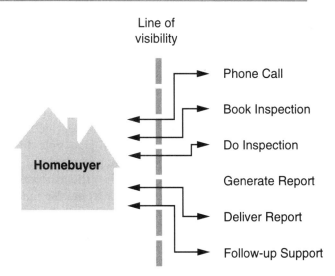

might cost a lot to set up. Don't worry about it. Just write down the ideas, no matter how difficult or even ridiculous they seem. You will have time to reject them in the next step. Brainstorming is a creative process, whereas evaluating each idea is an exercise in logic. Don't mix logic with your brainstorming or it will stifle your creativity.

Evaluate Your Ideas

The next step is to consider each idea, evaluating it on the

■ impact the strategy will have on your clients,

■ cost of implementing the idea, and

■ time commitment it requires.

Let's evaluate the idea of sending the report by courier. If you give your client a summary on site, they may not have a sense of urgency about receiving the report. Sending it by courier has little advantage and little impact, but it will consume a significant amount of profit from each inspection.

Now let's look at the Web site idea. Implementing the dynamic Web site reporting system may be expensive, but if it creates an extraordinary point of distinction for your company, it could launch your business to levels you never thought possible.

Spend Money to Make Money

Each idea has advantages and disadvantages. You need to weigh the long-term benefits, factoring your client's needs into the equation. Yes, you will save money if you decide not to implement a dynamic Web site system, but a dynamic site imparts distinction to your company and might make customers happy. **Customer satisfaction** leads to referrals that lead to increased business volume. More business means you can pay for your Web site. Once the initials costs are covered, Web sites are relatively easy and inexpensive to maintain. You can't always calculate the benefits based on cost alone. There are returns from customer satisfaction that don't always show up immediately as revenues.

In the previous example, we made a key assumption—we know what the customer wants. This is a typical but dangerous assumption. It's amazing how wrong we can be when we assume what customers want. For example, what if most of your customers do not have Internet access? Or, what if most of your customers think posting their report on a Web site violates their privacy? In the next section we will look at developing your ability to have the customer's perspective in mind.

CUSTOMER-CENTRIC BUSINESS

Think from Customer's Perspective

We looked at describing benefits, rather than features, in your marketing pieces. Benefits look at your service from the customer's perspective. This perspective should pervade all that you do, ensuring that the big picture encompasses a **customer-centric** philosophy.

Remember that the customer may include real estate professionals of all descriptions and anyone else that can send business your way. Everything you do should be evaluated with the following thought process:

- What's the benefit, or perceived benefit, to the customer?
- What can I do to make the benefit, or perceived benefit, more visible?
- Does this benefit result in a significant marketing advantage to me?

Perceived Benefits Have Greater Impact

Before we continue, let's define the term "perceived benefit" because it goes to the root of a customer-centric business. A **perceived benefit** is something that may or may not be a real benefit to your client, but the client thinks it is important. For example, let's take the idea of uploading the client's report to a secure Web site with lots of bells and whistles. Is this a benefit to the client? Isn't it simpler for the client just to get an e-mailed report? An e-mail does the job and saves the client the added step of going to a Web site. But the client often perceives the Web-based system as superior.

What Does Your Client Want?

How can you know what your client perceives as a benefit? Stop thinking like an expert and start thinking like your client. If you don't know what your client is thinking, ask. We will look more closely at how to obtain clients' thoughts and opinions in the section "Give Your Customers What They Want," later in this study session.

An Example

Here is a firsthand example. Our report-writing system is a 400-page binder. When we do a prelisting inspection for a seller, the report and the book are supposed to be left in the home for the person who ultimately buys the home. But we find that many sellers want to take the book with them to their next house, even though the report contents are for the home they are leaving! While our clients' perceptions are not what we expected, they have to be respected.

LEVELS OF SERVICE

Figure 3.2 summarizes four aspects of service you should strive for. We will look at each in more detail in the following sections.

Create Superior Service

Make Sure Customers Return

The idea here is to impress your customers in such a way that they will come back to you over and over, and/or refer you to others. A good home inspector does his or her job well and consistently. A good home inspector arrives on time

F I G U R E 3.2 Four Keys to Great Service

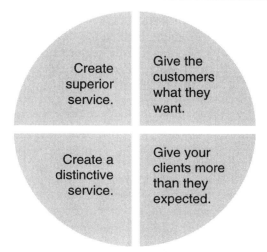

and delivers a professional report. Believe it or not, many home inspection companies can't even deliver on these basic services. If you deliver consistently good performance, you will be a contender. But a contender is not what you want to be. You want to be in the top-selling group of building inspectors.

The **Pareto Principle,** also known as the 80/20 rule, says that 80 percent of the effect is the result of 20 percent of the cause. Here are some examples from a paper by Arthur W. Hafner, PhD, MBA, Dean of Ball State University Libraries, Muncie, Indiana:

- 80 percent of advertising results come from 20 percent of your campaign.
- 80 percent of customer complaints are about the same 20 percent of your projects, products, or services.
- 80 percent of our personal phone calls are to 20 percent of the people in our address book.
- 80 percent of the outfits we wear come from 20 percent of the clothes in our closets or drawers.

While there are studies to prove it is true, it is easy to believe that 20 percent of home inspection companies perform up to 80 percent of the inspections in a given market.

Little Effort Goes Long Way

The fact is, to become part of the elite 20 percent requires being only a little better than the crowd. If you can analyze your service and figure out how to do it just a little better, you'll go far. How much faster is the winning time in an Olympic 100-meter sprint than the fourth place time: 20 percent, 15 percent, 10 percent? It's actually about 2 percent. Yet the fourth place person gets no medal, gets no parade or endorsements, and may be remembered only by family and friends. It is even more dramatic in business. The most impressive home inspection company gets the order with 100 percent of the rewards, and there is not even a silver medal for the second place finisher, who gets nothing.

Instead of being on time for the inspection, arrive ten minutes early. That way you can inspect the roof before your client and the agent arrive.

Does anyone really notice? During a presentation to a real estate office, an agent commented, "One thing I love about Carson Dunlop is I know when I arrive at the house with the client, the home inspector will have already finished inspecting the roof. The first time Carson Dunlop did an inspection for a client of mine, I was concerned when I got to the house at 9:00 A.M. and the inspector was not there. I called the Carson Dunlop office and they told me to look up. Sure enough, I saw the inspector finishing up on the roof."

You can't buy that kind of advertising. Special touches that make your service consistently better are enough to put you into the elite 20 percent. And what does it cost to arrive a few minutes early? Nothing!

Give Customers What They Want

How do you know what your customers want? Ask them. What's the best way to ask them? There are lots of ways, but we have found surveys the most effective.

If you **survey your client** on site during the inspection, you get a 100 percent response rate. Provide a clipboard with a pencil attached along with a simple questionnaire. Following are tips to help create a good questionnaire:

- Keep the questionnaire short (two to four questions only).
- Keep it simple.
- Don't ask questions to which you know the answer.
- Don't ask personal questions.
- Ask only questions that can be translated directly into a business decision. (In other words, ask yourself, "What am I going to do with the information?")
- Don't ask a yes/no question. (You want people to give you a better idea of how they feel about your question.)

The three different kinds of surveys you can use are as follows:

1. Likert scale (which measures the extent to which a person agrees or disagrees with a question)
2. Importance scale (which measures the importance of an issue to a person)
3. Semantic differential survey (which measures people's reactions to stimulus words and concepts)

Likert scale.   Here is an example of a **Likert scale** questionnaire.

Our business thrives on input from our clients. Please take a moment to help us improve our pricing structure.

Indicate your level of agreement to each statement by circling the appropriate number next to each question. Our rating system is as follows:

1 = strongly disagree
2 = disagree
3 = neutral
4 = agree
5 = emphatically agree

When I first heard your inspection fee, I was surprised how expensive you were.

1   2   3   4   5

Now that you have completed the inspection, I find that your inspection fee is very fair.

    1   2   3   4   5

If you had charged $50 more for the inspection, I would have still hired you.

    1   2   3   4   5

Here are a few notes about the Likert scale:

- Don't ask people to rate between 1 and 10. It's too big a range. For example, it is difficult to distinguish between 6 and 7 if the range is 1 to 10.

- You should decide if you want to provide a fence to sit on. For example, in our question above, we have used an odd number so that people could choose to be neutral and select 3. If you don't want a fence to sit on, use four or six numbers.

- These surveys can be quickly converted into a bar chart after you have a sufficient number of completed surveys.

Importance scale   An **importance scale** survey might look like the following example:

Our business thrives on input from our clients. Please take a moment to help us improve our service.

We provide many benefits that other home inspection companies do not provide. How meaningful are the following benefits to you? Put a check mark in the appropriate box.

	Not at All Meaningful	Not Very Meaningful	Meaningful	Very Meaningful
Use of digital camera during inspection				
Home Reference Book reporting system				

Here are notes on the importance scale:

- You can use numbers rather than boxes if you choose.

- Notice that we did not provide a fence to sit on. We want our clients to take a stand here.

Semantic differential survey   Following is an example of a **semantic differential survey.** This is a nice questionnaire because it is so simple to fill out.

Our business thrives on input from our clients. Please take a moment to help us evaluate our business. Place a checkmark in the appropriate box.

Carson Dunlop Home Inspection Service:

Inexpensive			✓		Expensive
Lacks Value			✓		Good Value
Unprofessional				✓	Very Professional

Narrative Survey

If you are looking for specific advice on how to improve your business, we like this three-question survey:

1. Was there anything about our service that you particularly liked?

   _____

2. Was there anything about our service that you did not like?

   _____

3. Is there anything that we could do to improve our service to you?

   _____

Don't Survey Agents On Site

Remember that because real estate agents are potentially your customers also, you should consider surveying them. Don't survey them on-site, though—agents don't want to fill out a survey during an inspection. They have work to do or phone calls to make. Furthermore, agents prefer not to fill out a survey in front of their clients.

Mail or e-mail the survey to the agent. Keep in mind that you will get a very low response rate with a survey that you mail to an agent. You may have to combine it with an incentive. For example, if they answer your survey, you will enter their name into a drawing. At the end of the month you will draw for a free inspection that can be given to a client.

Give Your Clients More than They Expected

You can achieve customer satisfaction simply by delivering what the client was expecting. If you deliver more than they were expecting, you not only have a satisfied customer, but you also have someone who will comment to others about your great service.

Many home inspectors take this information to mean they should show off their technical expertise during the inspection. But what you do technically during your inspection is lost on most customers. They don't understand it, and they have no way of knowing whether another inspector would have done the same or more.

Good Service Needs Creative Thinking

What does it take to offer a service beyond expectations? It takes imagination. If you think it also takes a lot of money, you're wrong. Yes, it is true that a big company can invest in systems that deliver a service beyond expectations. For instance, what does Carson Dunlop offer beyond our customers' expectations?

■ A free subscription to *managemyhome.com,* a customized online system that helps clients maintain and manage their home. For example, they will get an e-mail reminder to clean the filter in the furnace at the appropriate time, including tips on how to do it and an opportunity to contact us if they are unsure how to proceed. But they get the reminder only if they have a furnace. If they have a boiler, they will not get a message to clean the filter.

■ Customers get a follow-up e-mail asking if they were happy with the inspection.

■ Real estate agents get a thank you card from the home inspector for referring our service.

■ Clients are told that they can call us anytime about questions they may have about the house.

Courtesy Is Invaluable

Acts of courtesy such as follow-up calls cost nothing at all. The difference between you and the next inspector could hinge on something as simple as returning customer calls within three hours of receiving them. That kind of service has a tremendous impact on the customer, and costs you nothing.

Lest We Forget

Let us remind you once again that good service is not defined by the home inspector, it is defined by the customer. We talked about surveys, but only at the end did we focus on what questions to ask. Consider this one: "What could we do to make the home inspection experience better for you?" Or, if you are really bold, "What else could we do to help you?"

Create a Distinctive Service

Creating a distinctive service is often the result of the previous three steps. Over time, if you stay consistent in your good service, high-quality service will become your trademark.

Additional ways to help create a **point of distinction** for your service are to come up with unusual offerings, such as the following:

■ Provide each client with a free disposable camera at the beginning of the inspection to take pictures that they can show friends and relatives.

■ Provide each client the use of your digital camera during the inspection.

■ Deliver cookies to the real estate office once a month.

■ During the inspection, find out the closing date for the transaction. Send a welcome letter to your client the day they move in, inviting them to call you if they are unsure of how to operate any aspect of the home.

KEY TERMS

blueprinting your business process	Likert scale	semantic differential survey
customer-centric	Pareto Principle	service philosophy
customer satisfaction	perceived benefit	survey your client
customer service	points of contact	
importance scale	point of distinction	

STUDY SESSION 3 QUICK QUIZ

You should finish Study Session 3 before doing this Quiz. Write your answers in the spaces provided. Then, check your answers in Appendix A.

1. Each point of contact for your services represents (Circle one.)

   a. a service opportunity.

   b. your customer base.

   c. a number to add to your database.

   d. money well spent.

2. It's better to think like an expert than to think like a client. Circle one.

   a. True

   b. False

3. List two important things to remember when creating a questionnaire. We've given you an example to get you going:

   1. Don't ask a yes or no question.

   2. _____

   3. _____

4. When creating a questionnaire, don't give people an evaluation range that's too great, such as a range between 1 to 10. Circle one.

   a. True

   b. False

5. List two unusual service offerings that would make your service desirable to a client.

   1. _____

   2. _____

If you had trouble with the Quiz, reread Study Session 3 and try the Quiz again. If you did well, it's time for Study Session 4.

SERVICE PHILOSOPHY —PART II

Study Session 4 is a continuation of the discussion of customer service fundamentals started in Study Session 3.

LEARNING OBJECTIVES

At the end of Study Session 4 you should be able to

- describe in one sentence the importance of the inspection report;

- outline in one paragraph how to employ "risk reversal" to your advantage;

- describe five keys to dealing with a customer complaint; and

- outline your strategy for answering the phone while you are doing inspections.

Study Session 4 may take you roughly 60 minutes to complete.

In this section we look at some more aspects of providing excellent service to your clients.

THE IMPORTANCE OF THE INSPECTION REPORT

Make Intangibles Tangible

What a professional service offers is often intangible. A service professional works on the client's behalf to some end. While the service may result in a situation change, or a document, it is less about the end result and more about the process that takes you there. For instance, when you hire a lawyer, you may end up with a document, such as a will or a contract. When you hire a doctor, you may end up with a prescription. When you hire an engineer, you may end up with a design. But what you hired was the process that produced a result. Most people don't see the professional knowledge and process that goes into producing the end result. Fewer people appreciate the professional knowledge involved in a professional service. Nowhere is this more the case than for home inspectors.

In the home inspection business, the **inspection report** is the only tangible part of the entire process. Because the report carries the weight of proof of your professional abilities, it is extremely important. There are many reporting systems on the market to choose from. We encourage new home inspectors to buy one that's already out there. Unfortunately, most new home inspectors fall into the trap of reinventing the wheel.

Don't Reinvent Wheel

When you start a new home inspection company, you are not likely to have a full schedule of inspections. If you have two inspections per week when you first start, you're doing well. You may feel that your time is not worth much at this point, making you reluctant to spend money on someone else's reporting system. You go home after every inspection and diligently produce a written narrative, or you spend hours developing a checklist that you will provide to your client on site. What's wrong with this picture? Now is exactly the time that you most need a predesigned report. A professionally developed system makes you look good from the first day. It also saves time you would otherwise spend creating your own system. You have a precious nonrenewable asset called *time*. Any spare time you do have should go towards your marketing and sales efforts towards building your business.

REVERSING RISK FOR BUYERS

Have you ever watched late night television and seen a commercial for a product, such as a set of steak knives or a piece of exercise equipment? Who buys that stuff after seeing it on the television? How can they tell if the product is any good? To know its worth, you need to be able to touch it, to see how the parts are put together, then to try it out, and so on. So why would a buyer take that kind of risk?

Professional services are much the same. Your prospect can't evaluate your service with any accuracy, especially over the phone. Not only does your prospect have no idea what they will get from your service, but the prospect does not even know what you look like. The bottom line is, the prospect or client assumes all of the risk in the transaction. They take a leap of faith when they say, "Okay, I will hire you." Because there *is* risk involved, they may choose to call a few other home inspection companies until they get a good feeling from someone.

Remove Risk

How do you overcome this problem? The same way the late night television people do it. Do anything you can do to remove or reduce the risk. The television people tell you to order it and enjoy it for a week. If you are not happy, send it back for a full refund. You can do the same thing with your prospects. If they are hesitating, just tell them to book the inspection. If they are not happy at the end of the inspection, they don't have to pay. That is **risk reversal.**

Now the risk is all yours. You risk doing an inspection for a client who might not pay you at the end. Makes you feel a bit uncomfortable, doesn't it? Now you know how your prospects feel. But the risk to you is not as great as it seems. The fact is, almost every client is pleased with the inspection. Few people, if any, will tell you they are unhappy in order to get a free inspection. We have never had a problem with people taking advantage of this kind of offer. It's unlikely that you will, either. The upside far outweighs the risk that you may get cheated the odd time.

Risk reversal is a tool you should use in just about everything you do, not just when you are booking an inspection. Here are some steps you can take:

Step 1: For each transaction involving your business, identify the risk involved for the prospect.

Step 2: List as many ways as possible to reduce, or remove, the risk.

Step 3: For each of your ideas in Step 2, identify what the risk is to you.

Step 4: Select a strategy that has the best balance.

Here is an example.

Step 1: You've developed a strategy to get more real estate agents to refer business to you. You have decided that you will take one agent out for lunch per week. At the end of the lunch, you plan to ask the agent if he or she will refer their next inspection to you. What is the risk to the agent? The risk is substantial. The agent may already have a home inspector to whom they refer business. And the agent's home inspector is especially good because he or she doesn't alarm the clients unnecessarily. If the agent refers you instead, he or she risks that you will not be as levelheaded as the agent's current, preferred home inspector. You may kill the sale and cost the agent a big commission.

Step 2: How can you eliminate the risk for the agent? You could offer to pay the agent the commission if you end up killing the deal. Or, you could tell the agent that if the client is not happy with the inspection, the client doesn't have to pay. The second offer presents a more reasonable risk for you and no risk for the client, but it still leaves risk for the agent.

Step 3: What are the risks to you? Offering to pay agents their lost commissions if you kill the deal is too big a risk for you, not to mention that this offer has ethical implications. Offering to absorb the cost of the inspection reduces the client's risk, has little risk for you, but does not really reverse the risk for the agent.

Step 4: Strike a balance everyone can live with. Our strategy is a combination of reducing the risk for the client and quantifying the actual risk for the agent.

For instance, when you meet with the agent, explain how good you are with clients and how you put problems in proper perspective so that the client doesn't walk from the deal over small issues. Let the agent know that you understand the state of mind of someone buying a home, and that it helps no one if a client overreacts to a common, minor problem, and walks away from a good home. You may tell the agent that your role is to advise and help your client, not to impress them. You feel no pressure to find problems to help justify your fee. Then extend the offer so that if the client is unhappy for any reason, they will not be required to pay. You are not reversing the risk for the agent at all, but because you have explained your client-friendly approach, the agent may feel that your strategy does, in fact, reduce the risk of the client walking away from the deal.

You can make another point to the agent. If their client does not buy the home based on the results of the inspection, they will still buy a home. While the agent will have to spend more time with the client to find them another home and earn the commission, the agent/client relationship will be stronger because the client appreciates that the agent saved them from making a mistake by introducing them to you.

UNDER-PROMISE AND OVER-DELIVER

We mentioned earlier that you can achieve customer satisfaction by coming close to delivering what the client was expecting. Your goal now is to surpass client expectations. You have to find out what the expectation is and offer a little extra. Another way to accomplish the same goal is to reduce the client's expectations first, and then exceed them.

Don't let the real estate agent over-promise on your behalf. Even though the agent has been through many home inspections, most agents don't really understand the technical aspects of your service. We have found that agents may overstate what a home inspector does. For example, an agent will tell the client that a home inspection will uncover all of the hidden defects that the homeowner can't see. While we, as home inspectors, have lots of tricks up our sleeves for uncovering problems with limited visibility, we can't uncover hidden defects.

Agents often say things such as the following:

■ "The home inspector will look into every nook and cranny." Clients are then surprised that we don't move pianos and china cabinets.

■ "The home inspector will look at the heat exchanger in the furnace." Actually, home inspectors just look at the parts of the heat exchanger that are visible from the vestibule area in front of the burner.

Educate the Agent

If you have a working relationship with agents, it's a good idea to let them know the limitations of a home inspection so that they don't over-promise on your behalf.

Present Limitations Up Front

Another way to avoid the over-promise problem is to **under-promise and over-deliver.** Tell your clients about the limitations of a home inspection up front. Then the client will be all the more impressed with what you are able to do during the inspection.

Adjust Customer Expectations

Home inspectors are reluctant to explain the limitations of the inspection up front because they don't want to start discussing negatives as soon as they meet the client. However, explaining the limitations before you begin the inspection is a good strategy for the following reasons:

■ It supports the under-promise and over-deliver philosophy.

■ It increases the difference between what the customer expects and receives by reducing a client's expectations.

■ It reduces the chance that your client will sue you for something that you could not see during the inspection.

■ Clients are less likely to ask you to do something during the inspection that is outside the scope of a home inspection.

Here is a sample process and outline you can use, or modify, for your on-site explanation of the inspection limitations.

Step 1: Introduce yourself to the client. Exchange business cards.

Step 2: Explain to the client what you are going to do during the inspection. For example, say that you will inspect the roof first on your own, but from then on you would like the client to accompany you throughout the inspection.

Step 3: Ask the client if they have concerns about particular areas. Make note of what they say. This shows that you are taking them seriously. Explain that you will be sure to address those issues as you get to that area of the home.

Step 4: Suggest that they look at the contract while you inspect the roof.

Step 5: Explain your findings regarding the roof. This step establishes your credibility immediately. If there are no roof problems to report, then describe the roof system.

Step 6: Tell them that before you continue you would like to answer any questions they have about the contract. This is the time to explain that the inspection is a visual, nondestructive investigation, and that, as such, the inspection has inherent limitations. For example, if there is no access hatch to the attic, you will not be able to look at the roof structure. (Use an example that does not apply to the house you are inspecting.)

Step 7: Now go ahead and inspect the house and impress them with your talents.

By the way, we typically e-mail or fax our inspection agreement and a copy of the Standards of Practice and Code of Ethics to the client before the inspection. We have found it has at least five advantages:

1. Clients appreciate having the time to review the agreement.

2. Clients with expectations beyond a standard home inspection can call back and say this is not what they wanted.

3. The client can see that a large association, not an individual or a small company, sets the rules of the game. The association's presence helps assure the client that the rules are fair.

4. The inspector saves time on site, because the client already knows, and has agreed to, the rules of the game.

5. The inspector's liability is reduced because it is difficult for the client to argue that they did not know what they were buying when they arrived at the inspection.

Be prepared for the following question, "If you can't tell me every problem with the house, what's the point of a home inspection?" The answer is, "We promise to drastically reduce the risk of buying this home, but we cannot eliminate the risk completely." Depending on the situation we may also offer, "I am sure that by the end of the inspection you will have learned a great deal about the home and be in a much better position to make a well-informed decision. If this does not happen, you will not be asked to pay for the inspection."

Here is a simple way to go the extra mile for your client. After the inspection, send them an e-mail with an article that relates to something you discussed during the inspection. You can also send them a link to a Web site that may be useful to them. If there is nothing memorable about the inspection, pick a component of the house and send the client an article related to it. It could be an architectural explanation, a functional description, maintenance advice, design and planning information if they are remodeling, and so on.

You don't have to write the articles; you just have to find them on the Internet and send the link to your client. It won't take you long to develop a short list of things you can send clients. It takes about five minutes per client and will create a strong positive impression. And there is no hard cost!

CREDIT CARD PAYMENT

Offer Clients Several
Payment Options

If you take only cash on site, you may scare some people off. You need to be flexible about payment options or you risk losing clients.

From our experience, people prefer to pay by credit card rather than check or cash, especially if they get some kind of reward on their card. The credit card also allows the client to defer payment for some time.

Most small home inspection companies don't take credit cards. It's expensive to set up, and the credit card company fees cut into your profit. Some home inspection associations facilitate credit card transactions for members. This can be a valuable service. We do take credit cards, and some people choose us entirely on that basis.

FIX MISTAKES FAST

We have found that if you make a mistake and solve the mistake to your client's satisfaction, your client will sing your praises more than if you never made the mistake in the first place!

You Will Make a Mistake

Unless you are a machine, you will make a few mistakes over time. When you do, deal with them quickly. We will discuss your approach to mistakes in more detail in Study Sessions 9 and 10, but for now let's talk about the basics. Let's say a client calls back because they have just moved in to the house and discovered a problem that you missed. Here are a few tips to approach the situation:

Tip 1: Think about it from your client's perspective. Your clients have just invested all of their money in this home and are committed to spending more than they can afford every month for the next 30 years. They might even be experiencing buyer's remorse.

To you, this is just another house. To your client, it's their home, their nest egg, their retirement, their future. It's part of who they are. To the client, the value of the house is greater than the price tag alone.

Imagine after the emotional drain of moving, that on their first day in the house, they discover a problem with the house. You now have an idea of the emotional state the client may be in.

Tip 2: Empathize with the client.   Empathizing and sympathizing are not the same. To empathize means to understand them; to sympathize means that you share their feelings and opinions. At this early stage, you want them to know that you understand completely, but you don't want to tell them that you agree with their conclusion. Notice the qualitative difference between the two:

Empathetic response: "I know how discouraged you must feel."

Sympathetic response: "I agree that the leak in your skylight presents a big problem."

In the first response, you are not providing a diagnosis of the problem over the phone, nor are you agreeing that it's a problem. You are just telling them you can understand why they feel upset. In the second response, you risk making a wrong diagnosis, alarming the client, and making a mistake.

Tip 3: Don't comment on anything until you've reread the report.   Here is a common scenario: Your clients call you on your way to an inspection and tell you they are having a problem getting fire insurance because it turns out that the house has knob and tube wiring. The clients are in a panic because the insurance company has given them three months to rewire the home. The clients got three quotes that range from $6,000 to $10,000 for rewiring. The clients say this cost was unexpected and now they are concerned that they have just purchased a "money pit."

You try to calm the client down by telling them all about knob and tube wiring. You say that it's unfortunate the insurance company is taking this position because there is nothing inherently wrong with knob and tube wiring. As long as it has not been inappropriately spliced, it's perfectly good. It does not matter that it is an ungrounded system because today most appliances are double insulated and don't need a ground connection. The only areas that really need a ground are the kitchen and a home office.

This line of reasoning is unlikely to appease the homeowner because it does not solve their problem. You give up because you have to do your next inspection and you don't really remember the house anyway. You tell them that you will call them back in the evening to discuss what can be done. The client is unhappy with your response and with you. You now have an adversarial relationship with the client.

When you get home and flip through the report, what do you find in the first paragraph of the electrical section? You see the following paragraph:

> During the inspection, we identified knob and tube wiring through-out the house. While there is nothing inherently wrong with knob and tube wiring, if it has been tampered with there is a potential safety concern. During the inspection we identified a number of areas where the knob and tube wiring was inappropriately spliced. In addition, many insurance companies will not insure a home with knob and tube wiring. You should contact your insurance company to find out what their position is on the matter and contact an electrician to quote on repairs or replacement as required.

Do you think you should have looked at the report first? You bet! You should have empathized with your client by saying something like, "I can understand how discouraged you must feel. I'd like to give this problem my full attention, so I'll call you back this evening when I get back to my office." Now you have given yourself an opportunity to reread the report, remember the home, and make a plan of attack.

If you think this scenario is contrived, that nobody would call and complain about a problem clearly identified in the report, guess again. This scenario is more common than you think, and here's why. The inspection was done about three months before your clients moved in. Neither you nor your clients remember the details. Your clients have forgotten about the knob and tube issue because they had so many other things to deal with during the transaction. They were not worried about it because the agent offered at the time to give the client a list of insurance companies that insure a home with knob and tube wiring. Finally, your inspection report is still packed in a box with just about everything else your client owns. So the clients didn't reread the report before they called you.

The bottom line is this: Empathize, but don't get into any details until you have had a chance to go through the report again.

Tip 4: Most callbacks and complaints have nothing to do with the scope of the inspection.

For example, if the client finds a problem while renovating the home, you are probably not responsible because you advised your client before the inspection that a home inspection is visual and nondestructive. Again, the client doesn't remember this. You will have to remind them. Your best strategy in this case is to diffuse the situation:

- First, empathize with the situation.
- Then, explain how these things are impossible to detect during a visual inspection.
- Tell the client that their satisfaction is your prime concern.
- Finally, ask what you can do to help.

Ask What Client Would Like You to Do

More often than not, what the client asks for is less than what you imagine. We have used this technique many times and had the client say, "I just want you to advise me on what we should do next."

If you feel that asking this question presents too much of a risk, why not qualify it? "Because inspecting the clothes washer is not part a home inspection, I don't feel that I could buy you a new one, but is there anything else I could do that would help you?" If you are still worried about an unreasonable response, offer some reasonable suggestions that you can live with and that would make your client happy.

Tip 5: Get to the house before the lawyer does.

There is usually a way to deal with a situation to everyone's satisfaction if you do it quickly. Once a lawyer is involved, it is never easy.

We will look at handling complaints in more depth later in Study Sessions 9 and 10. To summarize, the key thing is speed. It takes no more time and costs no more to handle a callback quickly than to let it drag on. And with every passing hour, your client's frustration level rises, and your chances of an amicable resolution drop. Deal with it!

BOOKING INSPECTIONS

Booking the inspection may not seem like an area that needs much discussion. Your client, or the agent, calls. You agree on a time, and the inspection is booked. The mechanics may be simple, but the phone call is a key point of contact with the public. As such, it's an opportunity to offer exceptional service. It requires a certain amount of finesse.

For instance, who answers your phone? There are four common scenarios:

1. Your company is a multi-inspector firm, and you have people at your office that answer the phone and book inspections.

2. You are the sole proprietor, and you have a spouse or answering service to answer the phone.

3. You answer calls yourself, during inspections or between inspections, using a cellular phone.

4. Your calls go directly to an answering machine for follow-up later.

Keep It Professional

We encourage you to train anyone who answers the phone for you. If your spouse answers the phone, he or she should always introduce the business name as part of the salutation. For example, "Thank you for calling Head-to-Toe inspections, how can I help you?" It's one thing for people to know you have a home office, but it's another for them to feel they've disrupted your personal life. That's how they'll feel if they hear someone at the other end of the phone say, "Hello? No, he's out, don't know when he'll be back . . . oh, excuse me—no, Bobby, you can't have another cookie!" The caller feels awkward, and you look unprofessional.

This telephone point of contact presents an opportunity to demonstrate exceptional service. For instance, you may not be able to talk to your prospects the moment they call, but you can promise to return the call within four hours. You'd have to set up a system to have your messages directed to you, wherever you are, so that you can take note of the time the call came in and know when to call back. When you return the call, before the four hours are up, your customers know you mean business.

Don't Divide Your Attention

We generally don't recommend that you take calls on your cell phone during an inspection. Why? For three good reasons:

First, you could be on the roof when a call comes in. Answering the phone while you're on the roof is dangerous.

Second, if you are in the middle of an inspection and you answer a prospect's call, you divide your attention. Think of it this way. If you've made the effort to go to a store in person, you should get the salesperson's full attention. It's annoying when the salesperson focuses on the person who has called the store with questions. Give your full attention to your client and let the prospect leave a message. When you get back to the prospect, that's when they get your full attention.

Third, the person calling in will get better service if you are focused. You will be able to schedule more confidently with your material at hand in your office than if you were lying in a crawl space. You will do a better job in the privacy of your office than with a client, real estate agent, and seller listening to your conversation.

Nothing Beats a Live Voice

Of the four options listed above, a live voice is always the best. Consider a prospect with a list of three home inspectors. The prospect calls you first but gets your voice mail. There is a good chance the prospect will hang up and call the next home inspector on the list. If they get a live voice, even from an answering service, they are more likely to leave a message and wait for your call before committing to another home inspector. Of course, having a live voice that explains your unique selling proposition (USP), showing customers the benefits of working with your firm, and that books the inspection immediately is the best of all. But this may not be possible for a new home inspection company.

KEY TERMS

empathizing and
sympathizing

inspection report
risk reversal

under-promise and
over-deliver

STUDY SESSION 4 QUICK QUIZ

You should finish Study Session 4 before doing this Quiz. Write your answers in the spaces provided. Then, check your answers in Appendix A.

1. It's better to type each inspection report from scratch than to buy a ready-made reporting system off the shelf. Your client will be impressed by your effort. Circle one.

   a. True

   b. False

2. When trying to solicit an agent to refer your services, you can reduce the agent's risk by offering to pay for his or her commission if you kill the deal. This method of risk reversal is one we recommend highly. Circle one.

   a. True

   b. False

3. Give another example of risk reversal for either a customer or a client.

   _____

   _____

4. Give an example that demonstrates the difference between empathizing and sympathizing with your client.

   _____

   _____

If you had trouble with the Quiz, reread Study Session 4 and try the Quiz again. If you did well, it's time for Study Session 5.

PRICING YOUR SERVICES

Study Session 5 addresses your inspection fee.

At the end of Study Session 5 you should be able to

■ evaluate different pricing strategies;

■ determine if an inspection fee is too low;

■ outline the steps to setting an appropriate inspection fee;

■ describe one method of raising your fee without causing sticker shock; and

■ describe a few pros and cons regarding the use of coupons, discounts, and promotions.

Study Session 5 may take you roughly 60 minutes to complete.

Pricing is a fundamental component of marketing your business. In this section we look at issues to consider when pricing your services, with emphasis on the role of pricing in your business growth strategy.

STRATEGIES AND CONSIDERATIONS

Get the Price Right

If you price your home inspection service too high, the potential client might hire your competitor. If you price your home inspection too low, you might be selling yourself short. A common solution is to charge about the same as everybody else.

This solution would be fine if you were selling something generic. For example, if a home inspection were a series of steps and observations that everyone performed in exactly the same way, there would be virtually no difference between home inspector services and home inspection companies. Your report might then look something like this:

> Dear Ms. Smith,
> Here is our inspection report for the home at 123 Anystreet.
>
> **Inspection Report**
>
> | | | |
> |---|---|---|
> | Is there a roof? | Yes ☑ | No ☐ |
> | Is there a foundation? | Yes ☑ | No ☐ |
> | Does the house have walls? | Yes ☑ | No ☐ |
> | Is there an electrical system? | Yes ☑ | No ☐ |
> | Is there a furnace? | Yes ☑ | No ☐ |
> | Does the home have indoor plumbing? | Yes ☑ | No ☐ |

Even if every inspector were trained at the same school by the same teacher and achieved the same grade as everyone else, it's unlikely each inspector would share the same skill level and experience as his or her colleagues. Until all inspections are performed exactly the same way every time and offer exactly the same products, services, and support, inspectors don't have to all charge in the same price range.

Most professional services are cloaked in mystery. The client doesn't really understand what you are doing. They've hired you because you are the expert in this field. The more you convince your client that all home inspections are not created equal, the more room there is for a variety of pricing.

Expertise Comes with Price Tag

Clients are emotionally attached to the inspection. They are buying the home in which they plan to spend their leisure time, perhaps one in which they dream of raising their children and, possibly, retiring. In other words, the client is investing more than just money in the house. Their hopes, dreams, and fears are also wrapped up in the house. But the clients themselves cannot determine the condition of the house. That's your job. And because your client doesn't know anything about houses or home inspections, you are in a position to be the expert and to let them know if their investment is sound. As with any profession, expertise comes with a price tag, and different levels of expertise mean the price tag may vary accordingly.

A useful starting point is to research what inspectors in your area are charging. The average across North America was in the neighborhood of $290 as of 2003. There is a big spread on this average, however. For example, in our market, the average fee was about $350. Once you have this information, you can pursue one of several strategies to setting your own price.

Option 1: Charge the same as everybody else. Many new inspectors choose this option because it appears to involve little risk. But there is also little to gain from this strategy. If you price your professional services in a generic way, you come across as generic.

Option 2: Charge less than everybody else. This strategy is often used for new products and services. It gives new inspectors an opportunity to break into the market. The theory is to scoop the market share and then raise your prices.

Lowering prices below your competitor's may make sense for a new product, but lower prices for a professional service sends a negative message about your service. Lower prices suggest lower-quality service. You risk a reputation as the cut-rate inspector. Even if your strategy is to raise your prices later, you may get pigeonholed as the cheap inspector before you have a chance to prove your worth. Lower prices might also suggest that you're inexperienced. New-in-the business equals lack-of-experience which, in the client's mind, equals my-house-is-sure-to-collapse-shortly-after-I-buy-it.

Many consumers who hire professional services feel that the least expensive service has nothing to compete on except price, so it is not a wise choice.

Option 3: Charge more than average. For a professional service, a strong, perceived association between price and quality suggests you should put your prices up. For example, let's assume you are planning to have laser eye surgery. Who are you going to choose to perform the surgery, the cheapest surgeon, an average-priced surgeon, or a surgeon who charges just a bit more than everyone else? Even if the most expensive surgeon didn't have a compelling reason for you to choose him or her, you might pay the premium because the price suggests high-quality service.

Have you ever been to a restaurant with someone you wanted to impress and ordered a bottle of wine based on price rather than preference? If so, this proves that price does suggest quality.

Another strategic pricing issue is whether to charge a flat rate or use a price matrix. Some home inspection companies charge a flat rate regardless of the home size or age. The benefit of flat-rate pricing is that it's simple for your clients to understand. The rationale for this strategy is that even on a very large home, there is only one electrical system, one heating system, and so on. The actual open space in the home doesn't take much incremental time to inspect within a reasonable size range. Furthermore, on average, your time works out pretty evenly spread across many homes. Some houses take more time, and some take less time.

Flat-rate pricing might work in an area where you don't typically see many very large homes, or very old homes, but for most home inspectors, some kind of price matrix makes more sense for two reasons:

1. Big homes do take longer. In our area, most homes that are over 5,000 square feet will have two heating systems and two or three electrical breaker panels. In addition, there will be three to five bathrooms instead of one or two. And frankly, it does take more time to inspect 4,000 square feet of roof than 1,000 square feet.

2. Old homes take longer. Many home inspectors charge more for a home that is older than 25 or 50 years. There are more renovations, additions, wear and tear, and mixing and matching of different systems.

Even if the possibility of charging more does not interest you, once you get fully booked, you will recognize that the additional time on the larger and older homes will throw off your schedule, often making you late for the next inspection. From a scheduling perspective alone, you need to know the age and size of the home.

Two additional areas where you may want to charge more are

1. multi-unit residences, and

2. areas far from your territory, especially if there is nobody else servicing those areas.

There are other ways to set your fee. Many home inspection companies set their fee based on the selling price of the house. Because the scale is rough, people don't perceive that you are charging more just because they are buying an expensive house. The rationale is that a more expensive home in a given area is going to be larger. Further, many homebuyers don't know how many square feet the home is, so purchase price may be a better indicator than size in determining an appropriate fee.

For many years, Carson Dunlop based the inspection fee on the purchase price of the home. The price schedule looked like this:

- Homes under $350,000 were a flat fee of $350.
- Homes over $350,000 to $400,000 were a flat fee of $425.

This turned out to be a very good price matrix. We almost never ran into scheduling problems, and the fee was almost always justified by the size of the home. Occasionally we got into a home that was very expensive based on the location, but was actually a very small home. In this case, we would reduce the fee. We did this without a hitch for almost 20 years, with regular increases in fees and adjustment of the schedule.

More recently, we received some feedback from the real estate community who felt we were penalizing their wealthy clients. We had little choice but to change the price matrix to reflect the number of square feet.

Our biggest objection to the price-based-on-square-feet approach was many clients didn't know how many square feet the house was. Often we would arrive at an inspection to find that the 1,500 square foot home was actually 1,500 square feet per floor, not to mention that it had three stories plus a basement. While it's easy to reduce a fee on site, it's almost impossible to raise the fee on site!

If people don't know how many square feet the house is, we ask the following questions and make a best guess:

- Is it a big house or a little house?
- How many floors?
- How many bedrooms?
- How many bathrooms?
- Is the house as wide as it is long?

You can usually get a rough idea of square feet with this information. If a client says, "I think it's 1,500 square feet, but it has three bathrooms and five bedrooms and three stories," you might guess that it's 1,500 square feet per floor.

Our price matrix has looked like this:

For a single family home, or duplex, under 20 years old:

- Under 3,000 square feet—$380
- 3,000–4,500 square feet—$440
- 4,500–8,000 square feet—$600
- Over 8,000 square feet—$900

For a single family home, or duplex, over 20 years old (reducing the square foot break points):

- Under 2,500 square feet—$380
- 2,500–3,500 square feet—$440
- 3,500–5,000 square feet—$600
- Over 5,000 square feet—$900

A minimum charge for a three-unit residence—$430

A minimum charge for a four-unit residence—$600

As you can see, there are many ways to break down your fee. One strategy may make more sense than another in your area. Either way, the first thing you should do is find out how much other inspectors are charging.

Advantage to
Staged Pricing

Staged pricing allows you to quote a base fee that sounds reasonable. As you get more details, the price may increase, but by then you often have the client committed to your benefits. If your high fee prevents people from calling you in the first place, you won't have a chance to win them over.

PRICE COMPLAINTS

Have you ever had anyone tell you that your rates are too high? If you haven't, then you are definitely under priced!

If you experience no resistance from your prospective clients about your inspection fee, you are probably selling yourself short. Here is another way to look at it: If you fear losing business and risking complaints, offer your inspection service for free. You will get lots of business volume, and you won't get any complaints about your price. This example of selling yourself short might seem obvious, but you may be doing exactly the same thing to a lesser extent at $250. This concept is hard to grasp until you take the leap of faith and raise your prices. Strangely, we struggle with this every time we raise our prices, but every time we raise them, no one notices! And what's the worst case? You may do fewer inspections for more money and enjoy more free time without losing money.

In Study Session 6 of Section II, you will learn to handle price objections from your prospects. In the mean time, track how many of your prospects complain about your inspection fee or don't hire you because you are too expensive.

Some say that unless you have a complaint rate on pricing of about 15 percent to 20 percent, your fees are too low. They say that 10 percent of the people will complain regardless of the price. So add a little more (5 percent to 10 percent) to make sure you are not selling yourself short.

And remember, even if you lose business by raising your prices, you probably are further ahead because you will be doing fewer inspections at a higher price.

RAISING YOUR PRICES

*Don't Grow by
Doing More*

Raise Your Prices

*Keep Up With
Inflation*

This section assumes that you have already started your business. The quickest and most effective way to bring your business up a notch is to raise your prices.

Most people picture that growing their business means doing more inspections per day and, consequently, more inspections per year. Others grow their business by hiring and training other inspectors (multi-inspector firm). While these two examples may seem like the most reasonable ways of growing your business, guess again. They are the most difficult way to achieve your growth goal.

But what if you don't want to hire other inspectors, and you'd rather not do three inspections per day, six days a week? How can you grow your business, while maintaining little or no staff, and ensuring yourself a sane workweek? Simple: by raising your prices. As a one-person outfit, you have limited resources. Once you are booked, that's it! There's no one else to do other inspections while you go to a different job site. One good way to grow your business is to raise your prices. In fact, raising your prices may be a better way to achieve your growth goals no matter how you have configured your company.

Inflation is another reason to raise your prices. If you keep your prices static, you will make less and less over time simply because you are not keeping up with inflation. That's no way to reward experience! Furthermore, if you have staff, you can bet they will want raises. And other costs of your business, such as your car and your communications infrastructure, will also increase over time.

Pricing Versus Volume

Ratchet Up Your Prices

*Several Small
Increases Best*

*Work Less,
Earn More*

The question that inevitably gets raised is, "If I raise my prices, won't I lose clients?" Yes. But you should do it anyway and here's why!

Let's say you raise your prices and your business volume decreases by 20 percent. Guess what? You now have one day in five to do more marketing, sales, and promotion. In short order, your business volume will be back up to where it was before, only now your are making more money for your time. The process can then repeat itself. You will be using what's called a **ratcheting technique** to grow your business.

The premise is simple: Increase prices and business volume decreases. Market yourself well and business volume increases. Increase your prices again and so on.

In the sales and public relations discussion on Study Session 6 of Section II, you'll learn techniques that get sales volume back up quickly. But be warned, you may not have a chance to practice these techniques because increasing your prices does not always reduce your business volume!

We have found that raising our prices twice a year by a small amount is less likely to raise eyebrows than making one big increase every two or three years. It is easy to defend small increases as inflationary adjustments. It's much harder to explain a big increase. The argument that you have not raised prices for a long time and have fallen behind makes you sound like a poor businessperson at best, and less than honest at worst.

If you're now thinking, "I can't afford to spend one day in five marketing," think of it this way: Whether you choose to spend one day in five growing the business is up to you. But guess what? You have lost 20 percent of your business volume, yet you're probably making as much, or more, money than you were before because you are getting paid more for each inspection!

How much business volume do you have to lose before you are worse off than before you raised your prices? Let's look at a dramatic example.

This simple calculation gives you a general idea of what's at stake.

Let's say you presently do 400 inspections per year. You charge $250. What does the company gross? 400 × $250 = $100,000. That's great, why would we mess with that?

Let's assume you raise your price by 20%. Let's further assume that you lose 20% of your business volume as a result, and you never grow back to your original business volume.

Your new fee is $300, and your new business volume is 320 inspections. You now gross 320 × $300, which is $96,000.

Well, you are $4,000 short this year, but you are only working four days a week! You are working 80% as hard for 96% of the revenue. And your overhead went down because you are only producing 80% as many reports.

Here are a few other things to consider regarding the calculation in the example above: If you factor in your company's overhead and other costs, the calculation becomes even more dramatic in favor of raising your prices. A calculation done by accounting firm Vine and Partners, LLP, suggests that if your margin is 60 percent (meaning 40 percent of your income goes towards expenses, which is typical for the home inspection business), then you could raise your prices by 20 percent, decrease your sales volume by 25 percent, and still break even. If your margin is 40 percent (not unreasonable for a multi-inspector firm), you could raise your prices by 20 percent, decrease sales volume by 33 percent, and still break even.

If you are worried about the **sticker shock** of raising your prices by 20 percent, you don't have to raise them all at once. For instance, if you phase in the price increase over the course of a year, you will not lose a significant amount of sales volume.

Price Elasticity

Price elasticity of demand (or, price elasticity, for short) refers to the change in the number of units sold when the price of a product or service changes. This equation is based on the consumer's sensitivity to the price of a product or service. For example, if a box of cereal is $2.95 and you sell two million units per year, what would you expect to happen to the number of units sold per year if you increase or decrease the price by a dollar? That depends.

If the price increases, and unit sales decrease, it is an elastic price. If the price increases and the unit sales don't decrease dramatically, it is an **inelastic price.**

The price elasticity of demand is high when there are many equivalent options for purchase. This is true of commodities like bread, milk, heating oil, electricity, and gasoline for example, especially where the features and benefits are uniform, and consumers don't perceive a difference in value between one product and another. For instance, if a box of a certain cereal costs $2.95 at one store and the same cereal costs $1.95 at the store next door, the cheaper box will sell more units.

For your purposes, if you raise your inspection fee by 20 percent, what do you think would happen to your sales volume?

For a professional service, or for anything where there are intangibles, the price elasticity of demand tends to be inelastic. A home inspection service, as we have discussed, is an intangible purchase because it is difficult for the client to compare one inspector to another while talking to them on the phone.

Prestige Pricing

Prestige pricing refers to a strategy that convinces a client that a product or service is as high quality as the price tag suggests. This strategy is also called price signaling. The price signals the quality. Even if the quality of a product is low, the high price encourages people to buy it anyway. Cosmetics present the classic example for price signaling. Inexpensive cosmetics don't sell well. If you make cosmetics, don't worry about who or what it was tested on, just make it expensive and it will sell!

Every marketing textbook has the story about the store that can't unload their overstock of widgets. They are priced to sell but no one will buy them. Due to a miscommunication between management and staff, an employee raises the price of the widgets by 50 percent. Suddenly they start selling like hotcakes.

In the home inspection industry, the combination of prestige pricing and the inspection's highly intangible nature means the demand is not only inelastic, but sometimes, there is an inverse relationship between price and business volume. Depending on where you sit in the market, you may find that raising your prices *increases* your business volume.

Agent Reaction To Price Increases

Prospective customers don't generally have a problem with inspectors raising their prices periodically. Our experience, however, shows that some real estate agents react with temporary sticker-shock each time inspectors raise their prices. Although your prospective clients won't perceive anything out of the ordinary in your pricing (because they have never had a home inspection before), the agents know how much you charged previously.

The agents like to look good to their client. If the agent refers a home inspection company, and the client finds out that a different company charges $50 less, the client might wonder why the agent did not tell them about that option. The agent wants to be the one who gets a good deal for their clients on all fronts related to the house transaction.

Keep Your Agent in the Loop

The agent looks uninformed and sloppy if they tell their client that you charge $275 and you subsequently tell the client the price is actually $300. The agent's frustration with you is understandable. They are trying to look well connected and on top of the transaction. If you don't keep the agents up to date, you have hurt their ego, and possibly their pocketbook, if they lose the client's confidence. It's an issue of trust.

Keep Agents' Perspective in Mind

Educate the agent about your pricing. Remember, agents don't have to think in terms of increasing their fee because they generally get paid a percentage of the selling price. This pricing strategy guarantees that they always stay in step with inflation. In addition, though their commission is negotiable, the range is more or less within an industry standard. In short, agents do not function in the same world or in the same way as professional service providers who compete with other professional service providers. They don't rely on pricing strategies as a marketing tool that gets them a bigger piece of the pie. Some real estate organizations do use reduced rates as their marketing strategy. But these companies are the exception rather than the rule.

Whatever the cause of the backlash over prices from the agents, experience shows that it's temporary. If the agents are loyal, and are referring business to you, they will continue to do so in spite of your increased fees, as long as you keep them in the loop.

Experiment with Pricing

Why not experiment with increasing your prices? You have little to lose and a whole lot to gain. You can always go back to your original pricing, but you'll never know what it's like to earn more and work less, unless you raise your prices. But don't forget to keep everyone in the loop, except, of course, your prospective client. They didn't know what you charged before, so why inform them of a price increase?

COUPONS, DISCOUNTS, AND SPECIAL PROMOTIONS

Attract Customers with Incentives?

What's a good way to get people to use your service? How about offering a coupon or a discount? This promotional strategy comes so easily and quickly to mind that many home inspectors print coupons and distribute them without thinking of the downside to this practice.

Experience shows that coupons and discounts are not always a good strategy for inducing people to try your service. The losses may outweigh any perceived gains.

In this section we will

- define some terms and concepts,
- outline the theory of coupons and discounts,
- give you arguments for and against using coupons and discounts, and
- tell you how to do it right, if you decide to use them.

Definitions

Discounts, coupons, and sales are short-term incentives designed to increase sales. In general, a coupon provides a financial incentive for someone to choose you rather than the competition.

Discounts, coupons, and sales are all forms of **promotion.** A promotion can be price-based or non price-based. A price-based promotion refers to a coupon, discount, or sale. A non price-based promotion may be a contest or prize.

Front End or Back End?

A promotion can be front-end loaded or back-end loaded. A front-end loaded promotion for a home inspection would be something like a discount on the home inspection. A back-end loaded promotion would be something like a discount on a follow-up service, if the client first hires you to do the inspection at the regular price.

Theory and Practice

Promotions are designed to increase sales by

■ increasing existing customer loyalty. For instance, offer the customer what's called in-pack coupons. When the loyal customer purchases your product, they get a coupon for the next purchase. This strategy reinforces the buying behavior.

■ inducing customers to buy a larger volume. We have all heard of this strategy: Buy one and get a second one at half the price.

■ encouraging the customer to buy now. If there is a chance that the customer may need it in the future, they may choose to buy it now rather than later, if you offer a rebate with an expiration date.

■ persuading the customer to "choose me." A discount coupon might achieve this goal.

■ encouraging a potential customer to try your product or service. A free sample or a discount coupon would achieve this goal.

■ relationship building. You can build relationships by offering a prize or a sponsorship to a real estate office.

Coupons, Discounts, Sales Are Incentives

Theoretically, coupons are an inducement for someone to try something that he or she, after having tried it, will buy over and over again. The coupon is designed for things that are purchased frequently. A good example is a box of cereal. Because you get a discount coupon, you decide to give it a try. After trying it, you decide you like it and continue to buy it on a regular basis. In the case of cereal, the coupon achieves its desired effect. The cereal company makes up the coupon money on the repeat sales. Nobody expects that if they have a coupon for one box of cereal today that they should always get the same discount tomorrow.

Don't Choose on Familiarity

Many home inspectors offer discounts and coupons because it's a familiar marketing strategy. The two-for-one sale, on items ranging from oranges to jeans, has become a marketing standard. Because, as consumers, this is the kind of marketing we are exposed to, it's one of the first approaches we think of for our own businesses. We figure if it works for Nike, a company full of smart marketing talent, it should work for us.

In the world of retail, coupons are a good system for the following reasons:

■ The coupon acts as an advertisement for a company.

■ The coupon is focused; it goes directly to the person that is about to use a similar product.

■ The coupon can easily be tracked; the retailer knows if the coupon is doing its job.

These strategies do work in some situations, but it's important to know that they were never designed for a professional service, and they were definitely not designed for home inspections.

The theory of coupons does not apply to home inspections because people may get only one or two inspections in a lifetime. You are unlikely to make up the money in the long run from repeat business from the buyers. (One solution is to raise your prices and offer a discount to put you back where you were!)

Give Coupons to Agents

In the home inspection business, it's more effective to give the coupons to the real estate professionals that refer business to you for the following reasons:

■ It's too expensive to get the coupons in the hands of potential buyers when you consider the cost of distributing the coupons (delivering them to the buyers) plus the face value of the coupons.

■ The agents get a benefit from being able to pass a discount along to their client.

■ If you give the coupon to agents, it reminds them to refer you.

Arguments for Using Coupons

The coupon is a strategy for soliciting real estate agents. Practically speaking, you will need to go to real estate offices, offer the agent your coupons and suggest they consider referring you. If you are unknown to the agent, this approach alone will not necessarily induce the agent to recommend you.

But you can avoid promotional pitfalls while introducing agents to your business by framing your discount as a special promotion. For example, you can donate a free inspection as a prize

■ at a real estate office golf tournament,

■ to the month's top producer at a real estate office, or

■ in recognition for having referred 30 buyers to you this year.

In exchange for referring a large amount of their business to you, give the agents some discount coupons for their clients. The agent then gives the coupon to their clients, along with a recommendation. The client calls and hires you to do the inspection.

Arguments Against Coupons and Other Promotions

Coupons Can Devalue Your Service

Consider the long-term effect of coupon use. A coupon will eventually devalue your service by the value of the coupon. Here's how.

Let's assume you give coupons only to your best agents. Other agents will hear about it and ask, "Why can't I have coupons for my clients?" Real estate professionals have weekly meetings, and they discuss business with other agents. They have few secrets from each other. If you are giving coupons to your best agents, you will have to give coupons to all agents or risk a backlash.

If you give coupons to all agents, you will now be doing all your inspections for your regular fee, less the coupon value. You have just devalued your business by the value of the coupon.

Coupons Cause Sticker Shock

What happens after your promotion has expired? The same thing that happens when you raise your prices. Your agents will experience sticker shock. In fact, the sticker shock is much worse after a coupon promotion ends than when you raise your prices. Even though you are not raising your prices so much as returning to your regular price (which is now the cost of the inspection without the value of the coupon), what the agent experiences is not only a perceived higher price but also the loss of an incentive to give to their client.

Coupons May Not Be Worth Aggravation

The bottom line is, once you start using coupons, you've set up an expectation and practice that you might find yourself stuck with for good. In the short term, you could counteract sticker shock by setting your fee $50 higher than you actually want to charge and then give a coupon for a $50 discount. In the long term, however, this approach is counterproductive because clients and agents probably perceive the coupon as a price ruse anyway, and that your fee is inflated in order to accommodate the coupon. If you give a coupon to everyone, you may as well be charging your regular price.

Coupons and Discounts May Send Wrong Message

When a consumer buys a box of cereal with a discount coupon, they don't think the cereal is inferior in any way. A professional service, however, especially one that a consumer purchases once in a lifetime, may appear inferior if a discount strategy comes attached. You create a mindset that would not otherwise have been there. For instance, your client's unspoken thoughts might be, "You are not worth $350, but for $300 should I hire you?"

Another loss you may not have counted on is the loss of your referring agent. Although the coupon might have induced an agent to try you out, once the coupon is gone, the agent might go, too. The agent has relatively little invested in the coupon because it's not his or her money being spent on the inspection. The only benefit to the agent is that the coupon helps the agent look good when he or she gives it to the client.

Tips for Optimizing Coupons and Discounts

If you're still committed to some kind of discount strategy, back-ended promotions are a better way to go. Here are examples:

- Give a coupon to your client for a discount on a follow-up inspection. You will come back in six months or a year to update your report and to verify that the suggested improvements were done properly. This is a good back-end strategy that does not devalue your professional service.

- It would be unethical to give a kickback to a real estate agent for referring business to you, but it's not unethical to give something to one of your clients for referring business to you. It could be something small like a box of chocolates, movie tickets, or a lottery ticket. If you don't want to do this, at the very least, you should ask your current clients to refer business to you. Why? Most people buying a new house also have friends who are buying, or thinking of buying, a house. If your client is happy with your service, they are usually more than happy to refer you to their friends, but they sometimes have to be reminded. A short note to your client might do the trick, with or without an inducement. The note might read, "Our business is successful because satisfied clients refer us to their friends. If you have a friend who is buying a home, or thinking of buying a home, please pass on our business card. We will do our utmost to make sure your friend is as satisfied with their inspection as you have been with yours."

- Discount coupons to real estate agents could be made more effective by offering one discount coupon for every ten inspections they refer to you. This strategy is less likely to devalue your inspection fee, and you could offer it to any agent that wants to participate. The downside is you will have to carefully track every inspection referred by each agent.

To Coupon or Not to Coupon

It's not a decision to be made lightly. Once you start using coupons as a marketing strategy, it's hard to stop. It seems to please real estate professionals on one hand but

- if an agent is going to refer you because they have a $50 coupon to give to a client, what's to stop your competitor from offering a $55 coupon?

- because your service is devalued by the face value of the coupon, you would have likely done just as well by reducing your fee and selling your service as the reasonably priced alternative to your competitor. The strategy will save you the cost and aggravation of the coupon, both in terms of financial outlay and the spiraling effect of coupon psychology that does not, ultimately, work for a service-based offering.

- once your business is well established, you will have a loyal following. Because these loyal customers will refer you with or without a coupon, why get them stuck on a coupon?

KEY TERMS

discounts, coupons, and sales

elastic price

inelastic price

prestige pricing

price elasticity of demand

promotion

ratcheting technique

sticker shock

STUDY SESSION 5 QUICK QUIZ

You should finish Study Session 5 before doing this Quiz. Write your answers in the spaces provided. Then, check your answers in Appendix A.

1. When you first start out, setting your prices lower than your competitor's ensures that you capture the market. Circle one.

    a. True

    b. False

2. You can grow your business by doing less work and charging more. Circle one.

    a. True

    b. False

3. When you increase your prices, your sales will decrease. Describe the process of ratcheting up your prices as a business growth strategy. In other words, how can you raise your prices without losing sales volume in the long run?

    _____

    _____

    _____

4. All products and services have a price elasticity of demand. If the price increases and unit sales decrease, the price is elastic. If the price increases and the unit sales don't decrease dramatically, the price is inelastic. Is the demand for building inspection pricing elastic or inelastic?

    _____

    _____

    _____

5. Prestige pricing (Circle one.)

    a. suggests your product or service is high quality.

    b. signals a product priced out of anyone's range.

    c. refers to your competitor's price.

    d. decreases sticker shock.

6. In order to avoid sticker shock, it's better not to tell your referring agent when you raise your prices. Circle one.

    a. True

    b. False

7. If you decide to use coupons, you should distribute them to (Circle one.)

    a. your entire neighborhood.

    b. your referring agent.

    c. all your clients.

    d. your family and friends only.

If you had trouble with the Quiz, reread Study Session 5 and try the Quiz again. If you did well, it's time for Study Session 6.

MARKETING FOR GROWTH

Study Session 6 deals with the three ways to grow your home inspection business. You need to know these strategies before you can effectively decide on an overall growth strategy for your business.

LEARNING OBJECTIVES

At the end of Study Session 6 you should be able to

■ illustrate three ways to grow your business;

■ describe in one sentence the advantage to developing a back-end to your business;

■ outline three follow-up strategies;

■ list at least three ancillary services you could offer to diversify your home inspection business; and

■ list at least three extra services you could offer at the time of the inspection.

Study Session 6 may take you roughly 60 minutes to complete.

In this section we will look at growth from a marketing perspective. That is, what strategies and tactics should you pursue to reach more customers and make more money?

THREE WAYS TO GROW YOUR BUSINESS

At first glance, **business growth** might seem to be a daunting task. There are so many strategies to choose from. The sheer size of the task may paralyze you.

The good news is there are only three ways to grow your business. All marketing strategies and sales campaigns are just subsets of these three strategies.

The three strategies are as follows:

1. Increase the number of customers and clients.
2. Increase your fee.
3. Sell more services to each client.

The following sections provide a brief overview of these three strategies.

Increase the Number of Customers and Clients

This strategy includes

- finding new customers and clients,
- getting more people to refer clients to you,
- increasing retention rate of your referral base,
- improving sales techniques (increasing your conversion rate),
- diversification (thinking outside of the box for new inspection opportunities), and
- other strategies.

New Customers Only Part of Puzzle

This is the conventional way to grow a business. Because I need more sales, I will go and find more **customers** and clients. But this is the most difficult and expensive way to grow a business. You should do this, particularly when you are just starting out, but do not only this. Focusing on getting repeat business with an established customer, for example, is an efficient way to grow your business. There are other strategies that you can combine with this to build real strength into your company. We will explore some of these later in this session.

The next two strategies are more cost-effective ways to grow your business, yet they are overlooked by most home inspectors.

Increase Your Fee

We have talked about this already, but let's touch on it one more time. It's so easy, but so few do it. Nothing seems to scare home inspectors more than increasing their fees. The inspectors immediately imagine that nobody will want to hire them at a higher price and that they will lose much of their business to competitors.

But the following cannot be overstated: Demanding progressively more for your professional service is a highly effective way to grow your business.

Because we have already looked at how to set your inspection fee and how to raise your prices, we won't go through it again here. To summarize, here are some good reasons to raise your fee:

- There is a strong perceived relationship between inspection fee and quality of the inspector.

- If you have not changed your fee in a long time, you are effectively gaining more and more experience while getting paid less and less money over the years.

- You should keep up with **inflation.** This means raising your fee every year just to keep up. If you have been in business for five years and have never increased your price, you are likely making effectively $20 to $25 less per inspection than when you started.

- Your employees want more money.

- You can work less and make more money.

- You are in the knowledge and communication business, not the assembly line business. This means you should get paid for what you know, not how long you work. So when someone says you shouldn't raise your prices because your inspections don't take any longer than they used to, you can say that you know more than you used to know and are more valuable to your clients now.

Don't sell yourself short. You owe it to yourself to get paid what you are worth. Every day you pull off the impossible. Think about it: Home inspection is a business with unusually high liability, slim profit margins and limited economies of scale. We provide an incredibly diverse, multi-disciplined consulting service, under difficult in-field circumstances, in an impossibly short time frame, and we produce extraordinarily detailed technical reports, almost instantly.

Sell More Services to Each Client

This strategy may include

Sell More than Home Inspection

- additional services at the time of the inspection, like testing for lead paint, radon, asbestos, or carbon monoxide. This is called "upselling" or "cross selling."

- follow-up services once your client moves in, including an inspection to verify that your recommendations have been addressed correctly, or perhaps an indoor air-quality inspection

This is equivalent to the innocent question at the fast food outlet, "And would you like fries with that?" Upselling and cross selling are everywhere. At the carwash, have you ever been asked if you want the hot wax too?

If you can offer other inspection related services with your home inspection, you may find your revenues increase dramatically. When booking the home inspection, you might offer a water-quality test if the home has a well, a septic tank inspection, indoor air-quality test, swimming pool or spa inspection, and so on.

BRAINSTORMING AND EVALUATING YOUR GROWTH MARKETING

How do you generate your unique marketing strategies from the three main strategies?

Be Creative

Categorizing all marketing strategies into three general categories is not intended to limit your imagination. In fact, it should do quite the opposite; it should make you more creative. Use the categories as jumping off places. For instance, you don't have to list just strategies that you think are consistent with the category headings. You can brainstorm strategies that fly in the face of the main category suggestions. For example, don't get stuck thinking you have to find strategies to increase the number of customers you have. You also have to think about the strategies that will keep the customers you already have. At the end of the day, your brainstorm may generate ideas that are just plain bad, but cracking your imagination open to good ideas means you will be letting in the bad ones, too. And who knows, even the bad ideas may have a kernel of something brilliant.

Remember the following in your business growth brainstorming session:

- To brainstorm effectively, you need to write down ideas as they come to mind regardless of how ridiculous they seem.

- Have a separate brainstorming session for each of the three categories of business growth—increase number of customer transactions, increase your fee, and sell more services to each client.

Look at Each Idea Critically

Cost-Benefit Analysis

Once you have brainstormed and come up with a few dozen ideas to grow your business, it's time to evaluate each strategy.

To evaluate a marketing strategy effectively, compare the cost to the benefit. You are looking for the best return on investment possible. For instance, you need to know how much you can spend to acquire a new customer. How much can you spend to acquire a homebuyer? Not much. As we discussed earlier, there is not enough money in a single transaction to justify a substantial marketing effort targeted directly at the homebuyer. How much can you spend to acquire a new agent to refer business to you? Remember, the agent may refer many clients to you.

Value of Referral Source

How much is an agent worth to you? It's a good idea to do a rough calculation to find out how much you stand to gain from acquiring the customer (in this case the real estate agent). To do this you need to find out how much they are worth over a lifetime of business transactions. This calculation is called the "net worth" or "marginal net worth" or "life cycle value" of the customer. No matter what you call it, it is the profit that customer brings to your business over the whole term of the relationship.

Let's see if we can figure it out with an example using a hypothetical inspection company. We'll start with the following assumptions and one or two pieces of advice:

- Let's assume you think it makes sense to work with real estate agents.

- Let's assume you are going to focus on building relationships with top-producing agents who work primarily with buyers rather than sellers.

- Let's assume that a top agent refers 20 clients a year to a home inspection company, and that 15 of the clients get an inspection with that company.

- Let's assume that the average relationship between an agent and an inspection company is four years.

- And lastly, let's assume that the average inspection fee is $350 and the average profit is 20 percent or $70 per inspection.

We now have enough information to determine the net worth or life cycle value of one real estate agent to this hypothetical inspection company. We will make a profit of $70 per inspection times 15 inspections per year times four years = $4,200 from this relationship. We now know the benefit of a relationship to this company.

Now let's look at the cost. The question is, how much should the company invest to establish the relationship? In theory, they could invest $4,199 and be ahead of the game. But because we spend that money up front, and it takes four years to get $4,200, that seems like a bad deal. Every company will look at this slightly differently, but it seems reasonable to invest $2,000 to acquire a $4,200 profit. This represents a return on investment of over 100 percent ($4,200 ÷ $2,000) over four years. The $2,000 investment in the first year provides a return of over 25 percent per year for four years.

This seems strange. Do inspection companies really invest up to $2,000 to establish a relationship with one real estate agent? Well, let's look a little closer. The company will probably not be successful in establishing a relationship with every agent they contact. In fact, the company might only set up a relationship with one agent for every 20 they contact. This means that the $2,000 is invested in 20 agents, averaging $100 per agent.

If the assumptions are all true, we can spend up to $100 in marketing to every top-producing agent in the market. This is invaluable information because it allows the company to know what the return on investment is. They have done a cost benefit analysis and can set their marketing budget accordingly. The $100 per agent can be spent a number of ways, and good companies will experiment with different methods to try to improve the conversion rate of agents and to extend the length of the relationship. They may also invest more in agents who produce more than 15 referrals in a year.

Hard Costs and Soft Costs

The hard costs and soft costs should be included in any cost calculation. The hard costs for mailers, lunch bills, and so on, are easy to calculate. The soft costs—for the inspector's time for example—are harder to calculate. Most home inspectors don't recognize this cost because it does not show up on their financial statements. That's because the cost is what we call "opportunity cost."

Account for Opportunity Cost

An opportunity cost may be the soft cost of your time. When you take the time to meet with a real estate agent, you might have been doing an inspection instead. Your opportunity cost is the money you could have made while doing an inspection, for example. From now on, when you evaluate marketing strategies, factor in an opportunity cost. For many, this is roughly $30 per hour. Let's look at where that number comes from.

Again we will make some assumptions. Let's assume your goal is to take a salary of $60,000 out of the company. If you work 40 hours a week for 52 weeks a year, that is 2,080 working hours per year. If you earn $30 per hour, your annual salary would be ($30 per hour × 2,080 hours) $62,400. In the example above we allowed $100 per agent on average. This would include the $30 per hour soft cost or opportunity cost for your time.

The numbers are not as important as the concept in the example above. If you can train yourself to think in these terms when it comes to marketing, you will be better prepared for success.

For every idea that your brainstorming session generated, go through a cost-benefit analysis, such as the one in our example, and decide whether it is worth pursuing. In many cases you will have to make assumptions. That is part of the business world—you have to make decisions with less than complete information.

Brainstorm a Second Time

Once you have evaluated each idea in your first brainstorming session, it's time to brainstorm again. The goal of this second session is to see if ideas spawn other ideas or subsets of the ones in the first brainstorm session. You'll be surprised how many ideas you can generate from just three strategies!

SPECIFIC BUSINESS GROWTH STRATEGIES

This section covers some examples of specific strategies that take advantage of one of the three main strategies we listed:

1. Increase the number of customers.
2. Increase your fee.
3. Sell more services to each client.

More strategies will be covered in the sales and advertising discussion in Section II.

Follow-Up Marketing

Maintain Existing Customers

This strategy is a subset of getting more clients, but with a twist. **Follow-up marketing** relies on the business concept that it's cheaper to maintain a customer than it is to find a new one. For example, the cost to acquire a new agent to refer business to you is significant. The cost to maintain a relationship is less, but there is a cost. Many home inspectors fail to see this, and, as a result, relationships fail. Agents drift away often from sheer neglect. Many inspectors spend no time nurturing the relationship. This nurturing may be as simple as saying, "Thank you for the referral."

Hard to Fill Leaky Bucket

It may be helpful to look at business relationships this way. If you are adding new relationships into the top of the bucket, while neglected relationships are leaking out the bottom, you are working hard to maintain a half-full bucket. We have said it takes more money and time to develop a new relationship than to maintain an existing one, so doesn't it make sense to spend some time maintaining relationships?

Many inspectors proudly point out the ten new relationships they have developed, but fail to notice the 15 agents who have stopped referring them. This is no way to grow a business. And that's why follow-up marketing is so important.

Follow-Up Letter to Agents

One follow-up strategy is to write a letter to the agent. The inspector collects the agent's business card at the beginning of the inspection. If the inspector has not met the agent before, the inspector sends a quick letter to the agent after the inspection. You might develop some postcards for this purpose. It takes the inspector about a minute at the end of the inspection to fill out and mail a postcard to the agent. The postcard may say something like, "It was a pleasure to meet you at 123 Any Street yesterday. Please call me to help your next clients (or, I look forward to working with you again soon). Sincerely, Inspector." This strategy is cheap, quick, and has an impact.

Follow-Up Call to Agents

You can also follow up by phone. Follow-up calls to agents fall into two categories: (1) agents who refer you business and, (2) agents who used to refer you business but no longer do. Let's look at each case.

*Agents Who Refer
Business to You*

Call the agent periodically to find out if your services continue to be satisfactory. You don't have to call them after every inspection, just periodically. You can start by saying, "Thanks very much for referring Mr. Jones to us." Then you can ask the following:

- "Are you happy with the home inspection service?"
- "Are you happy with my answering service?"
- "What kind of feedback do you get from your clients about the home inspection?"

If you are brave, you can also ask what you could do to serve them better, although you always risk having to deal with an unreasonable request. You can make this decision on a case-by-case basis.

*Initiative as Important
as Content*

Most inspectors don't like to phone agents for fear that the agent may have something negative to say about how the inspector handled the inspection. This fear is understandable because we often have to take a stand on unpopular issues. The fear may be well founded, but the logic is not. You should phone regardless of how you think the agent will respond because the gesture is at least as important as the content of the call. The agent will recognize that you made an effort.

In order to put your fears to rest, think of it this way—there are only two possibilities:

1. The agent has good things to say, and your call reinforces your relationship.
2. The agent has negative things to say, and you now have an opportunity to mend the relationship. If you are unsuccessful, you will be no further behind. So it's a win-win decision. And even if you can't salvage the relationship, you can learn something from the experience that can be applied in future situations.

*Agents Who Used to
Refer Business*

*Answers Are a
Phone Call Away*

At Carson Dunlop we keep track of agents by using a database. The database tells us who refers business to us and who does not.

What do we do with this information? We identify agents who send us less business than they used to. This allows us to follow up with them. If you are an independent inspector, you may not have the benefit of a database. How else can you find out this information? There is a great low-tech way to gather information—make a phone call to the agent.

We call agents who have stopped sending us business and ask them why. Most of you are now thinking, "That's not a call I want to make." None of us likes making that call. But do it anyway. Why? Because there is no downside. You can't get any worse than an agent not sending you any business. You should look at this call as an opportunity.

You can start the call with, "I'm calling because we have not heard from you lately and we were concerned. Are you all right? (You may find out that they in fact have had to step away from their business for some reason.) If they say they are alright, you can say, "I hope we have not done anything to lose your confidence in us." If not, they will say why they have not referred as many clients to you. They may be concentrating on getting listings, for example.

If they have had a problem with you, it is great to find out about it so you can clear it up or fix the problem. We have found that often it is something as simple as another home inspector seemed to value their relationship more than we did. The agent felt neglected and unappreciated. Or perhaps the agent feels you caused a client to back away from a deal unnecessarily. No matter what, this is a chance to set things right.

What's the lesson here? No matter how many scenarios you invent for the dreaded call, there is only one that includes the agent never wanting to do business with you again. There are many more possibilities that could result in a relationship that is even stronger than before.

*Make a
Check-Up Call*

It may seem like these calls take a lot of work and time, but they provide great value. It does not take much time, and the opportunity cost is minimal compared to how difficult it is to acquire a new referring agent. It's a competitive market out there. You need to keep your referral base intact.

*Following Up
with Clients*

You may want to follow up with clients as well as agents. You have already done the inspection, why should you stay in touch with previous clients? There are at least three reasons:

1. To capture repeat business when the homeowner buys another house in five years
2. To remind the homeowner to tell their friends to hire you when they buy a house
3. To keep you in the forefront of the client's mind so that they are more receptive when you call to offer follow-up services such as a one-year inspection (an inspection of the home one year after moving in to verify that things have been improved or repaired properly)

Ancillary Services

*Sell More than
the Inspection*

Ancillary services are additional services that you can offer to your client at the time of the inspection. For example, when you get the inspection booked, you can then ask the client if they would like you to test the paint in the home for lead.

Ancillary services fall under the category of "selling more services to each client." There are two distinct categories of ancillary services:

1. Services to your client at the time of the inspection
2. Services to your client after they move into the house

An excellent example of an ancillary service is McDonalds' classic question, "Would like fries with that?" The people who serve you at McDonalds understand that once you are in a buying mode, it is very easy to get you to buy more. Most home inspection companies know little about this ancillary service concept.

Once you have made a sale and convinced the prospect to hire you to do a home inspection, it is very easy to sell the client something else.

Here is an example of this psychology in action. Have you ever bought a new car? If you have, there is no doubt that you have been fed through the new-car-buying mill at the dealer. Critical to the car dealer's pitch is to sell you a number of invisible options such as an extended warranty, undercoating to protect the frame from rust, clear coat to protect the paint, upholstery treatment to protect the upholstery, and many other similar options. These options make the dealer lots of money but are harder to sell than the visible options, like a sunroof and electric windows. The dealer's strategy is to sell the invisible options to you *after* you have already agreed to buy the car. Typically, you make the deal with the salesperson, but the owner or manager approves the deal in their office. Once the deal is all wrapped up, they send you to another office to finalize the paperwork for the financing or leasing. It is here that they sell you these options. They know you are in a vulnerable position psychologically because you are committed. To get you to agree to a few other relatively inexpensive options is easy, especially when they can just wrap it into the financing or lease. For $20 per month more, you can have the extended warranty.

It is universally understood in marketing and sales circles that once you are committed to a purchase, it is easy to sell you a smaller purchase related to the initial purchase. This works for the home inspection business, too. The following example illustrates this point.

> A home inspector in San Francisco, California, offers a home inspection that includes a number of ancillary services as part of the standard service. This inspector feels that these ancillary services should all be wrapped into the price of the home inspection. Sure, his inspection costs a little more, but clients get carbon-monoxide and lead-paint testing included.
>
> A home inspector in Cincinnati, Ohio, offers a standard inspection for $300. In addition, clients can choose optional packages. One package includes the standard home inspection plus carbon-monoxide testing. Another package includes the inspection, carbon-monoxide testing, and lead-paint testing.
>
> A home inspector in Boston, Massachusetts, offers a standard home inspection. Once the client agrees to hire him and the inspection is booked, he asks if they would like to have a carbon-monoxide test done while he is there. He then asks if the client would like the paint tested for lead while he is there.
>
> Which of the three home inspectors is the most successful? If you say the inspector from Boston, you would be correct.

Make Sure It's Profitable

Many ancillary services can be offered at the time of inspection. Most of these require some additional knowledge, training, and, in some cases, a license. You may also need specialized equipment. Investigate each of these to find out if it is a good fit with your company, personal comfort level, and profitability goals. Some home inspection companies have been very successful offering these ancillary services. They turn a $300 inspection into a $600 inspection with very little extra time on site. A service that is not profitable on its own may be profitable if you are already there and you remove the travel component. Look at what other inspectors are offering. Ask clients if there are other services they would value. Pay attention to current issues in the media. Is mold a big issue in your area? Make sure you will be able to perform the service competently.

Keep Client Relationship Going

Consider ancillary services to offer after the client moves in. The philosophy behind this strategy suggests that during the inspection, you spend 2½ to 3 hours with the client, developing a rapport. At the end of the inspection, you have become the trusted advisor. Most home inspectors just throw that rapport away at the end of the inspection. It's possible the inspector will get some referral business out of it. But it's more likely the inspector will get business if he or she keeps the relationship going.

Watch Back-End Business

In fact, the most neglected part of the home inspection business is the **back-end business strategy.** What is a back end? A back end to a business is the ability to sell to a client over and over again. Your business should have a back end because the cost to acquire the client is fairly high in the first place. At first glance, the home inspection business appears to have no back end. You acquire a client who is unlikely to call you back for another inspection in the near future. If you are lucky, you may get one more inspection in a lifetime out of that client. From a back-end point of view, this repeat rate is simply not good enough.

To summarize, offering ancillary services to your client after they move in makes sense on two fronts:

1. Your clients already know and trust you, so they are more likely to be receptive to your ancillary services.

2. From a business perspective, it's important to have a back end to the business.

What kind of services can you offer as a follow-up? Here are suggestions:

- Improvement Checks: Inspections to verify that all improvements that you suggested in your inspection report have been carried out properly.

- Seasonal Inspections: For example, you could offer to inspect seasonally relevant components of the home every year. You could have a checklist you go through in the spring and fall, for example.

- Periodic Inspections: Some clients have expressed an interest in having their home inspected periodically to help avoid costly repairs. Maybe you could develop the *Year Five Inspection,* for example.

- Indoor Air-Quality Inspections: Indoor air quality is a hot topic and will get more and more press over the next few years. Because indoor air quality is usually related to how the occupants use the home, the inspection is best offered as a follow-up service rather than at the point of inspection.

- Energy Efficiency Study: You can inspect the home and make recommendations relative to the energy efficiency of the home. You can project the payback relative to the cost of energy improvements.

Diversification

Think Outside Box

Diversification falls under the general category of getting more customers. Here's an avenue to explore that's a natural for home inspectors—brand new homes. Inspecting new homes falls into the following three categories:

1. Construction management and progress monitoring

2. Inspecting the new home prior to taking possession

3. Inspecting the new home prior to the expiration of the builder's warranty

All three categories of new home inspection require some knowledge and skill beyond the standard home inspection. Inspecting a new home is very different from inspecting resale homes. The main difference is resale homes are inspected using a performance-based inspection strategy, while new homes are inspected primarily against applicable codes.

A performance-based inspection means you are looking for evidence of nonperformance. You are looking for things that don't work. You have some code and construction knowledge that may help you predict nonperformance down the road, or point out safety concern issues, such as a reverse polarity outlet.

A new home does not have any history. You cannot evaluate its performance. All you have to go on is the codes and an understanding of construction errors that can lead to nonperformance.

Know Building Code Cold

Because of this basic difference, the inspection and the report are very different. You are not likely to run across a worn-out roof surface, but you are likely to see a roof/wall flashing that is not done properly. You have to know your code and reference your findings. You will be up against the builder!

We have found inspecting the home prior to the expiration of the warranty to be the most interesting from a profitability and a "good fit" standpoint. Here are six reasons why it's a winner:

1. There is some history to the home. It will have been through all the seasons, and the homeowner will have operated all the fixtures. You can use some of your performance-based inspection savvy here. You still have to be code proficient.

2. The inspection is a quick, checklist type inspection.

3. Because your client already owns the home, your inspection report will not be used to make a buying decision.

4. There are no real estate agents involved.

5. You can go after the business rather than waiting for a referral. You can aggressively pursue this business in your slow periods and ignore it when you are busy. It's like a faucet you can turn on and off.

6. The inspection is not time-sensitive. It can be done any time over a period of several weeks.

   Reasons 2 to 5 apply to all three types of new home inspections.
   We solicit this business in two ways:

■ We supply a list broker with a geographic area, and they send us a monthly mailing list of homes that are ten months old.

■ We send a mailer to each homeowner with a compelling reason to have us inspect the home prior to the warranty expiring.

This strategy has been successful and is a natural extension to what we already do.

Commercial inspections are another diversification opportunity. Again these inspections require a different skill set and reporting system than home inspections.

We hope this discussion on the three ways to grow a business has given you some food for thought and broadened your horizons. The key is to start thinking outside of the confines of the standard home inspection. We will be looking at many other ways to build your business in Section II.

KEY TERMS

ancillary services	business growth	follow-up marketing
back-end business strategy	diversification	inflation

STUDY SESSION 6 QUICK QUIZ

You should finish Study Session 6 before doing this Quiz. Write your answers in the spaces provided. Then, check your answers in Appendix A.

1. List the three ways to grow a business:

    1. _____

    2. _____

    3. _____

2. What does "net worth" or "marginal net worth" mean?

    _____

    _____

3. What is an opportunity cost?

    _____

    _____

4. If an agent stops referring business to you, there is no point in calling the agent to find out why? Circle one.

    a. True

    b. False

5. List three ancillary services you could offer.

    1. _____

    2. _____

    3. _____

6. What is a "back end" to a business?

    _____

    _____

If you had trouble with the Quiz, reread Study Session 6 and try the Quiz again. If you did well, it's time for Study Session 7.

REFERRAL NETWORK

Study Session 7 deals with assembling a referral network and joining with partners who can refer business to you.

LEARNING OBJECTIVES

At the end of Study Session 7 you should be able to

■ list three areas from which to solicit referral business;

■ describe how to solicit referrals from top-producing agents;

■ describe in a few sentences the advantages to joining a business meeting group;

■ describe the difference between a joint venture and a strategic alliance; and

■ explain why exclusivity is important in a strategic alliance.

Study Session 7 may take you roughly 60 minutes to complete.

		Quantity
0793195691	BUILDING YOUR HOME INSPECTION BUSINESS	1
1427787980	AHIT REFUND LETTER 4E	1
		2

Total Pieces:

Return Policy

Exam preparation products are not returnable. If non-exam prep items are returned within 30 days of receipt, a full refund will be granted. If items are received after 30 days, the following refunds apply:

- 75% refund after 30 days
- 50% refund after 60 days
- No refund after 90 days

Please include packing slip along with the returned items.

961202163276747017 8068

Printed: 3/17/2011 2:30:01 PM

[handwritten: q17 5q9o2q1]

KAPLAN

AEC EDUCATION

Packing List

Direct Inquiries:

Kaplan Schweser
Kaplan Financial Education
1905 Palace Street
La Crosse, WI 54603
(800) 824-8742

Order Number:	15625430
Client ID:	CS
Customer PO Number:	CONSIGNMENT ORDER
Order Date:	3/17/2011
Shipment ID:	SIB1752744
Case Identifier:	CTN1985590
KDC Carrier Code:	RP

Bill-To Customer:

American Home Insp. Training I
N19 W24075 Riverwood Dr.
Waukesha, WI 53188
UNITED STATES

Returns to:

KAPLAN DISTRIBUTION CENTER
901 BILTER ROAD
SUITE 150
AURORA, IL 60502

Ship-To Customer:

Donald Cruz
1032 West Wind Dr
Davenport, FL 33837
UNITED STATES

Target Agents

Why do you need a referral network? Many home inspectors focus their marketing dollars on schemes that target the client directly. This strategy requires identifying and connecting with people who are about to buy homes. The problem is that spending money targeting the client can quickly eat up the profit from an individual transaction. The bottom line is, the cost of reaching each individual client may be too high. While clients may be a source of referrals, they typically do not refer you a continuous stream of clients.

Another strategy is to target your time and money on a network of people who can regularly refer business to you. Every time you succeed in landing another referral source, you have the possibility of receiving several inspection referrals. In simpler terms, would you rather spend $100 to land one client or $100 to land 100 clients?

This section is about establishing this network of people to refer business to you.

TOP REFERRAL SOURCES

The first thing to do in networking is to make a list of possible referral sources. For home inspections, the most obvious are the following:

- Real estate agents
- Bank managers and mortgage brokers
- Real estate lawyers

Target Top 20 Percent

The next step is to identify the top 20 percent of the people in each of the categories. We've already talked in Study Session 3 about how, in any field, 80 percent of the business is being done by 20 percent of the people. While top agents do most of the real estate business, a whole lot of agents do very little business at all. You can't afford to be networking with agents who don't produce. The same goes for mortgage brokers and lawyers. Remember the discussion in the Study Session 6 about how much an agent is worth to you over the lifetime of the relationship. Now that we are going to spend all of our time and money on **top producers,** how do we identify them?

Real Estate Agents

From the list of potential referral sources, the real estate agent is the most likely to refer business to you. The critical point at which you need to influence a homebuyer is after they have made an offer, and the offer has been accepted, subject to a satisfactory home inspection. At this critical time, the homebuyer is in the care of the real estate professional. They are not at the bank, and they may not have spoken to their lawyer. The homebuyer often turns to the agent for a referral to a home inspector. So it makes sense to focus on the top 20 percent of the real estate professionals.

Target High-Profile Real Estate Offices

To identify the top real estate agents, start with well-known offices. Top producers may also exist in lesser-known real estate offices, but you are more likely to find them in a high-profile office.

Check the newspaper. Real estate agents advertise their listings in the newspaper. Look in the real estate section to see which names crop up the most. An agent who takes out a large block ad with a number of properties advertised is probably a good prospect.

Most real estate offices publish lists of their top producers and prizewinners at least once a year. A big office will often have an entire center spread in the real estate section of your city's newspaper.

Ask a Top Producer

Another way to find the top producers is to ask another top producer. Once you have a few top producers on your list, you can try asking them who in their office are top producers. Or, put another way, "Are there any other agents in your office that are as good as you?" Contrary to popular myth, flattery actually gets you everywhere.

A List

In some markets you may be able to buy a publication that ranks all agents and offices by sales and listings for both units and dollar volume. Needless to say, this is very valuable.

Bank Managers and Mortgage Brokers

Before we discuss how a bank manager or mortgage broker could send business your way, let's clarify the difference between a mortgage broker and a mortgage specialist.

Target Mortgage Specialist or Broker

When you go to a bank to get a mortgage, a bank manager, a customer service representative, or a dedicated mortgage specialist may handle your transaction. A dedicated mortgage specialist deals only with mortgages. In fact, some mortgage specialists will come to your house to discuss your mortgage. If you are soliciting referrals from a bank, your best bet is to find out if that bank has a dedicated mortgage specialist. A dedicated mortgage specialist is more likely to work with lots of homebuyers. Volume is what you need.

Mortgage brokers work independently and may represent many banks. The **mortgage broker** will discuss the needs of the client and find the best matching mortgage product at the best price. A mortgage broker is also likely to work with many homebuyers and is a good place for referrals.

Although the person who writes the mortgage is not positioned at a critical point of influence like the real estate agent is, there is an angle that may be worth exploring. Many clients are preapproved for a mortgage. *Preapproval* is a process in which the lender helps you determine how much you can spend on a house. The lender tells you how much they will lend you based on your financial situation.

Contribute to Bank Manager's Package

This preapproval phase happens before the prospect has found a home. There may be an opportunity to reach the prospect at this stage. For example, if the bank has an information package they give to each client at the preapproval phase, you may be able to get your information into this package. Your information should not be just a brochure of your services; it should be something useful to a homebuyer. For example, Carson Dunlop publishes a home improvement and construction-cost flyer that is very popular. That's the kind of marketing material a bank or mortgage broker would feel good about including in their information kit.

Real Estate Lawyers

Real estate lawyers don't usually get involved in the transaction early enough to have an opportunity to influence a prospect on your behalf. Real estate agents have standard offers to purchase and many standard clauses, and the lawyer is often not involved until well after the home inspection is done.

Some people have their lawyer draft or review the offer to purchase. In this case, the lawyer could influence the buyer and refer business to you.

Sometimes Target Lawyers

A lawyer may be a good contact, however, if you do inspections on new homes. Inspecting new homes is a different type of inspection, requiring a different skill set and inspection report. If you do these kinds of inspections, real estate lawyers are a good source for referrals because their clients often ask them to review the offer of purchase and sale. These offers on new homes are complicated, multipage documents that usually require a magnifying glass and a law degree to work through. Many buyers ask their lawyers to review this document.

You could introduce the inspection done at the expiration of the builder's warranty to the lawyer, for example. The lawyer may recommend it to his or her clients. Again, having some sort of informational flyer or brochure to give to the lawyer is a good idea. It's something the lawyer can pass along. If it comes from the lawyer, it has an added layer of legitimacy. The downside is the client may not remember in several months.

BUSINESS NETWORKING

The idea of business-networking and the **business meeting group** has spread across North America. Designed to foster business relationships and referral business, these groups are comprised of a variety of professionals who get together to share information. These groups may differ slightly from each other but they have the following common themes:

- Each meeting group typically has only one professional from each area of business. For example, there will be one real estate lawyer, one real estate agent, one bank manager, one dentist, one home inspector, and so on.
- The group meets weekly or monthly to share business ideas and strategies.
- The group members refer business to each other.

Build Network of Referral Sources

The idea behind this networking and referral group is that once you establish and grow the network, you will have a steady flow of referral business. All of the people in your group will be familiar with your service. They are expected to keep you in mind any time they have an opportunity to pass on the name of a home inspector to someone, whether it is a person buying a home or someone else who could refer business to you on an ongoing basis. In return, you are expected to do the same.

If there is no such organization in your city, or if the organization exists but it already has a home inspector, you could easily start your own group.

JOINT VENTURES AND STRATEGIC ALLIANCES

Joint ventures and strategic alliances make sense in many businesses. Let's look at each to see how they can help grow your business.

Joint Ventures

A **joint venture** is a strategy or plan you undertake with the help of, or in partnership with, another company in a related, but not competing, business.

The sole proprietor home inspector tends to be insular in his or her thinking. It's better to open your mind to how others can help you, and how you, in turn, can help them. This is a leap worth taking.

Work with Others

The thinking goes like this: First identify everything you do. Then identify all the other professionals and service providers with whom you come in contact in any way. Write this information down and rearrange your contacts into a pecking order. Ask in other words, which professionals and service providers rely on whom and at what time? Then identify which of these people or companies are at the same level or below you. Those at the highest level may refer business to others. Those at the lowest levels may receive referrals. Those in the middle may provide and receive referrals. Think of how they can help you, or how you can work together.

Here is an example. Let's say you identify the real estate lawyer as being at the same level as you. You might design a joint venture to target previous clients of his or hers. You tell the lawyer that you will pay for the costs of mailing a letter to each of his or her past clients who have purchased a new home in the past six months. The mailer advertises two services:

1. You advertise your inspection prior to the expiration of the new-home warranty.
2. The lawyer can advertise a special on wills. Most real estate lawyers also write wills as a secondary specialty.

You get your contacts; the lawyer gets a free mailer. Everyone is happy.

Why did we say that you should only contact people or companies at the same level or lower? If you contact someone higher, you become the hunted rather than the hunter. To a real estate agent, you are lower on the food chain. The agent might use you to cover the costs of some of his or her advertising. Here is a common scenario: An agent asks you to pay for an ad on the back of his or her business card, to pay for a link to his or her Web site, or to pay for putting your logo at a corner of their weekly ad in the newspaper. They know that they can tap you, a few other home inspectors, bankers, and lawyers. The agent ends up getting his or her ads, business cards, and Web sites for free. If that agent refers a significant amount of business to you, however, it is very hard to say, "No!"

If you can think of people at a lower level than you on the food chain (moving companies, locksmiths, carpet cleaners, alarm companies, landscapers, painters, etc.), you can ask them to pay to put their logo at the corner of your business card, report, or Web site. Be careful of professional association ethics rules. You do not want to cross any lines here.

A Strategic Alliance

Sell Other Company's Products

A **strategic alliance** is similar to a joint venture but it involves two or more companies that have products or services so compatible that one company can actually sell the other company's product or service.

For example, if you formed a strategic alliance with a company that installs alarm systems, you could literally make recommendations and quote a price for an alarm system for your clients at the end of the home inspection on behalf of the alarm company. You would get a portion of the alarm installation fee for your trouble.

Maybe the alarm company could advertise and offer a discount on a warranty inspection for all of the new houses that get an alarm system installed.

You have seen strategic alliances before. If you join a club, or buy a product, you get discount coupons on other related products or services that will save you more than the cost of the original product or service. For instance, an airline might advertise free flights to Hilton Head to play golf. Is the flight really free? No, in fact it's full price, but after all the associated discounts—50 percent off the cost of your hotel room, 20 percent off the car rental fee, and half-price golf lessons—the flight cost is effectively free. In other words, if you take advantage of all of these offers, you will have saved more than the cost of the flight.

It's easy to assemble a list of suppliers that would be willing to offer a discount to your clients in exchange for you inserting their coupons or flyers into the back of the inspection report. You could advertise that anyone who gets an inspection with you will save more than the inspection fee on things they will need to buy in the first year they are in the home.

Again, consider the code of ethics of your professional association, if applicable.

Exclusivity Is Key

The strategic alliance requires more than assembling coupons. You need to endorse the companies involved exclusively, and they need to endorse you exclusively. For instance, if you include a coupon to Acme alarm systems at the back of your home inspection report, *don't* include a coupon from Acme's competitor. You can only endorse one alarm company. Why? You undercut your alliances if you dilute the pool. In other words, why would Acme agree to offer your clients a discount if you are also offering clients access to other alarm companies? This exclusivity goes the other way, too. If Acme offers their discount to other home inspection companies, the widespread access to the discount dilutes the effectiveness of your campaign. Why would a client choose you if they can get the Acme discount with another home inspection company as well? Exclusivity, therefore, is required.

Which suppliers may be interested in participating? Think of all of the parties and processes involved in the transaction. Here are some to get you started:

- Real estate lawyer
- Mortgage financing company
- Insurance company
- Alarm company
- Moving company
- Carpet cleaning firm
- Painting services
- Locksmith shop
- Deck building company
- Basement finishing firm

Here are two cautions:

1. Don't step on any toes. If the agent is involved in strategic alliances, you don't want to interfere with their relationships. The agent may be your prime source of business. Some agents will resent you offering a coupon or endorsing a bank if the agent has a mortgage broker with whom they do a lot of work.

2. Don't form a strategic alliance with a company that could influence your inspection. For example, if you have an alliance with a roofing contractor, and you inspect the house and the roof is shot, your client, the agent, and the seller may be suspicious about your assessment of the roof. Is the roof shot because you want to send business to your friend, or is it really shot? Here are some alliances to avoid:

- Roofer
- Contractor
- Basement waterproofing
- Electrician
- Plumber
- Heating contractor
- Renovator

KEY TERMS

business meeting group	mortgage broker	strategic alliance
joint venture	real estate lawyer	top producer

STUDY SESSION 7 QUICK QUIZ

You should finish Study Session 7 before doing this Quiz. Write your answers in the spaces provided. Then, check your answers in Appendix A.

1. List two ways to identify a top producing real estate agent:

     1. _____

     2. _____

2. What is the difference between a bank mortgage specialist and a mortgage broker?

    _____

    _____

3. What is the difference between a strategic alliance and a joint venture?

    _____

    _____

4. List three companies that you could form a strategic alliance with.

     1. _____

     2. _____

     3. _____

5. List three companies that would not be good candidates for strategic alliances because of a possible conflict of interest situation.

     1. _____

     2. _____

     3. _____

6. Why is it a bad idea to contact people higher on the food chain than you when soliciting joint ventures?

    _____

    _____

    _____

If you had trouble with the Quiz, reread Study Session 7 and try the Quiz again. If you did well, it's time for Study Session 8.

WRITING YOUR MARKETING PLAN

Study Session 8 deals with writing a marketing plan.

LEARNING OBJECTIVES

At the end of Study Session 8 you should be able to

- define SWOT analysis;
- list one important reason for a marketing budget;
- create a marketing plan outline;
- flesh out each category of your marketing plan;
- estimate associated costs for each category of your marketing plan;
- list one good way to track your marketing strategy; and
- describe the importance of testing a marketing strategy.

Study Session 8 may take you roughly 60 minutes to complete.

This section looks at how to allocate your marketing dollars, how to analyze your business and competition, and, ultimately, how to write a marketing plan. By the end of this section, you will have all the tools you need to write a complete marketing plan. A number of templates and tools are available on the Internet (e.g., *www.entrepreneur.com/howto/mktngplan/*)—some for free and some at a cost. Keep in mind that many of the templates, and sections of templates, are not relevant to a professional service such as a home inspection business. Try to use a template that's flexible.

Regardless of the marketing plan template you use, a few fundamentals are required. In Study Session 8, we will look at some of the background work you should do, provide an example of a marketing plan, and show you how to put it together.

SITUATION ANALYSIS

Before we launch into the marketing plan, there are two processes you should know. These two concepts will set the stage for writing the marketing plan and will, ultimately, show up in the plan in one form another:

1. Situation analysis
2. Marketing budget

In this section we'll look at situation analysis and, in the next, marketing budget.

Do SWOT Analysis

Situation analysis is also called a SWOT analysis (pronounced like the police unit). **SWOT** stands for Strengths, Weaknesses, Opportunities, Threats. A SWOT analysis is a great exercise, especially for the home inspector who is just getting into the business or is considering getting into the business. SWOT analysis gives you an overview of the business in one neat, little package. It helps you see if the business is viable. If perspective is what you are looking for, SWOT analysis is for you. Following is an overview of the SWOT analysis.

List Your Good Points

"S" is for strengths.   Describe the positive aspects of your company and your service—your unique selling proposition (USP), value proposition, and other aspects of your service. To give you an idea, here is an example for a person who worked for a builder, pouring foundations for new home developments:

Foundation specialist: I am able to detect problems in foundations that other home inspectors would either never pick up or not analyze correctly. This detection could save a home buyer substantial money. I am also able to suggest simple solutions to problems that could otherwise kill a deal. This capability will appeal to the real estate sales professionals.

Over 20 years in the building industry: I know where the problems are and how to detect them. In addition, solutions to almost any problems are at my fingertips.

Specialize in newer homes: I will cover areas most home inspection companies are not familiar with, such as code and safety issues for newer homes. My company specializes in homes built in the last 20 years. This is a neglected market segment.

Charismatic: I get along well with clients and agents.

Good communicator: I can explain the details and answer questions, keeping problems in proper perspective.

List Where You Could Improve

"W" is for weaknesses.   It's time to be honest. List any areas in which you are weak. Most home inspectors getting into the business may be weak in some technical areas. Typically, the new home inspector is strong in a few areas but may not be knowledgeable about one or two others. The weaknesses will present themselves to your clients. For instance, say you spend lots of time and energy inspecting and describing every aspect of the home but when the client asks, "What about the electrical system?" you say, "Seems fine." After hearing your comprehensive reporting on the rest of the systems, your client will not be satisfied with "Seems fine."

Other weaknesses may be

- lack of funds for building the business,
- no contacts in the industry,
- an old car or truck that is not presentable,
- no business cards and no money to have them made,
- nobody to answer your phone,
- no sales or marketing experience, or
- no bookkeeping and accounting skills.

List Revenue-Generating Opportunities

"O" is for opportunities.   List how you think you can make money. Wherever you can, you should quantify things. Let's continue with the example of the foundation specialist who would like to specialize in newer homes, whose list might be as follows:

- Identified several areas that all have homes between 5 and 20 years old.
- In a small geographic region, with a less than half-hour travel span, there are approximately 8,000 real estate transactions per year.
- There are 32 real estate offices in this area.
- Four of the real estate offices are top offices with top producers. Hence a large portion of the market is concentrated in a relatively small area.
- This is an expanding territory. There are new houses being built on the outskirts. These houses will eventually be candidates for resale.
- Know the builders and soil conditions in these areas, so you know where problems are likely to develop.

Know Your Competition

"T" is for threats.   If you're looking for threats, start with the Yellow Pages. How many other home inspection companies compete in your target market? How long have these companies been in business? This might be a good time to spend some time looking at competitors' Web sites and making some anonymous calls to the home inspectors in your target market. When you are making these calls, don't forget about call display—call from an anonymous phone. Find out what they charge and how long they have been in business. What is their USP, and what is good about them?

Don't be discouraged when you finish writing up your list of threats. You will have identified competitors who seem to be much more experienced than you are and who have lots more marketing savvy. The fact is, very few people out there will know as much as you know when you finish this book. From our experience, most home inspectors spend their energies on technical issues and learning about new, neat inspection techniques. When it comes to running a business and getting more business, you will be miles ahead of most of your competitors.

MARKETING BUDGET

The **marketing budget** is something that gives most home inspectors chills because it seems to involve spending money. We would like to present the marketing budget as exactly the opposite, an opportunity to invest wisely. We have looked at the concept of return on investment and have learned how to evaluate each investment opportunity.

The larger marketing expenses usually involve advertising, but most advertising does very little to help grow a home inspection company. A marketing budget does not have to be money that you set aside at the beginning of the year to spend on marketing; it's just a realistic assessment of what you plan to spend.

Budget Approaches

How do you come up with an amount to spend in the first place? You do it with some educated guesswork. There are many approaches to finding your budget. You could try a mock calculation of what you think you stand a chance of earning in Year One. Or you could check the amount currently in your bank account and allocate a portion of it to marketing. Or you can wait until you finish your marketing plan, when you have a better idea of the costs involved. Whichever approach you take, keep in mind that you will have to make adjustments to your budget and to your marketing plan as you go. Tweaking the budget usually means you have to go back to your plan and reassess one or more of your marketing strategies.

In the marketing plan template we have provided for you, we put the budget up front to help you decide which marketing strategies to undertake. We suggest you write the budget first, then go back to modify it after you have finished your marketing plan.

Why do you need a budget? For a few very good reasons, of which the most important is controlling your expenses.

Control Expenses

Rule number one for controlling expenses is to have a marketing budget. It does not matter how much money you have decided to allocate to marketing—$10 or $10,000—you have to decide on the amount ahead of time. One good reason follows.

Have you ever had a company call to offer you a networking opportunity that requires you to advertise in a real estate presentation folder? For $500 per year, your business-card-size ad will be printed on the inside of the folder, which holds the agreements and documents for the agent's clients. If you have not been contacted to participate in one of these, you will be soon enough. We will talk about the effectiveness of this program in more detail in Section II. The sales pitch is always the same, "It only costs $500. After two inspections, you will have more than paid for the ad. Don't you think that your name on the inside of this folder will get two inspections in a year?" This seems like a compelling argument. Now you have to make a decision, do I spend $500 and hope to get at least two inspections out of it, or do I pass on the offer? Tough decision, isn't it? No, it's not—because you have a marketing budget!

How does the marketing budget help you make the decision? Establishing a marketing budget forces you to spend that money on the most effective strategy, and not on whatever new marketing "opportunities" come your way. If we go back to the example, you should not be trying to decide if you would get two inspections out of the presentation folder advertising, you should be deciding how you could best spend your money. If the salesperson says, "Don't you think you could get two inspections by advertising in this folder?" your answer should be, "Because I have a fixed marketing budget, I need to spend the money in the most effective way, not just in a way that may break even." In order to make this decision, think of all the other ways you can spend $500 and decide if the presentation folder is better or worse. For example, would you be better off spending $500 taking ten agents out for lunch?

By the way, if you only make $70 profit on a home inspection, as the hypothetical company did in our earlier example, how many inspections do you have to do to break even on a $500 investment? It looks like more than seven to us.

Many home inspectors are afraid to miss out on an opportunity. When offered the presentation folder, they take it because their competitors are in there, or might be, and they don't want to miss out.

Rule number two for controlling marketing expenses is knowing that there are no once-in-a-lifetime opportunities. You'll have many, many opportunities. You need to pick the best ones and reject the rest. Your marketing budget will help you do this.

Set a marketing budget and stick to it. If you are offered a new opportunity and have already allocated your marketing dollars for the year, you either have to bump a program you have already decided on, or you have to wait until next year to give the new opportunity a try.

Another benefit of the marketing budget is that it is now easy to say "No" to marketing pitches that don't interest you. It is hard to argue with, "Our marketing budget is fully committed for the next year."

How do you decide how much you should spend? Look at your marketing strategies from a cost-analysis perspective:

Step 1: By the time you are finished with this course, you will have so many strategies to choose from you can afford to pick the ones that seem interesting. Pick out a number of strategies you would like to try.

Step 2: For each strategy, determine how much it will cost you to implement.

Step 3: For each strategy, determine how much time it will take you to implement. Multiply by the hourly rate that you make while inspecting. For example, our hypothetical inspection company had an opportunity cost of $30 per hour.

Step 4: Add the numbers from Step 2 and Step 3 to find the total cost. Then estimate how much revenue and profit the strategy is likely to get you. Pick the strategies that provide the greatest return on investment. (This assumes you have an equal level of confidence in all of your assumptions. In reality, you may be quite confident in some assumptions and unsure about others. Select the strategies where you are most confident in your assumptions, and where the return on investment is good. Save the gambling for the casino.)

Here is an example.

Let's look at a plan to take one real estate agent out for lunch every week. Assuming we are talking about 48 weeks of the year, the cost analysis would go as follows:

- To implement the program may cost you $40 per lunch. It will cost you $1,920 to implement the program (48 weeks × $40). Let's add $5 to each lunch meeting so you can send a follow-up thank-you letter or two. This brings our cost to $2,160 to implement the program.

- The time needed to implement the plan is 48 weeks × 4 hours (setting up the appointments + rescheduling cancelled appointments + lunch + travel + phone calls + follow-up letters). If we use $30 per hour as our opportunity cost, we get $5,760 (48 weeks × 4 hours × $30 per hour).

- The total cost of the program is $7,920 ($2,160 + $5,760).

- Let's take a stab at how much business we might get from this strategy. These exercises often produce inflated totals due to overconfidence. Let's be conservative here. Assume that we convince 15 agents to give us a try. Say these agents are happy and refer us an average of five deals in the first year. We get 75 inspections out of this strategy. If we have targeted top producers, we should have no trouble getting five inspections out of each agent we convince to refer business.

- If the profit on each inspection is $70, you will make a profit of $5,250 on the 75 inspections. But we spent $7,920! The missing piece is the marginal net worth or life cycle value of the customer we spoke about earlier. Relationships established this year will pay dividends for a number of years. The key here is to understand that budgets are a one-year look at the world, but your marketing plan has to be longer term. Look at all of the possible strategies you may pursue from both perspectives.

Perform this cost-analysis calculation for every strategy that you are interested in. Then select the best few. You can now compare the real cost and the opportunity cost with what you were thinking you would spend this year. You can then adjust your budget, or your expectations, as necessary. If your budget was only $10 to start with, this exercise won't take you very long.

Remember to include in your decision the level of confidence you have in the assumptions used to evaluate the strategy. You might break possible strategies into groups of high, medium, and low levels of confidence that your assumptions are right. These groups translate into the probability of success for each strategy. A strategy with a high probability of a modest return may be a better choice in your marketing plan than a strategy with only a low probability of a great return. In the example we looked at above, you may question whether you would be able to convince agents to change their behavior over a single lunch. Is this a high, medium, or low probability?

Don't let cost scare you away from a strategy. Some strategies cost more than others and take a bigger bite out of your revenues, but these strategies may be worth the extra cost by generating even more revenues in the long run. This is especially true if your confidence level is high that your assumptions are good and that this strategy has a high probability of success. When assessing all your strategies, be sure you consider them from all angles.

A big cost with a small potential return may not make sense. A big cost with a big potential return may not make sense either, if the chance of seeing that return is slim.

Now that we have laid the groundwork, let's get into the marketing plan. We'll use the budget and SWOT.

WHAT IS A MARKETING PLAN?

You Have to Have a Plan

Keep the Plan Flexible

Impress a Lender

Avoid Overspending

A **marketing plan** outlines and organizes all the ways in which you intend to market your business. It often covers a two-year window, but you have flexibility here. Why is it necessary to create such a document? A marketing plan functions as a point of reference or guide; it reminds you of your goals and your action plan. It's a dynamic document that you modify as you go. As you gain experience in your business, you will find out what works and what doesn't. If an item on your plan doesn't work, you can change it or abandon it.

Over time, you will refine this document into something more like a reference of proven successful marketing strategies. Our goal is to help you focus your efforts on strategies that work and avoid the pitfalls that take many home inspectors years to figure out. We will present what we feel is the path of least resistance. Some marketing strategies will have a better fit with your personality, ability, budget, market, and goals than others.

Another good reason to have a marketing plan is to show a third party such as a bank. If you are trying to get a business start-up loan, for instance, the marketing plan gives you legitimacy in the bank's eyes—it shows the bank you are serious about your business.

A marketing plan helps to prevent you from trying every marketing opportunity that comes along, without regard to budget. If you follow your plan, you will realize that adding a new activity means dropping a planned activity or changing the budget.

A marketing plan is a subsection of a business plan. As a service-intensive business, your marketing plan is likely the most important section of your business plan.

The good news is you already have the content for your marketing plan at your fingertips. All you need to do now is organize this information into a plan of action.

Remember, a marketing plan is just that—a plan. It is not a guarantee of profit. But with a plan, you stand a better chance of realizing your financial projections. The plan gives you a foundation upon which to build your business.

Remember too, that plans make you no money until they are well executed. There are those among us who are wonderful planners but hopeless implementers. If you know deep down, that you won't follow through on the items in your plan, save yourself a lot of time and don't bother with the plan.

Not only do you already have the content for a plan, but you also have a basic template for your plan. There are also many marketing-plan templates on the market, online and in book form. In the bibliography, we have listed a few books that will be helpful here. An Internet search will bring up plans you can purchase and plans that are free. Most plans assume you have a product to sell. You are looking to build a plan for a service business.

General Principles of a Marketing Plan

Marketing plans vary widely depending on where you find a template and what you are offering. But they all share some general principles. The following list highlights the general principles that your marketing plan should include:

- General overview and mission statement
- Features and benefits of service
- Unique selling proposition
- SWOT
- Budget
- Target market segments
- Market size and penetration
- Competitive analysis
- Service pricing and financial projections
- Distribution channels
- Marketing methods
  - Advertising
  - Public relations
  - Sales

General overview and mission statement. This is the basic information you need to know about your company. Start by asking yourself the following simple questions:

- *Who* is the company, including principals and employees?
- *What* is the product or service? What is the company's goal?
- *Where* is the location of your business and what is the service area?
- *How* does the company plan to accomplish its objectives and sales volumes?
- *Why* is your product or service superior to existing services?
- *When* are your services purchased and who does the purchasing? For instance, the client purchases your service on site, but, in a sense, it is the agent who sets up the purchase beforehand.

Once you've written your general overview, you are ready to dig into the meat of the plan.

Features and benefits of service. We have talked about these. List the features of your service and the related benefits for customers. Does your service meet the demands of the public who uses these services?

Describe what agents look for in an inspector and what homebuyers look for in an inspector. Then describe how your services meet those needs.

Unique selling proposition. What is the one benefit of your service that others cannot offer?

SWOT. You've already done the work on the section that looks at your strengths, weaknesses, opportunities, and threats. Just take that exercise and plug it in here.

Budget. As we said earlier, take a stab at a budget before you get into the rest of your plan so that you have an idea of what you have to work with. But be prepared to adjust your budget after you have developed your plan and to add or take out any strategies that you've changed your mind about. If you've already made a tentative budget, insert it into this section of your plan.

Know Your Target Market

Target market segments.   Describe your target market. Home inspectors have to break these into segments. Those segments may include homebuyers, homesellers, homeowners, real estate agents, lenders' title companies, real estate lawyers, and others. You may break some segments down further. Homebuyers may include buyer of new homes, first-time homebuyers, buyers of condominiums, and so on.

Market size and penetration.   For every market segment, define the total potential sales within this proposed market. This includes all the possible home inspections in the segment, for example. Then project your penetration into the market over 6 months, 12 months, 18 months, and 24 months. This will be based on your estimate of how much demand you can create for your service in the market segment.

A business operations survey is available from the American Society of Home Inspectors (ASHI). This may help you come up with reasonable numbers. This survey addresses average inspection fees, business volume, and other insights into the profession. You can obtain this valuable document from the ASHI® through *www.ashi.org* or by calling 800-743-2744.

Compare your service output capacity to your estimate of market demand. This is a check to make sure that if you create the demand, you will be able to provide the service.

Know What Market Wants

Know Your Competition Cold

Competitive analysis.   This section outlines what your prospects want and the competition you face while you try to respond to that demand.

Who is the competition? Other home inspectors. You are competing with inspectors who already have established relationships with agents. Ask yourself the following questions in order to know more about your competition: What are your competitor's service areas? Number of years in the business? Who they get referrals from? Features and benefits of their business? What is their unique selling proposition?

How does their service compare in quality, pricing, and packaging to yours? You'll have to do some research here. You might want to visit real estate offices and see if there are brochures from other inspectors. Or you could take an agent out for lunch and ask. The more you know about your competition, the better your chances of knowing how to overcome the hurdles.

Find out what market share your competitors enjoy. One way is to conduct an informational interview with an inspector who works in a completely different service area. That way, they won't feel like you're encroaching on their territory. But you'd have to make sure the service area shares the same qualities of the service area you intend to break into. For instance, both areas have a large proportion of old homes.

What are your strengths and weaknesses compared to your competition? Consider location, size of resources, reputation, services, report type, speed of delivery, flexibility of hours, and so on.

Here are other questions to consider about your competitors:

- How many firms offer your service?
- Is your desired service area saturated with building inspectors?
- How many of these firms look prosperous?
- How many services such as yours went out of business in this area last year?
- Can you find out why they failed?
- How many new services opened up in the last year?
- Which firm or firms in the area will be your biggest competition? Why?

*Get Paid Properly—
Cover Your Costs*

Service pricing and financial projections.   When you get to this part of your plan, you need to consider four main elements:

1. Labor
2. Operating expenses
3. Planned profit
4. Competition's prices

*Don't Sell Yourself
Short*

These elements will help you develop a pricing structure that is fair to the customer and to you. Not only must you cover all expenses, but you must also allow enough to pay yourself a salary. Remember our discussions on pricing—don't sell yourself short.

ASHI® did a survey of inspection fees across North America. The average fee in 1999 was about $250. The problem with this figure is that the inspection fees vary dramatically geographically. For example, in areas that have no basements and no fossil fuel furnaces, the inspection tends to be a little faster and the inspection fee tends to be a little lower. Florida tends to have lower inspection fees than Vermont. Fees also vary with the cost of living. More expensive places to live have higher inspection fees.

To get a better idea of inspection fees, you should do a survey over the phone. You can do this anonymously.

Analyze the particulars of your pricing by doing the following:

*Work Out All Pricing
Costs*

- Describe the generic price range and rationale for home inspection services. You can look at this in a few different ways. If you've decided to go for a price higher than your competitors, show how you might lose a percentage of sales volume, but that you will make up any financial shortfalls through the price you charge. Remember from our pricing discussion that charging more than the competitor sends the message that your service is high quality. That's not to say that your prices should say one thing while you do another—live up to your message and offer high-quality service! If you are planning a promotion, show how you have modified your price structure to accommodate your promotional prices, discounts, or coupons.
- Show how this price covers your expenses and has appropriate margin for profit. You need to know what your costs will be in order to ensure you can cover them. Because "Murphy's Law" says hidden expenses will crop up when you least expect them, build in room for incidentals. Include a breakdown of all service costs in your plan. The more detailed you get about the following for example, the better idea you'll have of how to price your business and ensure profit:

- Operating expenses
- Computer, printer, and software
- Inspection tools
- Insurance (property, auto, general liability, errors and omissions, health and dental, etc.)
- Association dues, training, and continuing education
- Communications expenses, such as telephone, fax, Internet hookup, and Web site
- Marketing materials, including business cards, brochures, stationery, inspection report system, etc.
- Car expenses, such as gas, repairs, and reserve for replacement, etc.
- Inspection time
- Administration time
- Incidentals
- Profit

- Provide a sales forecast of the market share you think your company can realistically expect to generate. It's a good idea to set up a financial projection page. Some items to consider are the following:

  - Sales forecast

  - Budget

  - Profit margins, including variations due to promotional pricing or coupons

- Provide a projection of the next few years of your business.

Distribute Your Service to End-User

Distribution channels. Analyze your distribution channels by asking the following questions:

- How do you plan to get your service to the end-user? This is an especially important question in the home inspection business. Your end-user is your client, the homebuyer. But getting to the homebuyer directly may be an inefficient use of your resources. Many inspectors reach their clients through real estate agents. Here is where you describe that process.

- How do these channels help you meet your time frames? In your case, developing a relationship with agents may save you time because you don't have to solicit homebuyers directly. Once you've invested time pitching agencies and agents, you will be able to decrease that time investment in the future, and increase your inspection time availability.

Distribute Materials Strategically

- How does your distribution channel display your materials? You might want to put together a package of your marketing materials to be kept at the agency or with the agent. It might include your business card, a brochure, a sample report, any promotional material, such as coupons, and even a customer feedback form.

Summary

Remember that your marketing plan will be a living document. You will make changes from time to time. And remember that no matter how good the plan is, it in itself won't make you any money. Only the effective implementation of the plan will lead to success. And speaking of success, how will we know when we get there? Let's look at tracking our progress.

TRACKING AND TESTING YOUR PLAN

Re-Evaluate Your Marketing Plan

Once you start to implement your marketing plan, you can evaluate how your marketing strategies are working. As discussed, your marketing plan is a dynamic document. Be critical, particularly of where you are spending your marketing dollars. If a particular strategy is not performing, abandon it. If another strategy is doing well, do more of it. The goal is to optimize your return on your marketing investment. How do you know if your strategy is working? Tracking and testing will help you find out.

Tracking

Tracking means determining exactly how much profit you gained from a particular strategy. Here are examples to get us thinking:

> You decide to place a display ad in your local Yellow Pages. It costs you $500 per month. At the end of the year, you have spent $6,000. The sales team from the Yellow Pages contacts you and asks if you would like to place a larger ad for the upcoming year. You, of course, have no idea whether your $6,000 generated 5 or 50 inspections for you. How do you decide if you want a bigger ad or whether you want to remove the display ad all together? If you have not tracked the effectiveness of the ad, you are in no position to make a decision.

> You decide to distribute flyers to every house in your area that comes up for sale, believing that if they are selling their house, they are probably going to buy another. At the end of six months, you are trying to decide if you should continue with this strategy, but you don't know if these flyers brought you inspections or whether your clients are getting to you through another channel.

These examples illustrate that you need to track the effectiveness of your marketing strategies. There are so many ways to grow your business; it doesn't make sense to spend money on strategies that are not paying off handsomely.

How do you track the effectiveness of a marketing strategy? The tracking procedure has to be built into the design. Some strategies are easy to track, while others are difficult. Let's look at some tracking methods.

One easy to track strategy is coupons. You just count the number of coupons that come in.

Always Track Marketing Performance

How do we track the example we started with—the Yellow Pages advertising? The only good way to track advertising is to ask every customer or client how he or she heard about you. You can do this when they book the inspection, on site at the inspection, or both. We recommend both. You then need to keep track of this information. At the end of the month, you will have a list of all of the ways your clients heard about you. If you know where all your clients heard about you, it is easy to find out which marketing strategies are working.

Questionnaires

Another style of tracking you can use is the questionnaire. Some inspectors ask clients at the inspection to fill out a simple survey, and one of the most important questions is to ask how the client heard about you.

Three other tracking strategies are the following:

1. Discounts or offer numbers
2. Separate phone numbers
3. Tracking business volume

Discount or Offer Numbers

You might get customers to refer to a discount or offer number. For instance, if you write a column for the local paper on home maintenance, tell the public that if they refer to offer #21 they will get a free disposable camera to use during their inspection. Then use different offer numbers for different newspapers or advertisements.

Separate Phone Number

You may choose to have a separate phone number installed. For a major promotion or marketing strategy you may even want a number with a distinctive ring. You will know that all the calls that came in on that number are from that strategy.

Tracking Business Volume

Tracking business volume is less accurate at pinpointing effectiveness, but it may give you a general idea. We have used this method to track the effectiveness of office talks. We track how much business is referred from a particular real estate office, so we know approximately how much business we can probably expect from the office in the upcoming months. We then unleash a marketing campaign on that office, such as making a series of presentations in the office. We can then monitor the increase in business as a result of the campaign.

You can increase your accuracy by tracking one more thing. At Carson Dunlop we track our business as a percentage of all the real estate transactions in our area every month. These figures are available from the local real estate board. The advantage is that we can track our increase in market share rather than absolute numbers. This can help make good decisions. For example, if home sales in your area are up 30 percent in a month, and your sales are up 10 percent, you may actually be losing market share. On the surface, a 10 percent increase in business is encouraging and you decide to continue your current marketing efforts. The reality is you are inspecting a smaller percentage of the sales, and your marketing program may not be working.

The same thing may be true in the other direction. If you try a marketing strategy and your sales stay flat, you may be discouraged. But if you know area real estate sales dipped 20 percent during that period, you are gaining market share, and your marketing program is working well.

Tracking Inquiries

You should also have a list of inquiries you can cross reference with your client list. You can find out which strategies generated the most inquiries and which actually produced results. For example, you may discover that the leads you get through the Yellow Pages are more price resistant—they are price shopping. But the leads you get from the mortgage broker convert easily to inspections. This is the kind of information you need to track.

Don't Use Untrackable Strategy

Some marketing strategies can't be tracked. How do you deal with such a strategy? You don't use it! Don't participate in marketing efforts that can't be tracked with a high degree of reliability. Most good marketing strategies can be tracked, although it might take some creativity.

Testing

Once you become proficient at tracking, it's time to add another level of sophistication to your marketing mix: **testing.** The mantra is: "Test everything." If you launch a marketing campaign that seems to be paying off well, don't be satisfied. Try tweaking it a bit and then track it closely to find out if your tweaking made the strategy work better or worse. If it works better, throw out the old way and use the new. Here is an example. When we launched a warranty inspection (inspecting new houses near expiry of the warranty), we designed three different mailers and sent them to different areas to find out which one would "pull" the most. We found out which of the mailers worked best and used it on the next mailings. Every few months we try again with different wordings and continuously refine and improve our marketing.

Test Strategy in Low-Risk Market

If you are trying something new and feel unsure, test it in a market that is not going to hurt you if it fails. Let's say you are thinking of testing a completely new pricing strategy, or a new inspection report format. Try it on a segment of your market rather than on all of your clients at once. Maybe you would use the new format for five referring agents only. Then monitor the reaction. Because it is difficult sometimes to predict the reaction of your referral base, take it slowly.

One Thing at a Time

Sometimes you are excited about trying several new marketing strategies. Resist the temptation to implement them all at once because you won't be able to tell which is effective. For example, you introduce new features and your market shares go up 10 percent. That's great, but maybe one of the strategies alone would have caused this jump. Worse, maybe one of the strategies would have cause a 15 percent jump, and one of the other strategies is actually driving people away. Measuring one thing at a time is effective. Measuring several strategies at once is impossible.

THE MARKETING CYCLE

Marketing is not a static process. Most people picture a single event. They devise a strategy and launch and reuse the same strategy as is down the road. The reality is that marketing is a continually changing entity. As such, it needs your attention.

Picture the marketing process as a cycle, as shown in Figure 8.1. The four steps of the cycle are as follows:

1. Build a strategy, tactic, or process.
2. Implement what you built.
3. Measure your results.
4. Refine based on measurements.

F I G U R E 8.1   The Marketing Process Cycle

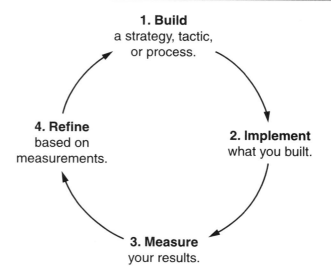

The cycle emphasizes that marketing is a process and not a single project. If you can remember that, you will stay flexible, changing your strategies as necessary, instead of getting locked into something that may work now but not later.

KEY TERMS

financial projections	marketing plan	testing
marketing budget	SWOT	tracking

STUDY SESSION 8 QUICK QUIZ

You should finish Study Session 8 before doing this Quiz. Write your answers in the spaces provided. Then, check your answers in Appendix A.

1. What do the letters in SWOT stand for?

   _____

2. A marketing budget helps you (Circle one.)
   a. get money for printing.
   b. pick the best marketing strategy and reject the rest.
   c. write your business plan.
   d. choose a good marketing-plan template.

3. It's a good idea to position yourself as "a home inspector" if you are not sure which market you want to attract. Circle one.
   a. True
   b. False

4. If you want to find out what your competition is like, what kinds of questions would you need to ask? List three good questions.
   1. _____
   2. _____
   3. _____

5. There are no "once in a lifetime" marketing opportunities. Circle one.
   a. True
   b. False

6. Explain the difference between tracking and testing.

   _____

   _____

7. List the four parts of the marketing cycle?
   1. _____
   2. _____
   3. _____
   4. _____

If you had trouble with the Quiz, reread Study Session 8 and try the Quiz again. Before proceeding to Study Session 9, do Assignment 1.

ASSIGNMENT 1

DEVELOP A MARKETING PLAN

Assignment 1 is designed to help you develop your company. We are going to ask you to do some research and make a few phone calls.

You should allow yourself three to five hours to complete Assignment 1.

1. Do an Internet search for free marketing plans that come close to your business. If you do not have access to the Internet, contact your bank or go to your local bookstore and find some sample business plans.

2. Brainstorm the categories headings and content for your marketing plan.

3. Write up a marketing plan.

When you are finished with Assignment 1, you're ready for Study Session 9.

HANDLING COMPLAINTS—PART 1

Study Session 9 introduces you to resolution techniques for complaints.

LEARNING OBJECTIVES

At the end of Study Session 9 you should understand how to

- handle callbacks;
- determine complaint validity;
- chose the best resolution technique to use; and
- decide if you should get your insurance company involved.

Study Session 9 may take you roughly 60 minutes to complete.

What does handling **complaints** have to do with marketing your home inspection firm? The way you receive and resolve complaints from clients can work for you or against you in retaining those clients and attracting new ones. Remember, marketing is an activity designed to encourage prospective customers to contact your company. It is also inherent to inspections themselves, including the way you handle problems when something seemingly or actually goes wrong. Without trying to sugarcoat the situation too much, you can turn a complaint into a marketing opportunity. And because every home inspector eventually gets complaints, you might as well polish your skills. In Study Session 9 we look at the first steps in handling complaints, including your initial response to the unhappy client and the information-gathering process. In Study Session 10 we continue the discussion, with a look at how best to resolve the complaint.

ART VERSUS SCIENCE

It is appropriate for this topic to start with a disclaimer. Explaining technical aspects of home inspection is easy. Research can be done, and technical issues are anchored in physics and building science. Explaining complaint resolution is more challenging. There is little authoritative material, and we are dealing with the art of human relations rather than a science. As a result, no definitive answers exist. Our goal is to make you think. We encourage you to challenge everything presented in Study Session 9 to take away any of the ideas that work for you.

One Size Does Not Fit All

When dealing with communications and human emotions, there is one thing we can be sure of—one approach does not work equally well with all clients. You will need more than one strategy to be successful. We have learned this lesson the hard way. For instance, we handled a complaint beautifully with a specific strategy in June, but when a similar situation arose in September, the same approach backfired, becoming a lawsuit.

IDENTIFY YOUR PHILOSOPHY AND APPROACH

Your personal and business philosophies play a role in how you handle complaints. We find that, in general, there are three types of home inspection professionals:

1. *The hardliner.* These home inspectors defend themselves against any and all complaints vigorously, never admitting any mistake.

2. *The validater.* These inspectors defend complaints vigorously when they feel unjustly accused, but they respond if there was a valid problem with the inspection.

3. *The conciliator.* Some inspectors try to satisfy every client and may pay to make a problem go away even though they made no mistake.

There is no right or wrong approach, but you should recognize your philosophy and develop your approach accordingly before you are in the midst of a complaint.

Your philosophy of complaints might depend heavily on whether or not you have errors and omissions insurance. If you do have this kind of insurance, you have to decide whether you are willing to submit a claim and risk increased premiums.

There are three schools of thought regarding handling **complainants** who ask for money:

1. Deny all requests for financial compensation.
2. Pay all requests for financial compensation.
3. Pay only the valid claims.

The deny-all-requests supporters believe that every complaint is a negotiation, and you have to start from a tough posture.

Those that follow the pay-all-requests approach believe that goodwill is more important than the claim. The downside to this approach is it does not take long before you have a reputation for having deep pockets. People will complain knowing you will grease any squeaky wheel.

Paying only the valid claims seems like a good approach, but how do you determine which claims are valid?

Complaint Validity Is Grey Area

In reality, we believe that you can't take a black-and-white approach to the situation because different strategies work for different situations. Furthermore, callbacks and complaints are rarely black and white. They almost always involve shades of grey. From our experience, the client is clearly wrong about 10 percent of the time, and it's easy to show them why. About 10 percent of the time, our inspector just missed something and we have to decide how to resolve the issue to everybody's satisfaction. But 80 percent of the time, the situation is a grey area. Later we will look at approaches to determining the **complaint validity** and the responsibility for the problem.

To start down the road to effective complaint resolution, there are two things you should keep in mind:

Complaints Are Opportunities

1. It's just business—don't take it personally or it will consume you.
2. A complaint is an opportunity. Someone who has a complaint resolved to their satisfaction becomes a more loyal client than a client who never had a problem to start with. Nine out of ten clients who have a complaint resolved to their satisfaction will tell five people about the positive experience, whereas the average client that was satisfied from the start tells only two other people of their satisfaction.

For more on this see *Basic Facts on Customer Complaint Behavior and the Impact of Service on the Bottom Line* by Jack Goodman, President of e-Satisfy and former President of TARP, a company specializing in the measurement of customer satisfaction and loyalty. See *www.tarp.com.*

COMPLAINTS ARE OPPORTUNITIES

A complaint is an opportunity to do the following:

- Satisfy your client. You will probably be referred business from a satisfied client.

Generate Goodwill

- Generate goodwill. Do this with all parties involved in the transaction. The agent, the seller, and perhaps even the lawyer, will see how professionally you handled the situation.

Avoid Bad Publicity

■ Avoid bad publicity. Whether you are right or wrong, a complaint handled badly could end up losing you lots of business if a disgruntled client decides to sink you at all costs. A disgruntled client could write to the newspaper, tell 100 friends, or register a Web site called *www.thisinspectorsucks.com.*

If you handle a complaint well you may

■ save money;

■ save time;

■ prevent the situation from turning into a lawsuit, which is bound to cost you more than the original complaint, even if you win;

■ keep your insurance premiums down; and

■ take the stress out of your life.

A complaint is also an opportunity because many clients who have had a bad experience will *not* complain to you. Instead, they will just tell an average of ten other people about the bad experience. Thank people if they complain. Consider it a chance to turn a client around. If you end up paying out, consider it a learning experience.

In the following sections we look at a few techniques to

■ avoid complaints from the start,

■ competently deal with the complaint, and

■ handle yourself competently at a revisit, or callback.

AVOIDING COMPLAINTS

*Explain Scope of
Your Inspection*

Obviously, the best way to deal with a complaint is to prevent it. Some novice inspectors say the best way to avoid complaints is to never make a mistake. The fact is you don't have to make a mistake to get a complaint. Many complaints we get are not the result of inspectors making mistakes; they are a result of clients not understanding the scope of work. When a client books an inspection, they have their own idea what their $400 gets them. They often think they paid you $400 to ensure they would not have any problems with the house. They don't know that the $400 will get them a specific scope of work that excludes a number of areas.

Wouldn't it be nice if people could pay $400 one time and get an insurance policy that nothing would ever go wrong with their home? There would be no deductible, no exclusions, no limit, and no expiration date. Just call the home inspection company, and they will take care of it! Clearly you cannot afford to offer this, but unless you tell your client otherwise, they may assume that is exactly what they are buying. If you ever see an insurance policy like this, buy it for yourself, and then let us know where to buy it!

Have a Good Contract

One of the best ways to avoid complaints from the start is by using **a good contract.** Is the focus of the contract to limit liability? Your lawyer might say, "Yes—a good contract should limit your exposure." Your lawyer's one responsibility is to give advice to protect you as well as possible. You have other responsibilities including building a successful business. While your lawyer's advice is valuable, remember it is narrow in focus. Your focus has to be broader. The lawyer's protection is of no use if people will not use your service because they perceive that you will not stand behind your work.

In our opinion, the main purpose of the contract is not to limit liability, but rather to ensure that the client understands what we do, and what we don't do. In other words, we set up a contract so that the client and the home inspection company can agree on the scope of the inspection.

You need to consult your lawyer when it comes to designing your contract. The problem is that most of the contracts we see are designed to stack things in your favor should you end up in court or in a legal dispute with your client. While this approach protects you, these contracts often do little to avoid the problem in the first place. Most complaints do not go to court, and many do not involve a lawyer. You handle most complaints face to face with your client. You should consider how your contract helps in this situation.

You've seen how most contracts work. Someone hands you a three-page contract and shows you where to initial and sign. You usually go ahead and sign without reading it because it's a condition of commencing a job. These contracts do not help to create an understanding between you and your client. Our contract, on the other hand, clearly communicates what we do, and what we *don't* do, in a few short lines. We try to use everyday words and sound reasonable in the contract. When our clients sign this contract, they are effectively agreeing that they understand

- the scope of the inspection,
- that a visual inspection is not exhaustive, and
- that the home inspection is not a guarantee or warranty for the home.

But more than that, we want our client to feel that our agreement is fair and reasonable. We believe that people will deal with you differently if they feel you are being fair, than if they feel your contract is one-sided and adversarial. It sounds old-fashioned and perhaps a little naïve, but we believe that it is good business to treat people as you would like to be treated.

We don't list every exclusion on the contract because we want the client to understand the general concept. In discussion with home inspectors over the years, we have found that many find it embarrassing to highlight what they don't do. They don't like to arrive on site with the client and begin by telling the client all the things the inspection doesn't cover. You can certainly start with what you are going to do, and then give some examples of things you do not. There is no need, in our opinion, to list everything you do not do. Can you think of any other business service that describes in detail at the beginning of the work all the things they don't do? There is no need to apologize for your service. It's valuable and it's extensive.

We have found that it is better to adjust the client's expectations from the start then impress the heck out of them in the delivery. In other words, we underpromise and over-deliver. We always find that clients are more than impressed with what we are able to do during an inspection.

There are many contract wordings, and we encourage you to check with your attorney before settling on any. However, remember that attorneys have a specific goal—to minimize your liability. As we said, their goal is not to build your business success, and an attorney typically has no role in your marketing or customer service activities. Your goals may include business growth as well as liability control.

Contract Limitations

Many contracts have clauses to minimize the inspector's exposure. These clauses include

- a monetary limit on your liability, such as the amount of your fee (if allowed in your jurisdiction);

- a statute of limitations that sets a restriction on how long people have to come after you for a problem (if allowed);

- a counterclaim clause that tells the client that if they sue you and lose, they will pay your costs;

- an option for a technically exhaustive inspection at a considerably higher price, which is designed to reinforce the idea that a home inspection has a limited scope; and

- exclusions for everything you can think of (radon, lead, mold, building codes, engineering work, concealed items, environmental issues, operating costs, acoustical properties, etc.).

Contracts may use statements similar to the following to clarify scope and minimize your exposure:

- The inspection is visual only.

- There is no inspection of concealed areas.

- The inspection identifies only conditions that are both present and apparent at the time of the inspection; intermittent problems are not covered.

- Our professional opinions are often based on inference because there is no direct evidence or incomplete information.

- The inspection is not a guarantee or a warranty.

- There is no responsibility if repairs are done before we can examine the property.

- We are not responsible for betterments that put the client further ahead of where we told them they were. For example, if we say the roof has five years left and it has to be replaced immediately, we should not be responsible for a new roof with a 15-year life expectancy. We should only be responsible for a roof with five years of life remaining.

- The inspector is not liable for any consequential loss (if the roof leaks and destroys a $20,000 piece of furniture, the damage to the furniture is not our responsibility).

- The contract is the entire agreement (anything we say in our advertising does not matter).

- This contract replaces all previous representations (including what we may have said on the phone or on our Web site).

Here are additional tips involving your contract:

Give Client Time with Contract

- Make sure the contract does not look too one-sided. If it is, it's more likely to make the client hostile, and a court may dismiss your contract as being unfair.

- Get the contract or agreement to the client before the inspection. Consider e-mailing or faxing the contract to the clients so they can look it over, sign it, and fax it back. There are several benefits to this approach. One is that the client cannot claim that they had to sign the contract under duress. Signing under duress means that your client has little or no choice but to agree to the contract. A client can claim that they had to sign the contract under duress if we arrive at the inspection, present a contract they've never seen before, and imply, "Sign this contract or I won't do the inspection, and because this is the last day before you have to waive your condition with the seller, it's unlikely that you'll be able to find another inspector."

- If the client does not fax the contract back, we call and ask them to bring the signed contract to the inspection with them. Either way, they have had ample opportunity to read the contract, sign it, and ask any questions.

- At the beginning of the inspection, we ask if the client has any questions about the inspection agreement. It's not a bad idea to explain once more, at the start of the inspection, what you will be doing, including the scope of the inspection.

Booking the Inspection Is a Risk-Management Opportunity

Booking the inspection is an opportunity to ask the client some risk-management questions. This is a great time to ask about and document specific concerns. Concerns outside the scope of the inspection can be identified at this stage, and clients can be advised about where to get answers to these questions. We prefer to avoid telling clients, "We don't inspect for that." We try to tell them where they can get answers to their specific issue. We also make it clear that when clients ask for things outside our scope, this is not part of a professional home inspection. We don't want to leave the impression that other home inspectors may perform those services and that they have chosen a poor firm.

A conversation might go something like this:

Client: "We are concerned about the septic system."

Inspection Firm: "The evaluation of a septic system is not part of a home inspection. There are firms that specialize in this and we can coordinate a septic system evaluation for you, or refer you to a firm."

In this example, we have explained to the client that what they are asking for is outside of what any home inspector does, but we have offered to respond on their behalf. No doubt you can think of other questions and service requests that should be responded to in this way.

Encourage Clients to Attend

We have found that most of our complaints come from clients that did not attend the inspection. Having the client with you helps them understand the scope of the inspection. For example, if they are following you around, they will see that the basement floor is finished and that there is no way to verify if there is a floor drain. When the basement floods, you and your client can commiserate together that you were unable to verify the presence of a drain. The client who was not present during the inspection may say, "All I know is that I paid you to make sure something like this didn't happen." This statement is completely unfair and suggests you are that all-encompassing insurance policy that no one has ever seen.

In addition to understanding the scope of the inspection, there is another reason your client should be there. After two-and-a-half hours together, you have developed rapport. You have taken on the role of trusted advisor. When the client has a problem, they will be more likely to call for your advice rather than to complain. You have, in essence, developed a friendship. It's much harder to be unreasonable to a friend than someone you have never met.

There is a corollary to this that says if the buyers are a couple, and only one attended the inspection, the more aggressive one in a callback is always the one who did not attend. It is better for you to communicate with the one you worked with, wherever possible.

Stay Within Your Scope

Inspect with Even Hand

Don't underestimate the **in scope, out of scope** problem. A classic scenario with home inspectors is that the inspector is a hands-on expert in one area of house systems. For example, the ex-electrician will spend far too much time inspecting the electrical system and perform tests well beyond the scope of the inspection, often citing code references. If you spend too much time on one area, you may create an expectation of extreme inspection for the other systems of the home. The client could then come back later and ask why you did not strip down the furnace and find a crack in the weld where the primary heat exchanger joins the secondary heat exchanger.

Inspect all systems and components of the home to the same depth and stay within the scope of the inspection. Offer other services beyond the inspection if you choose to and are qualified, but don't confuse your client about what an inspection is.

Don't Over-Promise

Under-Promise and Over-Deliver

If you promise too much, you raise the client's expectations too high, and your client may use it against you later. For example, if your brochure says that you offer "complete peace of mind," your client might come back later and say, "You promised peace of mind, and what I have is a stress-inducing money pit."

The real estate agent often over-promises on your behalf. The agent has a client that is nervous about buying the home so the agent says, "Don't worry, this inspector will find any problems."

Disclose Your Errors and Omissions Insurance with Care

Many home inspectors say you should not advertise your **errors and omissions insurance.** Talking about your insurance may seem tempting if it distinguishes you from your competition. For instance, if inspectors in your area don't have insurance, you may use your insurance to demonstrate that you are a professional company, looking out for your client's best interest.

But advertising errors and omissions insurance can be like a lightning rod. People who never would have considered blaming you for a mishap may do so because they can justify that it's "just business." We have had clients say, "It's not that we think that you did anything wrong, it's just that someone has to be responsible for this and you have insurance, so there's no downside to you, right?" But there is a downside—you pay the deductible, your premiums go up, and your policy may be cancelled. Are you ready to say that to a client?

This one is a tough call, but that's what business is about. You need to evaluate your market conditions and weigh any marketing advantage of telling people you have insurance against the risk of increased complaints.

Ask Clients About Their Concerns

Ask Questions

We ask clients about their concerns at the time of booking and again at the beginning of the inspection. We listen carefully, and we write them down. This gives us another opportunity to explain what we can and cannot do. For example, a client might respond to your questions with the story that in the last house they owned, they had a huge problem with the main drain that runs from the house to the city sewer. Because the roots from the surrounding trees blocked up the drain, sewage backed up into the basement. The client says that they are worried about the situation repeating itself in this home.

Now you have the opportunity to tell the client that you won't be able to inspect the main drain as it is buried eight feet below the ground and is not visible. You can explain that if the main drain is a prime concern, they can have a specialized inspection done. There are companies that have video equipment that they can run inside the drain to see if there are any problems.

Value Your Own Service!

If you ever start feeling that you spend more time telling clients what you can't do than what you can, just remember this: A home inspection is a high liability, in-depth, multidisciplined technical analysis conducted under adverse in-field circumstances, requiring the generation of an incredibly detailed written report in an unrealistically short time frame for an inconceivably low fee. You're the one with the handicaps, not the client!

Document your clients' concerns and your responses. We have had more than one client come back to us and say that we told them the drain under the front lawn was fine, when we actually said we could not tell them about the drain, but there were specialists who could. People's memories are not perfect, ours included. Write your client's concerns and your responses in your report. If there is a problem later, it does not matter what was said on site. The only thing that matters is what is written in the report.

So far we have looked at ways to avoid complaints before the inspection starts. Now we will show you what to do, and what *not* to do, on site. Aside from performing a good inspection, you can do other things to reduce the likelihood of getting a complaint.

Document Any Special Limitations

List the Limitations

Your reporting system should be divided into each of the house systems you look at, and relevant limitations should be part of each section. For example, if you do a roof inspection when the roof is covered with snow, you should document this in the roofing section of your report.

If the house presents any special or unusual limitations to your inspection, these should be highlighted in some way. For instance, if the basement is a finished living space, document the lack of visible foundation. You might go so far as to indicate the percentage of the foundation that is visible. Or if the house has a crawlspace that's completely inaccessible, give it a check mark in the limitations section indicating that you had no access to the crawlspace. No access to a crawlspace is a big problem and should be discussed with your client. If you document the limitations now, you will do much better later if you get a complaint.

Deliver Consistent Information

Communicate Limitations

Keep Messages Consistent

It's a mistake to say one thing to your client and put something different in the report. Say what you write, even the bad news. Most inspectors have a tendency to "soft sell" the problems when explaining them to their client. Then when the inspector sits down to write the report, they think, "I'd better cover myself on this," and they write something more serious in the report. It's better to find a way of presenting a problem, even if it's serious, the same way when speaking to a client and when writing it in the report.

Don't Guess

If there is something you don't know, don't guess; telling a client that you don't know the answer is the only fair and professional thing to do. If you guess based on incomplete information, you are sticking your neck out. For example, say you see that the trusses in the attic have been modified. You have no way of knowing if they were modified properly. You don't want to say, "It looks like this has been done professionally." The carpentry might be professional, but there may have been no engineering done. Just say that you can't determine from a visual inspection if the modifications were done properly.

Don't Ignore Things

Get Advice

If there is something you don't know but think you should, don't brush it off. Get some help. There are ways to do this without saying to your client, "I don't know what I am doing, so I need to get someone else to look at this." You might say, there is something you would like to verify. You can go the extra mile for your client. You can then look it up in a technical reference, call another inspector that knows about it, or call a specialist in the area. Of course, good training up front will go a long way to reducing how often this happens.

This may make you feel a little better about not knowing something: First, no inspector knows everything there is to know. Second, no one can keep in his or her head all of the knowledge a home inspector has to have; it's just fine to know there is an issue, and you have to look it up or call someone to get the details. Third, your clients have no idea what you should know and what you shouldn't. Don't let your professional insecurity allow you to guess at or gloss over something. If clients could see the wealth of knowledge in a home inspector's mind, they would be overwhelmed.

Don't Show Off

Keep Your Language Simple

Fancy terms and technical jargon may make you look smart, but the home inspection business is about communication. The more your client understands, the better off you are and the less likely you are to get a complaint. Take the time to explain things in a way your client will understand.

Remain Impartial

Be Impartial

Remaining impartial is very important when it comes to avoiding complaints. Not only do you have a duty to your client to do the best you can for them, regardless of who referred the business to you, but you also need to be impartial when it comes to representing your findings. If you are unreasonably harsh about a particular condition, you may not be acting fairly to the seller. For example, if you find a few miswired electrical outlets in the basement, and you try to help your client out by saying the entire house should be rewired, you may get a complaint from the seller. In fact, we do get complaints from sellers and sellers' agents.

Our Loyalty Is to the Home

Don't be unreasonably soft on an issue either. This will come back to you as a complaint and possibly a lawsuit. We have been asked many times where our loyalty lies—to the buyer, to the seller, or to the agent. After several years we now answer, "Our loyalty is to the house. Our goal is to represent the condition of the house as accurately as possible."

Consider a Home Warranty

A number of **home warranty** products are available on the market. Some have so many exclusions and exceptions that they are not worth the paper they are written on. Others offer some measure of assurance to the home owner, especially when used in conjunction with a thorough home inspection.

We offer a home warranty product to clients that can be purchased at the time of the inspection, or after the inspection. This policy does three things for us:

1. When we get a complaint, the first thing we do is check if the client has purchased the warranty. If they have, we may find that the program covers the problem. End of problem.

2. The warranty allows us to explain that the warranty covers things we cannot inspect. Here is another opportunity to make your client understand the scope of the inspection. The client then understands that the home inspection itself is not a warranty on the home.

3. If the client did not buy the warranty, we can point out that had the client purchased the warranty, they would have been covered. In essence, when the client turns down the offer of the warranty, they are turning down any recourse on items covered by the warranty and not covered by the inspection.

Many companies ask the client to acknowledge that they were made aware of the warranty by initialing a sentence on the contract.

Offer a Prepossession Checklist

Share Responsibility

Another technique some inspection companies use to resolve complaints is to give the client a prepossession checklist. This list tells the client what to check before moving into the house. For example, the list tells them to look for evidence of dampness in the basement, and the client verifies that there's no evidence of dampness in the basement. It's then very hard for the client to come back three months later and claim that the inspector should have noticed the dampness in the corner of the basement. There was no evidence of the problem at the time of the inspection, and there was no evidence when the client did the prepossession walk-through. The condition only became apparent later. Inspectors cannot be expected to predict the future. In effect, the checklist gives some responsibility to the homebuyer.

HANDLING THE COMPLAINT CALL

Be Prepared for Complaint Calls

Avoiding complaints altogether is the ideal, of course, but not the reality. This call could happen to you: "Hello, you inspected the house we bought back in October and we moved in at the beginning of December, and two days later, it rained and the roof leaked into the family room and totally destroyed the hardwood flooring, and it got all moldy and the dog, who has asthma, had a bad reaction to the mold, and when my sister came over during the holidays, she slipped, and . . ."

Handling the call properly from the first moment it comes in is critical. Proper procedure can make the difference between a quick **resolution** of the problem and a lawsuit. Here are a few methods we have developed over many years.

Call Back Right Away

If the call was a message left on your voice mail, get back to the client as soon as you can. You want to show the client that you are interested in them and concerned about the problem. There is nothing worse than calling back a day or two later. Delayed **callbacks** send the message that you don't care. Further irritating an unhappy client makes no business sense to us. We would always rather speak to the client before they decide to call their lawyer.

Don't Be Defensive

Be Open

Being open is perhaps one of the most difficult things to do. A complaint about the inspection is indirectly, or directly, a complaint about you. Defensive behavior is almost sure to make things worse. It may help to keep telling yourself that the complaint is just business and that the call is just a business communication.

Thank the Caller for Calling and Listen to the Complaint

Recognize that calling you with a complaint is also difficult for your client. Thank them for calling and drawing your attention to the problem. Recognize that this was a difficult call for them to make. Thanking the client often defuses the situation.

Likely, the caller will launch into the problem right away, but if they don't, encourage the caller to explain exactly what happened. Listen carefully without interrupting. Take notes. Resist the temptation to speak up as soon as you hear something with which you disagree. Not only is this more likely to make the caller angry, but you are also more likely to say something that you will wish you had not said after hearing the rest of the information.

The more your client speaks, the better. We have often found that the client eventually says something that you can use, or is helpful to your cause. There is no downside to letting them speak their mind completely.

Once they are finished, repeat the situation back to them from your notes, to be sure you got it right. A good technique is to paraphrase what the client said. It shows that you listened, and that you are actively trying to understand their position. They will usually clarify or add some detail. Make notes of these comments as well.

Ask Some Questions

After the client has had a chance to explain the situation, and you have reiterated what they said, you should ask some questions. We often empathize with the client by saying something like, "I'm sure this is very frustrating for you. Let's see if we can get it resolved." This makes the client feel a little better. You are not brushing them off and are acknowledging they have a problem. Although you have not taken responsibility, their attitude often changes noticeably. It is good to slip into the role of consultant and to focus on solving the problem rather than worrying about who is to blame. The client has a problem in their home, and their first priority is to solve the problem, not ruin your day.

The next step is to drill down into the situation to get more information. We say, "May I ask a few questions to make sure I understand completely?"

You should have a standard list of questions to ask. These include the following:

- What was the date of the inspection? (Is there a limitation period in your contract?)

- Did you attend the inspection? (If the client accuses you of doing something at the inspection, it may not be true if the client was not there.)

- Can you remember the weather conditions at the time of the inspection? (The client's memory on this may be helpful. You can check the weather records. If the client does not remember the weather correctly, they may not remember other details as well as they claim.)

- Was the house vacant or occupied at the time of the inspection? (If the house was occupied, the carpets, furnishings, or storage may have concealed the problem. If the problem makes the house inhabitable, it is hard to believe people would live in the home, during winter in Minnesota with no heat, for example. It is also possible the house suffered damage by the occupants between the time of inspection and the time your client took possession.)

- What was in this area of the home during the inspection?

- When did you take possession of the home?

- Did you make any changes to the home before moving in?

- Did you do a prepossession walk-through just before closing? (If yes, Did you note this condition then?)
- Did you ask the seller about this situation?
- What does the inspection report say about this part of the home?
- Had anything about the house changed from the time of the inspection until the time you took possession? For example, had the house been left vacant, or had anything been removed from the house?
- Has anything in the house changed since you took possession? For example, have you done any repairs or made any improvements at all?
- Can you give me more some details about the problem? Where is it? How big is it? What does it look like?
- When did you first notice the problem?
- How did you find the problem? (Removing broadloom carpeting, stripping wallpaper, demolishing a wall, etc. If the problem was discovered during the work, ask if the contractor mentioned this problem before starting work. The idea is that if the contractor did not mention it when he or she quoted on a job, and discovered it once he started work, that suggests it was not evident to the contractor either until the work began.)
- Are you aware of any previous problems in this area?
- Has anything about the problem changed or been disturbed since you discovered it?
- Have you done anything to correct the problem? (If yes, What did you do? When? Who did the work? And so on.)
- Has the problem been constant or intermittent?
- Is there a home warranty?
- Have you contacted your home insurance company?
- Can you remember the weather conditions when you found the problem?
- Did you find any evidence that the problem has been there for some time? Or, Did you find evidence of a previous problem or repair?
- Did you receive a seller disclosure form? Did it say anything about this situation? (This looks for others who may be more responsible or jointly responsible for the condition.)
- Have you had any other contractor or consultant look at it? What were their opinions?
- Have you checked with the city regarding any permits for work on this part of the home?
- What does your inspection report say?

Document the answers to all of these questions. You may come up with additional questions, and not all of these questions will be applicable, but this is a good starting point.

Once you have asked these questions, a picture will start to emerge. You may have some follow-up questions as a result. Ask these and document the answers.

Take everything with a grain of salt. We often find that a substantial amount of what we are told is not true or is distorted. Take nothing at face value, and check everything without being confrontational about it.

Review the Report

Reread the Report!

Now that you have listened to the client attentively and have shown that you understand the situation, tell them you will pull the file and call them back in 60 minutes. If you are about to go into an inspection, tell them that you will call them back in three hours.

The golden rule of complaints is: *Never make a comment until you have read the report.* Even if you think you remember the house, reading the report will remind you of what was visible and what was not. You have probably inspected many homes since the home in question.

If you are a multi-inspector firm, speak to the inspector who wrote the report before you speak to the client again. The inspector may remember something about the house, or about the client, that sheds some light on the issue.

After you've reviewed the report, call the client back earlier than you promised. If you said you would call them back by 3:00 P.M., call them back at 2:30 P.M. Don't leave them waiting. Calling back early has significant value. Calling back late can do significant damage.

When you call the client back, you will have developed an opinion of the situation. There are only four things you may have concluded:

1. You need to go back to the home to get more information.
2. The client doesn't have a problem. The situation is normal or typical. (You will need to prove this to them.)
3. The client has a problem, but it was documented in the report. (Tell them where.)
4. The client has a problem, but it was not in the scope of a home inspection to discover it. (Show them where your contract or standards exclude it.)

An Alternative Strategy

If Asked to Write, They May Drop It

One strategy to handling a complaint call is to request a formal, written complaint. The logic here is that some people will call to complain about the most trivial things, but when you ask them to put it in writing, they see how trivial it is and abandon the complaint altogether. This is not a strategy that we have used because we worry that if you ask for the complaint in writing, the client may be more likely to ask their lawyer to write the letter for them.

HANDLING WRITTEN COMPLAINTS

A written complaint from a client should be taken seriously. The letter may come directly from your client, or it may be from the client's lawyer.

Read the Letter Carefully

First read the letter very carefully and then pull the report. If you are a multi-inspector firm, talk to the inspector after you've read the letter and pulled the report. Letters require the same thought process as calls—find out if the report addresses the problem and if the problem is within the scope of an inspection.

Call the Client

You can proceed in a number of ways from this point, but we have found the best approach is to phone the client directly, even if the letter came from a lawyer. Here are reasons why we like this approach:

- Calling has no downside. If the client does not want to speak with you and wants the lawyer to handle it, they can just say so.
- There is a chance that you can re-establish your relationship with the client and meet them face-to-face.
- It's difficult to get an accurate gage of emotion from a letter. The client may be very upset, or only a little upset but likes to write letters.
- The client may have been very upset when they wrote the letter, or when they passed the issue along to the lawyer, but the client may have cooled off during the time it took for the letter to get to you. They may be willing to talk to you about resolving the problem.
- It is harder to be unreasonable when you are speaking to someone than if you write to them. It's harder still in a face-to-face meeting.

Gather Information

When you call, follow the procedure we discussed for handling complaint calls. Gather information, then set up a revisit, if appropriate.

Remember that the closer you are to someone, the harder it is for them to be mean to you.

Calling Reduces the "Mean Scale"

This is our mean scale:

- It's easiest to be mean in writing.
- It's harder to be mean on the phone.
- It's hardest to be mean in person.

Replying to a Written Complaint in Writing

If your client does not want to speak with you, or if for any other reason you choose to respond to a complaint in writing, here are some tips:

Keep Your Letter Professional

- Choose your words very carefully. Assume that a lawyer will read your letter, and that it will be evidence in a court case.
- Don't be defensive or aggressive; it will not help your cause, even if it makes you feel better. Even if your client is behaving badly, you should be a consummate professional every step of the way.
- Avoid sarcasm. We know how tempting it is, especially when the client buries themselves in sarcasm in their own letter.
- If the problem is out of scope, or is documented in the report, follow the template we discussed for addressing complaint calls. If the problem is not covered in the report, and it's not out of scope, set up a revisit to the property.
- Do not reply by e-mail. E-mail circulates too easily and is too informal. If someone e-mails you a complaint, it is informal and you should follow it up on the phone, not by replying to the e-mail.

"Without Prejudice"

"For Settlement Purposes Only"

In Canada, if you put the clause *"without prejudice"* or *"without prejudice to any party"* at the top of your letter, it renders the letter inadmissible in court. This clause allows you to make offers or recommendations without committing yourself to anything. In the United States, it is customary to include a header on the letter that simply says FOR SETTLEMENT PURPOSES ONLY. The rules of evidence exclude any evidence relating to settlement discussions between the parties, so a header like that on a letter is sufficient to exclude the contents of the letter from any legal proceedings that may ensue as a result of the dispute.

Say you get a letter from a client who claims their roof leaked after they moved in. Instead of calling you, they went ahead and got the problem fixed for $5,000. The client believes you are responsible and requests that you cover the costs. There's no point in doing a revisit because the problem has been fixed. If you decide it's better to just offer to defray some of those costs as a goodwill gesture, you can write a letter saying that although you were not given the opportunity to assess the problem area to see if it was something you missed, you understand how upsetting it can be to have a leaky roof when you buy a new house. You offer $1,000 towards defraying those costs, but you don't want that offer to look like you feel responsible. The *"for settlement purposes only"* phrase, in the United States, or the *"without prejudice"* phrase, in Canada, covers you. It's like saying, here's some compensation, but it's not an admission of guilt.

You can also use these clauses for items that are clearly not your fault. For instance, if you get a letter of complaint about a central vacuum system that broke the day the owners bought the house, your letter would empathize with the client but reiterate that central vacuums are not within the scope of home inspections. You can then refer the client to the agreement they signed regarding the limitations of the inspection. It's still a good idea to put the appropriate phrase at the top of this letter.

Written Complaints from Lawyers

Consider Options Before Calling Insurer

If a lawyer sends you a letter on behalf of your client, you could turn the issue over to your insurance company or to your lawyer. Our feeling is that this tends to escalate things and takes control of the situation out of your hands. This may be the right thing to do if you are not comfortable dealing with complaints, but it can also be expensive. You will have to make a business decision about this.

Many errors and omissions insurance policies require you to inform the insurance company upon receipt of a complaint that might lead to a claim. Check your policy.

At Carson Dunlop, we call the client directly, regardless of whether we receive the letter from the client or from their lawyer. We have found that calling the client improves our chance of defusing the situation.

Respond to Lawyers In Writing

If you choose to respond to the lawyer rather than the client, do it in writing, not over the phone. If you live in Canada, use the *"without prejudice"* clause; if you live in the United States, use *"for settlement purposes only."* You can be sure that the lawyer has heard only one side of the story. The client will have described the situation in the most dramatic fashion possible to support their argument. The lawyer is clearly at a disadvantage.

You should assume the lawyer has not seen the report or the inspection agreement. You must respect client confidentiality. Only discuss the report with the lawyer or attach a copy of the report and the inspection agreement if you've received the client's permission first. You may point out the agreement, the limitations, limitation of liability, if applicable, and any arbitration clauses that your client may have signed.

We have found that there is a higher risk when we communicate directly with the lawyer. A lawyer may feel that it doesn't matter if their client doesn't have a logical and rightful claim because the insurance company may pay out anyway, assuming you have insurance. Clients and lawyers may spend some time and effort finding out if you have errors and omissions insurance. We talked about not advertising it earlier. This is why.

HANDLING AGENT COMPLAINTS

Exclude Agents But Keep Them Informed

Sometimes a client complains to the real estate agent about a problem. In turn, the agent contacts you to complain. In this case, our advice is to deal directly with the client rather than the agent. But keep the agent informed. If you offer to contact the client to work towards a resolution and promise to let the agent know how it's going, most agents are satisfied.

Tell the agent what actions you have taken and why. Don't ask the client to tell the agent because something will likely be lost in the translation. Use the opportunity to educate the real estate agent. Agents may be overselling what you can do. Make sure the agent knows how quickly and professionally you responded. It sounds strange, but this has helped us in some large real estate offices in our market. Agents respect the fact that you resolve problems quickly; they don't focus on whether you paid or not. It's about client satisfaction for agents, not finding a soft touch inspector.

PERFORMING THE REVISIT

While you can deal with some complaints over the phone, you may determine that you should **revisit** the home. We encourage you to build procedures for doing this now, not when you are in the middle of handling a complaint. Here is what we do when revisiting a home.

Take the Inspection Report with You

Bring the Report

There is a good chance that the client will not have the report available at the revisit. You need this information in case you have to point out that you did cover things during the inspection. It is also common that when you get to the home, the client has come up with other issues as well. For example, the original complaint may be about a shower stall that leaks. The client might be so upset about it that they start to doubt the quality of all the information that you provided. They then start to see defects everywhere, real or imagined, within scope or out of scope, inspected or not. This kind of reaction is entirely understandable, but you will be more ready for it if you have the inspection report, the standards of practice, and your inspection agreement handy.

This barely needs to be said, but we'll say it anyway. Review the report, your booking information sheet, and inspection agreement before going to the home. You need to know your report and the circumstances around the inspection. Who attended the inspection? What was the weather like? Did the client have any specific concerns? And so on.

Take the Inspector with You

Bring the Inspector

If you did not do the inspection personally, bring the inspector along. It's too easy for the client to be tough on someone who is not present. In addition, your inspector can verify what the conditions were during the inspection. For example, your inspector might remind the client that the previous owner had extensive storage in the corner of the basement where a dampness problem was subsequently discovered.

If you bring your inspector, coach him or her about not being defensive in front of the client. Tell your inspector that he or she will have ample opportunity to discuss things with you in private. You and your inspector have to work as a team. Decide ahead of time who will lead the discussion. It is usually best if the person who did not do the inspection conducts the discussion.

Take a Colleague

Bring a Colleague

If you are the inspector, it is a great idea to bring a colleague to the revisit. Saying, "It's just business and this is not personal," is easy, but keeping your emotions out of the situation requires almost superhuman control. Someone has attacked the core of who you are, and you feel the need to defend yourself. The fight or flee instinct is not dead! The presence of a colleague provides a neutral perspective and helps you stay calmer.

The severity of the complaint will influence this decision; it's probably not worth bringing a colleague to a revisit that might amount to a claim of $500. But if the client is claiming that the entire foundation will have to be replaced for $35,000, a second, unemotional opinion is very helpful.

What is the role of the other inspector? One of the questions you should be considering the whole time is whether a reasonable, competent inspector would have seen the problem given the conditions. It's very difficult to be unbiased about this. Another inspector you know and trust, and who is not personally implicated, can bring objectivity to the situation.

Ask Lots of Questions

Ask More Questions

Presumably you have already spoken to the client at length on the phone. You have gone through your list of questions and/or some kind of information-gathering routine. But it's still a good idea to ask questions again. In our experience, we sometimes get a different answer when we look the client in the eye, and when we have brought along the inspector who did the inspection.

Getting the client to explain the problems, and show you the problem area, while asking questions, shows the client that you are interested in getting to the bottom of the issue rather than going for a quick fix.

One thing to watch for where the buyers are a couple is that you almost always get different information from one than the other. This can be very helpful, because clients have a natural tendency to tell the story to their advantage and do not like to look foolish. When one person tells you something, we often paraphrase it and look at the other person to see if we got it right.

One goal of all these questions is to make sure there isn't a piece of the puzzle that you are missing. So even after you get more information, ask more questions as needed.

Give Direction and Be Helpful

Act as a Consultant

When we arrive at a revisit, we go into our helpful and trusted advisor role. Often this role is enough to satisfy a client who has a complaint. In our experience, many problems can be solved easily with a little common sense. The problems are often smaller than the client believes them to be. Your advice may include options that a contractor is unwilling to try because they don't make the contractor as much money, and won't solve the problem with 100 percent certainty. For example, a client has a ten-year-old, high-efficiency furnace and discovers that the induced draft fan has started leaking condensate. A furnace technician may suggest replacement of the furnace to the tune of $3,000. You come in and say, "Why not replace the gasket or, if the motor is shot, replace the fan." Now the bill is only $500.

The client might say that the contractor suggested it does not make sense spending $500 on a ten-year-old, high-efficiency furnace. Making that decision is your client's responsibility, not yours. You have added options to their list of solutions. Now they have to choose which option to pursue. But you can point out to them that you told them they have a ten-year-old furnace. If they buy a new furnace, that is their choice, but it is a big improvement to the home. You should not be responsible for improvements to the home. But more about that later in Study Session 10.

Bring a Camera

Photograph the Problem

Taking photographs is a good idea. If you are unable to come to an agreement with the client for some reason, having pictures will be helpful. You don't want to be in a situation in which the client fixes the problem and you have nothing to show what it looked like before.

If you decide to bring a camera to the site, be cautious how you present it. If you arrive looking like your whole goal in revisiting the house is to figure out how to document things for the upcoming lawsuit, you may set the wrong tone. A big fancy camera, with flash equipment and tripods, is more likely to invoke this response. A small camera that you have in your pocket is the way to go, but make sure it's good enough to get a quality image.

Note well that some courts will not accept digital photos because they are so easy to alter. A 35mm camera may be better if this is the case in your area.

Don't Bring Fancy Equipment

Don't bring any equipment to the revisit that you didn't use in the original inspection. Let's say you are investigating a damp basement complaint. If you used a moisture meter during your inspection, bring your moisture meter. If you didn't use a moisture meter during this inspection, don't pull one out during the revisit. Your client will wonder why you didn't use this piece of equipment in the first place.

Meet with Contractors on Site

Invite Client's Contractor

If there is a contractor involved, ask for the contractor to be there during the revisit. This is helpful for at least four reasons:

1. It's a good idea to form a professional relationship with the contractor. This contractor is probably telling your client that the inspector should have seen the problem. If the contractor is there, you have the opportunity to tell the contractor that there was snow on the roof at the time of the inspection, and that your original report recommended further evaluation by a roofing contractor in the spring. This might get the contractor on side.

2. In addition, you have the opportunity to bounce ideas off the contractor. If the contractor has indicated replacement of some component, you can ask how much it would cost to repair.

3. The contractor will have a tougher time being mean to you in person.

4. The client is not an effective communication conduit between you and the contractor. It's much better to speak to the source. You may look at your list of questions, and ask the contractor several of these. For example, it's often revealing to learn how the contractor found the rotted bathroom subfloor. If it was found after the toilet was removed and the vinyl floor covering pulled off, you may have a reason to say it was not visible during the inspection. If it were visible, why didn't the contractor tell the client before work started that the subfloor was rotted? It may sound like we are speaking from experience here. We are.

Bring Your Own Contractor

You may want to have a trusted contractor available on site to look at things on your behalf. This works particularly well if you feel you missed something. Your contractor also may be able to think of a repair strategy that is more reasonable than what the client or his contractor is suggesting.

If you have a relationship with a contractor, you may be able to get the work done for a better price. At the very least, you will know whether the client's contractors are charging fairly.

Don't Decide on Site

Give Yourself Time

Once you have finished your revisit and collected information, you don't have to give your client a decision about your position on the spot. Tell your client that you will get back to them at the end of the day or the following day. This gives you time to collect your thoughts, consult with a colleague, or do some research.

You then can complete your consultancy role and advise your client on how to correct the problem, if appropriate.

KEY TERMS

a good contract	errors and omissions insurance	in scope, out of scope
callbacks		resolution
complainant	for settlement purposes only	revisit
complaint		without prejudice
complaint validity	home warranty	

STUDY SESSION 9 QUICK QUIZ

You should finish Study Session 9 before doing this Quiz. Write your answers in the spaces provided. Then, check your answers in Appendix A.

1. When dealing with communications and human emotions, it is always better to use the same approach with all clients. Circle one.

    a. True

    b. False

2. The focus of a contract with a client should ideally be one of the following. Circle one.

    a. To limit your liability

    b. To maximize your client's understanding of what you can and can't do in the inspection

3. You should let your client know up front that you have errors and omissions insurance. Circle one. Explain.

    a. True

    b. False

    _____

    _____

4. Which of the following statements is true? Circle one.

    a. Documenting limitations of your inspection is something you should do only if you think the client is litigious.

    b. When speaking to a client, "soft sell" anything harsh you wrote in the report.

    c. If your report skills are good enough, your client doesn't have to come to the inspection itself.

    d. What you write in your report should be a reflection of what you tell your client in person.

5. If an inspector defends complaints vigorously when he or she feels unjustly accused, but responds if there is a valid problem with the inspection, he or she is most likely a (Circle one)

    a. Hardliner.

    b. Conciliator.

    c. Validater.

6. What two things should you keep in mind in order to deal with complaint resolution effectively?

    1. _____

    2. _____

7. List three ways in which a complaint can be used as an opportunity?

    1. _____

    2. _____

    3. _____

8. It is always better to have your client attend the inspection. Circle one.

   a. True

   b. False

9. Where should our loyalty lie? Circle one.

   a. The house

   b. The seller

   c. The agent

10. The best way to respond to a written complaint from a client is to reply with a written message. Circle one. Explain.

    a. True

    b. False

    _____

    _____

If you have trouble with the Quiz, reread Study Session 9 and try the Quiz again. If you have no trouble, you are ready for Study Session 10.

HANDLING COMPLAINTS—PART 2

Study Session 10 completes the discussion of resolution techniques for complaints.

LEARNING OBJECTIVES

At the end of Study Session 10 you should understand how to:

- determine responsibility;
- choose a course of action to pursue;
- protect yourself;
- avoid paying out; and
- handle complaints based on case studies.

Study Session 10 may take you roughly 60 minutes to complete.

Having completed your revisit, you are ready to take the next steps in handling a complaint. First, you need to determine responsibility, given all the information you have acquired. Then, you need to take action. In Study Session 10 we look at these steps, plus overall tools and resources that you can use throughout the complaint process. We conclude with two case studies so you can see how the approaches we've discussed might be applied.

DETERMINING RESPONSIBILITY

Determine if Mistake Was Yours

When you go to a revisit, you should give serious consideration to whether you, or your inspector, have made a mistake. Your first instinct may be to justify yourself, but if you were at fault, it's worth knowing. We are not suggesting that you admit you were wrong at this stage, even if you feel the admission is a business decision. We are suggesting that you may choose to handle things differently if you know you are wrong. For example, you may choose to pass it on to your insurance company to handle, or pass it to your lawyer to negotiate on your behalf. At Carson Dunlop, we are more inclined to try to come to an agreement that is satisfactory to everybody rather than pass it to the insurance company because most problems can be solved for less than the typical deductible.

We have developed what we call the **responsibility yardstick.** We go through the following thought process:

- Is there a problem? Sometimes a client perceives a problem. Often clients come to the conclusion that there is a problem based on having a particular and unreasonable expectation of their home. For example, the client complains that the water pressure is poor. When you revisit the home, you find that the pressure and flow is not only ample, but better than typical for homes in this area. What is the reason for this disparity of opinion? The client lived in a high-rise condominium before moving into this house. High-rise condos typically have much better water pressure and flow than houses. But the average homeowner has no way of knowing that.

- Is the problem in the report? If so, show the client that the report addresses the situation.

- Is the problem within the scope of the home inspection? If not, help the client understand why a home inspection would not reveal this problem.

- Would a competent inspector have found the problem under the same circumstances? If not, help the client understand that no home inspector would have discovered this.

- Was it visible at the time of the inspection? Consider the weather conditions, if stored material may have been in the way, and how any other special condition might have impeded access. For example, if the furnace burner cover is rusted into place, the inspector can't take it off and can't look for cracks in the vestibule of the furnace. If we arrive on site, and a technician has the furnace partially disassembled, and shows you a crack in the heat exchanger, you should be ready to point out that you have documented in the limitations section of the report that you were unable to remove the burner cover at the time of the inspection. There are many other cases in which the problem may not have been visible.

- Did the condition exist at the time of the inspection? There may have been two or three months between when you inspected the home and when your client moved in and discovered the problem. It is entirely possible that this is a new condition that did not exist when you were there.

- What were the circumstances? There may have been limitations that prevented you from performing your job to the best of your ability. For example, the basement might have been rented to tenants, preventing your access. You need to get into the basement to get to the heart of the home systems. It's not unusual for the homeowner to fail to give the tenant proper notice about your inspection. When you get there, the agent and the tenant have words. The result is that you have five minutes in the basement before the tenant sets his dog on you. Most experienced home inspectors will document limitations like this directly in the report.

- Did anyone else do something wrong? What we are looking for is any way to share responsibility or divert the responsibility. Was there a contractor who did something to cause the problem? Did the seller do something to cause the problem? Was the homeowner asked about this problem in the seller disclosure statement, for example? There is a high probability that the new homeowner has had a contractor in. Many people try to get work done before they move into a home. Always ask if the client has had any work done on the home. Even if the work seems unrelated to the problem, you should know. Most homeowners will not understand the cause-and-effect relationship between home systems.

After thinking through the responsibility yardstick questions, you should be able to determine either who is responsible for the problem or if it is a case of **unclear responsibility.** Either way, this will give you direction in your next step, which is to resolve the problem.

RESOLVING COMPLAINTS

Once you have revisited the house and determined whether or not you are responsible, the next step is to figure out what you are going to do about it. Don't expect every case to be clear-cut; most are shades of gray.

Rely on Your Company Philosophy

We talked earlier about a **company philosophy** to use as your starting point when deciding what to offer, or not offer, to your client to resolve the complaint. This will be helpful to you at this point.

There are probably only three possible positions to find yourself in:

- You are not responsible.
- You are responsible.
- You are not sure.

If you are not responsible, your challenge is to explain why to your client. If you are responsible or not sure whether you are, you can make an offer to settle, turn things over to your insurer, or tell the client they are not getting anything from you, and hope they go away. (In our experience, they rarely go away.)

Let's look at how the discussion may go if you have decided to meet the client to try to resolve things.

Meet or Call Client

This discussion is best held face-to-face, but we understand this is time-consuming and challenging. (We'll explain why this is better in a minute.) A phone call may be more convenient, and many discussions take place this way. A phone call is much better than anything in writing, including an e-mail.

The Discussion

If you want to make some points that will help your position, start by restating the situation and the client's position. If there are problems with the home, acknowledge them. Then explain what you have found in the home, in your contract and scope of work, in your report, in your research, and elsewhere that leads you to a different conclusion than the client's. We like to start with the facts and logic, and finish with our position. Then we ask if that makes sense. If the discussion is long, we stop along the way and ask if everything makes sense to this point.

A face-to face discussion allows you to gage your client's reaction to what you are saying. If the body language is receptive, you can keep going. If you sense they are not following you or disagree, stop and clarify. If people don't accept your facts, your assumptions, your premises, or your background information, how can you expect them to agree with your conclusions? You need to get agreement along the way to get agreement at the end.

A phone call does not provide the same dynamics as a meeting, but it is better than a letter. It is hard in a letter to stop and get agreement or clarity on a contentious point in the first paragraphs, because you don't have any interaction.

You may also have some documents that support your points. Put these on the table now, and leave a copy for the client. This is another good reason to meet rather than chat over the phone.

Emotions Get in the Way

In this discussion we are considering the facts, not personalities or emotions, and we are certainly not assessing or shifting blame. Because this is an emotional issue for the clients, their response may not be logical. But you need to remain professional and logical. If the client is irrational or abusive, end the discussion and leave quickly, offering to pick up the discussion at another time or to communicate in writing.

See it from the Client's Perspective

Get into Client's Shoes

Another rule of complaint resolution is to see it from the client's perspective without getting trapped. Remember that the goal is to come out the other end of a discussion with a satisfied client to the extent possible. If you can't see their point of view, it's unlikely that you will come to an equitable agreement. It's entirely possible that the problem is not your fault and that you have documented it adequately in your report, but you need to remember that the client still sees it as a problem. So, instead of insisting that you are not to blame, empathize with the client. The bottom line is this: From the client's perspective, they are now stuck with a problem they hired you to avoid.

Explain Your Position Carefully

Remember that what seems obvious to you may not seem obvious to your client. Some clients assume that a home inspection is a guarantee that nothing will ever go wrong with their house. You may have to remind them about the contract and the scope of work described in the ASHI® Standards of Practice.

Explain the Sampling Aspects of Home Inspection

It may be hard for clients to understand that a home inspection is, in many ways, a sampling exercise. We look at some bricks but not all of them. We look at some electrical outlets, but not all of them. We look at and operate some windows but not all of them. This may not seem right to clients, but it is the only way the home inspection can be offered for a few hundred dollars. A technically exhaustive inspection would take much longer and cost much more.

It's more complex than this because, while an inspection is a sampling exercise in many ways, in other ways it is not. We do not do a sampling inspection of the plumbing fixtures, electrical panel, the furnace, and the water heater, for example. The reason for this is that we are looking for big issues in the home. As we are doing that, we often come across smaller issues. While these are not the focus of the inspection, they are documented as a courtesy. Clients should not conclude that because we reported on some minor issues, we should have found all of them. We simply won't. Is this easy to explain to clients? No. Is it important to explain to clients? Yes. Is it easier to explain before or during the inspection than when trying to resolve a complaint? Absolutely.

By the way, we always cringe when one home inspector says he or she came through a house behind another inspector and found some things the first inspector missed. Of course he or she will. His or her sampling selection will almost certainly be different than someone else's. So the results will, of course, be different. This does not make one inspector better than another. The sooner that clients, real estate agents lawyers, judges, insurance companies, and home inspectors realize this, the better off we will all be.

Compromise When Responsibility Is Unclear

How do you handle a situation where it is unclear if the condition existed at the time of the inspection, or if, in fact, it could have been detected given the conditions surrounding the problem? Explain to the client why the fault for the problem is unclear. Consider a compromise. You could accept partial responsibility or you could accept no responsibility but agree to compensate the client partially.

Ask What's Fair

Ask the Client

If you believe the client has accepted your explanation, now may be a good time to ask your client what they think is fair. We prefer to ask what is fair, rather than what would make them happy, because the response is more likely to be reasonable. Don't ask this if you are not prepared to pay anything. We have a 100 percent satisfaction guarantee, and our clients can get their inspection fee back any time. We are always prepared to offer this.

By the way, we always ask what is fair before we make an offer. It is nonconfrontational, you don't have to accept what they say, and sometimes their expectations are lower than what you are prepared to offer. This has surprised us more than once.

Make an Offer

Making an offer to your client could affect your insurance coverage. Make sure you know your risks. For example, if your deductible is $5,000, and the issue you are negotiating with your client is a $2,000 issue, there seems to be little risk in cutting a deal with your client. But consider if your insurance company will then refuse any responsibility for this client when the client has another claim a year later. Make sure you know every detail of your insurance policy and speak to your insurance advisors.

Make the offer on a "without prejudice" or "for settlement purposes only" basis (see Study Session 9). If you put the appropriate language at the top of an offer letter, you are saying to the client that although you are making an offer to solve the problem, the offer does not constitute an admission of guilt on your part.

Ask the client if they think the offer is fair. Only settle if the client is satisfied. If you settle and the client is not satisfied, you have parted with money but have not solved the problem.

Get the client to sign a **release form.** The release says that the client will never ask you for anything as a result of this home inspection.

The following is an example of a release that we use. Please do not use this or any other legal document without the advice of a lawyer.

RELEASE

IN CONSIDERATION of payment to me, [client name], [refund amount in text and numbers], I hereby release and forever discharge ABC HOME INSPECTIONS from any and all actions, causes of actions, claims and demands, for damages, loss or injury, howsoever arising, which heretofore may have been or may hereafter be sustained by me, in consequence of the building inspection and report for [inspection address](our Report # [report number]), including all damage, loss and injury not now known or anticipated but which may arise in the future and all effects and consequences thereof.

AND FOR THE SAID CONSIDERATION I further agree not to make any claim or take any proceedings against any other person or corporation who might claim contribution or indemnity under the provisions of The Negligence Act and the Amendments thereto from the person, persons, or corporation discharged by this release.

IT IS UNDERSTOOD AND AGREED that the said payment or promise of payment is deemed to be no admission whatsoever of liability on the part of the said ABC HOME INSPECTIONS.

_____	_____
Date	Date
_____	_____
Signed	Signed
_____	_____
Witness	Witness

Don't Pay for Betterment

Don't Pay for Improvements

Betterment refers to a situation in which your client asks for compensation that results in bettering the client's original component. This is not a cost you should pay, but you may have to explain this to your client because they think they are being fair. The concept is best explained with an example:

> You inspect a home and find that the roof is in fair condition. You tell the client that the roof will likely be fine for another five years. The client then gets a roof leak, and the roofing contractor says the roof surface should be replaced now. The client calls you asking you to pay the $5,000 roofing bill because you said it would last another five years.
>
> Let's assume that during your revisit it turns out that the roof is old and should be replaced. Does it mean that you have to buy the client a new roof?
>
> There are a few ways to look at it. Your client might claim that they were not expecting to spend $5,000 now and you should pay the whole shot. But if you pay $5,000 for a new roof, the client is in a much better position than you told them they were in your report. What would be fair is to give them a roof that will last for five years. But, you can't buy a roof like that, so they will buy a 15-year or 20-year roof. And they are ahead of the game.

Offer Percentage of Cost

> Your client was going to have to resurface the roof in five years anyway, so why should they get a new roof for free? You could argue that because the typical life span of an asphalt shingle roof surface is 15 years and you indicated that it would last five years, you should pay one-third of the bill. Another way to look at it is that because your client would have had to pay for the roof in five years anyway, you are only responsible for five years of interest on money borrowed to pay for the new roof.

We have found that courts do consider the issue of betterment in arriving at settlements. But more about that later.

One of the most common examples of betterment occurs when the client wants you to pay for a new furnace because the furnace technician found a crack or hole in the heat exchanger. You told the client that the furnace was 20 years old and that it had a 25-year life expectancy. (The wisdom of this kind of reporting is a whole different issue.) Not only is the client going to get a new furnace that has a typical life of 25 years, they may also upgrade to a high-efficiency furnace. Should you pay for a high-efficiency furnace? Should you pay the total cost of any furnace? Should you pay for $5/25$ of the cost of a furnace similar to the one that is there now? It's up to you to negotiate.

In short, the betterment concept suggests that you are not responsible for putting the client into a better position than you told them they would be. You may only be responsible for putting the client into the same position that you told them they were in.

Identify Other Sources of Compensation

Share Costs

Whether the problem appears to be your responsibility or not, consider whether anyone else could compensate your client or **share costs** with you. One classic example is the homeowner's insurance policy. For example, the client calls because the roof leaked. They want you to pay for the repair to the roof, replacement of drywall, replacement of hardwood floors, and cost of repainting. Many homeowner insurance policies will cover the damage due to the leak but not the cost of repairing the leak. You may be able to cut your bill dramatically if the client has a policy that covers leakage.

What about a home warranty? Is there one? Is this problem covered? How about the contractor who installed the system? If your client is asking for compensation for a defective furnace, maybe the installer is at fault, or partly at fault, for installing a defective furnace. Maybe there is a manufacturer's warranty or recall that could take care of the bill. Perhaps the utility responsible for inspecting gas appliances is at fault. Perhaps a municipality signed off on a permit without doing a final inspection.

What about a seller or real estate agent who misrepresented the home? What if the seller ignored a recall notice on a furnace and failed to pass the notice to the buyer? There is often more than one contributor in a settlement.

Work with Your Insurance Company

How do you decide when to call your insurance company? The insurance company's policy will partly dictate your own company's policy. Many insurance company policies require notification of any potential claim. But when do you make a claim: after a complaint, after a demand for compensation, or after a lawsuit?

Speaking to your broker or insurance company when you are not involved in a complaint is a great idea. This is new to you, but not new to them. You can learn how these professionals feel, and perhaps get some good advice from them.

Resolving Complaints Yourself

At Carson Dunlop we do not call the insurance company every time we get a complaint because we resolve most complaints ourselves. But we understand that we take a slight risk in doing so. The insurance company does not want us to start to handle a complaint and then turn it over to the insurer when it gets out of hand. We may have done things they would never do, like admit fault, and as result, we may have reduced their chances of a successful result. In these cases, we may not be able to rely on our insurance. So when we handle things ourselves, we have to be comfortable that the dollar amounts are not too big for us and that we are comfortable that we can resolve it.

Talk to your insurance company about what level of control they give you in the handling of claims. For example, they might tell you that any complaint you think could result in a claim should be directed straight to the insurance company. It's fair at this point to ask how much control the insurance company will give to you. If they give you no control, and their policy is to settle for anything less than the deductible, regardless of the situation, then you may have an unacceptable situation.

Work with the Insurer

Our insurer will take our advice on any claims that we pass to them. If we say, "This one is clearly not our fault and we should fight it," the insurer will consider taking that course of action. An insurer should be ready to work with you in dealing with complaints and claims.

Have a Company Policy

How do we decide what goes to the insurance company? Our rough rule is that when a written or verbal request for compensation reaches half the amount of our deductible, we report the incident to our broker. If the claim is not serious, it is filed as an incident with the broker rather than a claim with the insurer. This arrangement has worked well for us. We are perhaps lucky to have a good broker who takes some responsibility by helping us decide when to make a claim with the insurer.

TOOLS AND RESOURCES

When dealing with complaints, you need to know every tool and resource that might help you resolve the situation fairly. Over the years, we have found that the following have been enormously helpful.

Tape Recorder

Focus on Conversation

A tape recorder that connects to your telephone is a great tool. If you take your calls from a cellular phone, attaching a recorder is a little more difficult. Recording your conversation guarantees that you don't miss anything the client told you because you can replay the conversation afterwards. It also allows you to devote your entire attention to the client. You don't have to focus on writing things down.

Weather Records

Discuss Unusual Weather

The most common complaints involve water infiltration of one form or another. If it's not the roof, it's the basement. Often these conditions are dependent on the weather at the time. Maybe the inspection was done in the middle of a four-week dry spell, and now your client has a leaking foundation in the middle of an exceptionally rainy period.

We know that after every major rainstorm we are going to get some calls from clients. For these kinds of problems, we always pull out the weather records for the inspection date, and for the date that the client had the problem. What good does this do you? We explain to our client that these problems often do not manifest themselves unless there are very specific weather conditions, and if we have not had those weather conditions recently, it is impossible to detect the problem during a one-time visit to the house. A source for weather records is the National Climatic Data Center (*www.ncdc.noaa.gov/oa/ncdc.html*).

Client Feedback Questionnaire

How can a client questionnaire help you handle a client complaint? We get a fairly high response rate to our client questionnaire. We insert the questionnaire in the front of the inspection report with a self-addressed, postage-paid envelope. We might get a 10 percent response rate. The respondents are primarily complimenting us on a job well done. People that take the time to fill these out usually write at length about what a great job our inspector did and about how thorough he or she was. Here are some excerpts:

"Your inspector was so thorough, he looked in every nook and cranny."

"It was such an education, we covered every corner of the home from top to bottom."

"Your report is incredible."

Now imagine one of these same clients complaining that the inspector did a substandard job.

You could point out to the client that their own words indicate they thought the inspection was "thorough." The fact is the condition was probably not detectable at the time of the inspection.

When Things Go Wrong

Every Home Has Problems

One of the best ways to handle complaints is to anticipate them. We include a document called "When Things Go Wrong" in our reports. We remind clients of this document when complaints come in. It is very nice to be able to say, "We told you this might happen." The script is included in the companion CD to this book. Feel free to use this document or any parts that you find helpful.

Drawing your client's attention to the "When Things Go Wrong" document is a good approach. We have found that the wording works in many situations.

Previous Reports

Know the Report History

Sometimes we inspect a home that we have inspected before. The longer you are in business, the more likely this is to happen. Our policy is that inspection reports are confidential. Even the fact that we have inspected the same home previously is confidential information. This does not mean that we don't look at the previous inspection report before the inspection. Getting as much information as possible to your inspector is critical. With an old report in hand, you can get a better idea of the things that have been covered up.

Make sure you have a system to notify you that you, or one of your inspectors, have inspected the home before.

Reference Material in the Report

Put Information in Clients' Hands

Most inspection reports include identification of conditions and some support material. Your client may never read the support material. For example, the *Home Reference Book* is Carson Dunlop's reporting system. The support material in the *Home Reference Book* has been carefully crafted and modified over the years to not only provide a valuable reference to our clients, but to help resolve problems later when our clients have a problem. The text has many references to problems that may be experienced that would not be identified in a home inspection. Drawing a client's attention to this reference material is sometimes all that is necessary when we are trying to resolve a complaint.

Contracts, Limitation of Liability, and Arbitration

Have a Contract to Fall Back On

Although your goal is to handle a complaint in order to get a happy client, you will sometimes, despite your best efforts, still have a completely unreasonable client. In these cases, you need a contract to fall back on. We can't advise you on this matter because a contract that works in one locality may not work in another. Here are things that have worked for some people.

Refund the Inspection Fee

Some home inspection companies have a clause that limits the liability to the inspection fee or another modest amount. Courts in some jurisdictions have accepted this clause. You should find out the situation in your market. This approach has worked well for some people.

There is at least one downside to the limitation of liability. Your clients, and indeed people who refer business to you, may take exception to such a clause. It does not feel like great customer service to some. You and your lawyer should decide whether to use this clause.

Seek Arbitration

Another clause that has worked for some inspectors sets arbitration as the conflict-resolution method of choice. **Arbitration** is a method of obtaining an impartial third party to make a decision when there is a stalemate. The benefit of arbitration is cost. When you get lawyers involved, costs go up and the litigation process is never simple. One of the downsides of binding arbitration is that there is no appeal process. An arbitrator who is not knowledgeable about home inspection and makes a poor judgment can hurt you and leave you no recourse.

Another possible disadvantage to arbitration is the tendency in some arbitrations to split the claim. This is not a great solution if you believe you have no responsibility. You may want to speak to specialists in your area to learn the pros and cons for your business.

What Courts Think

While we are not lawyers, and do not want to play amateur lawyers, this overview may be helpful as you think about complaints, and how a court may look at things if you end up there. In most of the United States you may have a complaint based on either contract law or tort law. A *contract law complaint* would mean that you are being accused of breaching your contract. You did not do what you committed to do in the contract. This is less common than a tort law complaint.

A *tort law complaint* in the home inspection world usually means negligence, and a contract is not necessary here. A tort is an injury or wrongful act. It simply means that you are being accused of doing something that hurt someone. In home inspection this is usually negligent misrepresentation. That means you did not do your job properly, and you did not tell the client what you should have. The act is typically unintentional and is the result of failing to act to protect someone, rather than committing an act that hurt someone.

The person making the complaint has to prove five certain factors were present to meet the test for a successful negligent misrepresentation claim:

1. There has to be duty of care between the parties. (This means one party's actions injure the other party.)

2. The information must be untrue, inaccurate, or misleading.

3. The home inspector must have been negligent in giving the information. (It's not enough that the information was wrong. It also has to be negligent. That means that the test is not met if the information, although incorrect, was logical and reasonable, given the situation.)

4. The client must have reasonably relied on the information. (If the information did not affect the client's decision to buy the home, the test is not met. If the client firmed up the transaction before getting the inspection results, they did not rely on the information.)

5. The advice must have resulted in a financial loss for the client. (If the problem does not cost the client anything, this test is not met. It may be because the client was remodeling the room anyway, and the damaged material was scheduled to be replaced. Perhaps the problem was covered by a manufacturer's warranty or a home insurance policy.)

A client making a complaint against a home inspector must meet all of the factors above to be successful in a case. It is not always easy for a person to prove all of these things. But before you draw any conclusions from this, let us reiterate. If you are examining these issues closely, you are probably involved in a legal dispute and should rely on professional advice.

Tracking Forms

Track Complaint Progress and Outcomes

It is a good idea to make up a form on which you record the particulars and outcomes of a complaint. This form is for internal purposes only. It's your way of tracking issues with a particular house and/or client. Covering all of your bases when you get a complaint is important. We have a system for tracking the progress of a complaint called the "Call Back Notice." After the complaint has been resolved, this notice gets attached to the inspection report and is filed. If you ever get another complaint for the same property, you can review the discussion(s) you had at the time.

CASE STUDIES

Here are two case studies from our files to sharpen your skills. We will take you through the complaint, what we discovered on the revisit, and the interaction with the client. As you read the case studies, focus on how the situation was handled rather than whether or not the inspector made a mistake.

Case Study #1: The Inspector Clearly Made a Mistake

We inspected a house with two attic spaces. The inspector only found and inspected one attic space. The inspector did not note in the report that there was a second attic space that was not inspected.

The client called after moving into the home, saying that there was considerable rot and water damage in the attic. A contractor who was preparing to do some remodeling found the problem. The contractor said that the entire roof structure would have to be replaced at a cost of roughly $8,000.

During the initial call, we told the client we would check with the inspector, look at the report, and get back to them later that day. The inspector was not available for two days, and we got back to the client on the third day after the initial call. The client was more frustrated than during the initial call. We arranged to get out to the home to have a look at the situation the next day.

The inspector and company owner went back to the home. We confirmed that the inspector missed the second attic, and we found the damage. However, the damage was not nearly as extensive as the contractor had suggested. We told the client we would be happy to take care of the problem, but that the repairs would cost more like $1,000, rather than the $8,000 the contractor had indicated.

The client was understandably suspicious of our estimate. We offered to have an independent structural engineer specify what repairs were needed, and we suggested that the client get three other contractors to quote on the work.

Although the engineer's report cost us $600, he agreed that the repairs were as we described. The repairs were carried out for $1,100, and we paid the entire cost.

We followed up to ensure the client was satisfied with the resolution of the situation. They were appreciative, although they reminded us that in the beginning it seemed we were dragging our feet and trying to duck the problem.

At the next company meeting, the situation was discussed in detail, including the resolution.

Here are ten key points to note about this case:

1. Get back to people when you say you will, even if it is to explain there will be a delay.

2. Do not accept or deny responsibility during an initial call.

3. Check the report.

4. Speak to the inspector if you did not do the inspection.

5. Always go look at a reported problem.

6. Have two people revisit the home, if possible.

7. Do not accept what contractors or other specialists say without confirming it.

8. Understand that your client has received different advice than what you gave and that the client may have trouble accepting your word. Get authoritative support for your position in a dispute situation.

9. If you agree to solve a problem for a client, make sure you have removed their frustration and recreated the goodwill.

10. Share the experience with other inspectors in your firm to minimize the chance of repeating the problem and to reinforce how problems should be addressed.

Case Study #2: The Inspector Clearly Made No Mistake

We inspected a home in the summer and found the plumbing system to perform properly. The clients did not attend the inspection, and our contract did not get signed until after the inspection.

The next February, following an unusually cold January, the clients contacted us through their lawyer saying we had missed obvious defects that resulted in freezing pipes and extensive water damage throughout the home. The problems had been corrected, and repairs had been made at a total cost of roughly $17,000.

Again, we took the details and told the clients we would get back them later that day after reviewing our files and speaking to the inspector. The report did not suggest a freezing pipe problem. The inspector did not recall any vulnerability in the home.

We contacted the clients through their lawyer and asked to visit the home even though the repairs had been completed. This gave us a chance to do an in-depth investigation and get more history from the clients. Details from the clients were sketchy, and we asked to speak to the contractor who had repaired the home. We spoke to the general contractor and subcontractors, including the plumber.

It turned out that second-floor bathroom pipes had frozen because they were run on an exterior wall with little or no insulation around the pipes. It was clear to us that no home inspector could have predicted this problem. It was not clear to us whether the problem had occurred previously because the bathroom had been recently remodeled. We did not know whether the sellers were aware of the problem and concealed it, or whether the problem developed because of the severe cold.

We explained to the client and their lawyer that we could not possibly have reported this situation because we could not see. It. The clients filed a lawsuit, and we went through the defense process and to trial. The clients claimed they hired us to find exactly this kind of problem, and they did not have any idea that our work would be so restricted. They expected much more than a visual inspection and the operating of fixtures using normal controls.

Knowing that there would be a cost to defend ourselves, we offered a settlement of $1,000 as a goodwill gesture, without accepting any responsibility. This was rejected.

We won the case, but our total costs were $6,500, exclusive of inspector and management time (which together totaled 54 hours). The court found that although the contract was not signed before the inspection (a clear mistake on our part), the client's expectations were not reasonable and that no inspection company would have predicted this series of events. The court also found that the clients were wrong to contact us only after the problems were corrected. We were denied an opportunity to inspect the problem and determine what happened. (In this case we were lucky that the contractors made it clear that the initial problem was concealed. That does not always happen.)

At the end of the process, the clients were not happy with us, although we were shown not to be responsible. We were not happy, having spent lots of time and money to defend ourselves when we did not make an inspection mistake.

Here are seven key points to recall from this case:

1. Get the inspection agreement signed before the inspection.

2. Try to be sure that your clients understand that you cannot find hidden problems or predict future difficulties.

3. If clients cannot attend the inspection, you are more likely to get a complaint. They did not see how much you did for them.

4. Do not accept the client's word or their lawyer's word for what happened. (In this case the problem was not obvious, although the client and their lawyer maintained that it was.)

5. Try to speak to the client to get as much of the story as possible, even when the lawyer is the one who contacts you initially.

6. Go back to the home even if repairs have already been made.

7. Understand that, when you are accused, there are often costs associated with proving you are right. This is a cost of doing business.

Understand that while customer service and satisfaction are very important to most businesses, you have to make the best business decisions you can. In this case, we did not want to fight our clients, but the compensation they were looking for was not reasonable. It was more cost-effective for us to fight and win, while losing the client's goodwill, than to pay what they insisted on. Had the clients' financial request been reasonable, we would have settled, even though we made no mistake in the inspection process.

KEY TERMS

arbitration	release form	unclear responsibility
betterment	responsibility yardstick	
company philosophy	share costs	

STUDY SESSION 10 QUICK QUIZ

You should finish Study Session 10 before doing this Quiz. Write your answers in the spaces provided. Then, check your answers in Appendix A.

1. List the four components of the "responsibility yardstick."

   1. _____

   2. _____

   3. _____

   4. _____

2. When you go to a revisit, you need to give your client a decision on site or else the client will think you are waffling. Circle one.

   a. True

   b. False

3. Why do you want your client to sign a release prior to compensating them?

   _____

   _____

   _____

4. Limiting your liability to the inspection fee in your preinspection contract works every time because once they sign it they are stuck with it. Circle one.

   a. True

   b. False

5. Explain the concept of betterment.

   _____

   _____

6. Why is it a good idea to make up a tracking form on which you record the particulars and outcomes of a complaint?

   _____

   _____

   _____

If you had trouble with the Quiz, reread Study Session 10 and try the Quiz again. If you did well, it's time for Study Session 11.

MARKET DIRECTIONS

Study Session 11 looks at the future of the home inspection profession.

LEARNING OBJECTIVES

At the end of Study Session 11 you should be able to

- list six issues that will influence the future of the home inspection business;

- give an example of how a home inspection might be bundled or allied with another service or business;

- define, in one sentence, the concept of consolidation and explain how it may affect home inspection businesses; and

- list six tactics you might use to compete more effectively with consolidated home inspection businesses.

Study Session 11 may take you roughly 30 minutes to complete.

As in any business, the home inspection industry is subject to the ebb and flow of change. What kinds of change? Anything from shifts in consumer expectations to shifts in the ways businesses are conceived and run. By completing this course, you are already more prepared than 99 percent of the home inspection companies out there and will be able to deal with changes as they arise. In this section we will look at some of the current and emerging pressures on the home inspection business.

Whither Home Inspection Business?

Here is a list of issues that may affect our future:

- The Internet
- Changes in consumer behavior
- Diversification in the home inspection profession
- Changes in the real estate profession
- Bundled services and strategic alliances
- Consolidation of the profession

Knowing what's coming may help you take steps to make your business vital and viable. Some of these changes may, at first, threaten to turn your world upside down, but it doesn't have to be that way. There is no perfect set of conditions in which to start and maintain a business. You cannot control all the variables. But you can be prepared with a little research and foresight. "Chance favors the prepared mind."

Let's look at each item on the list above to explore the change and to determine what you can do to make it work for you.

THE INTERNET

The information age is here. Thanks to the Internet, knowledge is easier to acquire than ever before. The Internet is a powerful communication tool that makes it easier, and less expensive, to communicate one-on-one and in groups. What are the implications for home inspectors?

Clients will expect us to be accessible on the Internet so they can

- evaluate and compare inspection companies when deciding whom to hire;
- check our availability and set up appointments online;
- receive their reports online; and
- receive ongoing support online.

The Internet makes it easier for customers to find out about us, but it also means it is easier to challenge our position as experts, because consumers can research a topic quickly and easily. That's why we suggest you have a good Web site, one that's easy to navigate and gives good information in a concise way. We will examine this in more detail in the next section.

The Internet is a powerful marketing tool. For instance, Internet-based contractor referral services have proliferated. As the name suggests, this online service offers consumers a way to connect to contractors. Many of these online referral services are trying to get home inspectors to list with them online. If you have a Web site and a listing with an online referral service, you have many more opportunities for contact with your public.

Associated with the Internet are immense database capabilities. Some say inspection reports are a treasure chest of information about homes, to which home inspectors hold the key. The Internet provides a way to unlock that chest.

CONSUMERS HAVE CHANGED

Consumers are better informed because access to information is easy, quick, and cheap. As a result, **consumer behavior** has become more demanding and less patient. As home inspectors, we need to keep up with expectations. For instance, in terms of response rate alone, a quick response to inquiries is no longer a competitive advantage; it's a minimum standard.

Knowing who your customers are, and what they want, will help you stay ahead in the business. We've given you a number of ways to find out what your customers want, all of which play out a single theme—ask.

HOME INSPECTORS ARE CHANGING, TOO

Many inspectors now offer more **diversification** through services such as termite detection; well and septic inspections; urea formaldehyde foam insulation (UFFI), radon, asbestos, and lead testing; indoor air-quality, mold, and carbon monoxide testing; swimming pool inspections; as well as inspections of new homes during construction, or before the warranty expires. Some firms are branching out into commercial inspections.

These added services help increase the profitability of our businesses, but in some cases, conflict with our codes of ethics. Can we refer a responsible tradesperson? Can we form strategic alliances? In our opinion, the codes of ethics guiding home inspectors need to be revised to reflect current market realities, while still protecting the consumer through proper disclosure and freedom of choice.

If a home inspection company is able to establish a relationship with a home warranty company to offer warranty coverage to clients at a discounted rate, based on the prescreening afforded by the inspection, should the company be able to pass this information along to a consumer who would benefit from it? We believe most people would say that is fine.

If the home inspector received a fee for connecting the client to the warranty company, some would see a conflict. The home inspector may not be sending the client to the best warranty company but to the one that pays a referral fee. But if the home inspector discloses that they receive a referral fee, the client can make their own informed decision about whether to accept the referral or check with other warranty companies. Transparency is the key in our opinion. As long as the client is not subject to abuse through undisclosed relationships, we do not see a problem. As home inspectors offer more services and refer more services to their clients, this issue becomes more important.

Not only have the types of service offerings increased, but the time frame for inspections is changing as well. For instance, prelisting inspections have become popular. Prelisting inspections make great sense in facilitating the negotiation by simplifying life for buyers, sellers, and real estate agents, as well as by speeding up the sale process. There are a number of benefits for inspectors as well. While a detailed discussion of this issue is beyond the scope of this book, the point is that changes to the home inspection are inevitable over time, and you will be well served to stay current with these and to think about how you want to position your company. You can ensure your business stays vital by carefully choosing which road you want to go down with respect to the services you want to offer.

THE REAL ESTATE PROFESSION IS CHANGING

Real estate agents and brokers are looking at significant upheavals in their world. For instance, the **RE/MAX effect** has changed the working relationship between agents and brokers. RE/MAX agents pay a "desk fee" to the broker, but then pay nothing or only a small fraction of the commission on each sale to the broker. This has moved the bulk of the commission revenue to the agent. Brokers now face the reality of doing more work for less money.

In addition, the Internet enables consumers to shop for real estate more effectively. Studies by the National Association of REALTORS® and the National Association of Home Builders show that over 35 percent of North American homebuyers are now using the Internet in the home purchase process. More and more consumers are unwilling to pay traditional commission rates. As a result, the role of the real estate agent is changing.

For the first time, agents and brokers are looking beyond their historic function, and beyond the transaction event, for sources of revenue. "Total home service" and **concierge service** programs have been popular for some time. These programs amount to providing other products and services to the client. For the client, it's one-stop shopping. For the broker/owner it means added revenue. These products and services are offered through a network of approved suppliers who ultimately feed a portion of the revenue back to the broker.

If most of your business referrals come from real estate agents, you need to know how their world is changing in order to adjust yours accordingly. How can you find out? Ask.

BUNDLED SERVICES AND STRATEGIC ALLIANCES

Grocery stores now offer dry cleaning and film processing services right inside the grocery store. Building supply chains not only sell you carpeting and cabinets, they will install them as well. Title insurance companies are helping homebuyers set up mortgages and home warranties. Major retailers are selling home furnishings, maintenance services, home improvements, home and auto insurance, home inspections, and so on. Banks want to not only handle your money, they also want to sell you insurance and stock brokerage services. Fast food restaurants are showing up inside hotels. Automobile manufacturers are partnering with entertainment companies to provide on-board recreation.

The world is moving toward one-stop shopping through **strategic alliances** and **bundled services,** and everyone wants to control the customer.

CONSOLIDATION

We've touched on five issues so far. The last one may be the most important—**consolidation** in the profession.

There is a good chance we will see consolidation in the home inspection profession over the next few years. Some people call it the "Wal-Mart phenomenon."

There will always be room for the small boutique inspection company with exceptional people who provide great and unique service. But these may no longer be the typical home inspection operations. And these players may have to evolve to survive.

Home inspection has become a target for many big North American companies. In its early years, home inspection was protected by its insignificant size and limited impact. That's changing. Here are examples:

- Major retailers have tried the home inspection business.
- Building material sellers have looked at the home inspection business.
- The largest private mortgage lenders and title companies have explored home inspections.
- Utilities struggling with deregulation are looking at getting into home inspection.

Many of these organizations have gotten it wrong in terms of setting up and delivering high-quality home inspections, but they have virtually unlimited resources. It's only a matter of time until they get it right.

Too Small to Matter?

Some people feel that the home inspection industry represents such a small sector that they don't know why big business would be interested in it.

And home inspection is still a relatively small business. Carson Dunlop's numbers show that as of 2003 it was a $1.3 billion-per-year business across North America. Comparatively, the home improvement industry was a $250 billion-per-year business.

There were roughly 25,000 home inspectors in North America in 2003, averaging 270 inspections a year, at about $290 per inspection. Throughout North America, home inspection is a fragmented, cottage industry. Most companies are one-person or two-person operations, and many inspectors still work part-time.

Too Difficult to Bother with

Other people maintain that home inspection is a difficult, personality-based business. Why would the big corporations want to be in it? It's about leverage. Big business is less interested in home inspections than in how to leverage home inspections to build their other businesses. They know that most homebuyers regard home inspectors as trusted advisors. They also know that homeowners spend more money on their homes in the first two years of ownership than over the next ten years. If a company can get an inspection business going, they stand to capture a larger market for the home improvements that new homeowners will make in their first two years of ownership. It's not the revenues that come from the home inspection that interest big business; it's the revenues from the related products and services that make up their core business.

Home inspection is important strategically because of the nature and timing of our work and of our relationship with homeowners. We are the first technically savvy people to get into the home.

We are now big enough to matter. Our profession is becoming an accepted practice, with inspections performed on roughly 75 percent of the 6-million resale homes in North America every year as of 2003, and the numbers are growing.

Some say that only the independent, dedicated expert can perform home inspections. They feel home inspection is special, and our role of impartial advocate is unique. Our distinct position as consumer guardian will protect us from being swept aside by big business. Besides, our codes of ethics prohibit offering the products and services that big companies will want to offer.

But there are four reasons why big companies will be able to take on home inspections:

1. **Big companies play by different rules.** As the big players of the world get serious about the home inspection business, our code of ethics will not deter them. They will let the market decide what it wants. There may be no perception of conflict of interest in the consumer's mind. The consumer knows that big retailers provide many home products and services. But, if the retailer also provides the best home inspection value, many consumers will choose them.

2. **These players are already a market force.** The big companies are already viewed as reliable and enduring. The public recognizes and trusts their brands. Most of us agree that the reputation of the home inspection profession is not unchallenged. The biggest and best among us are still not household names. Many consumers will be more comfortable dealing with a big corporation that has a reputation for standing behind its work, than a one-person operation with limited resources that may not be around in a year.

3. **The big companies compete on price.** Consumers may also see great value in the large corporate inspection because the price will be low due to economies of scale and the systems they already have in place. They may use home inspection as a loss leader to drive their other businesses.

4. **The stakes are high.** Homeowners are a huge market, and the big guys want access to the customer. Perhaps more accurately, they want to own the customer.

What should we do? First of all, don't panic. Every small business faces big business at one point or another. Better to know and be prepared than to remain ignorant. We can also work together to come up with different ways to handle our business in these changing times.

Our preliminary ideas include such things as the following:

- Diversify and create other revenue streams.
- Make yourself more valuable to buy out than to compete with.
- Build value into your business that goes beyond your personal reputation.
- Become part of an alliance or network of inspectors.
- Look for economies of scale.
- Build strategic partnerships with others outside of home inspection (relationships that have their own value).
- Gather your data into a database.
- Make yourself more valuable through ongoing and specialized training.
- Avoid spending time inventing the same wheel as everyone else.

SUMMARY

Home inspection is a young and exciting consulting service that plays a pivotal role in consumers' lives, affecting the largest purchase most of us ever make, at a critical time. The opportunity for this young profession is mind-boggling if it is approached with vision and respect for the world around us. We hope you will play a role in making home inspection the breakthrough professional consulting service of the 21st century.

KEY TERMS

bundled services
concierge service
consolidation

consumer behavior
diversification

RE/MAX effect
strategic alliances

STUDY SESSION 11 QUICK QUIZ

You should finish Study Session 11 before doing this Quiz. Write your answers in the spaces provided. Then, check your answers in Appendix A.

1. In what way can the Internet help the home inspection profession, in one sense, and harm it in another?

    _____

    _____

    _____

2. How has the Internet contributed to consumers becoming more demanding and less patient?

    _____

    _____

    _____

3. Why is big business interested in the home inspection business?

    _____

    _____

    _____

If you have trouble with the Quiz, reread Study Session 11 and try the Quiz again. If you have no trouble, you are ready for the Final Test and to begin Section II.

SECTION II

ADVERTISING, PUBLIC RELATIONS, AND SALES

Now that you have a solid understanding of the theory and practice of marketing a home inspection business, we can look at advertising, public relations, and sales. In a way, these are all extensions of your marketing plan and practice. Advertising and public relations are tactics for marketing your business. Sales is an inherent aspect of your business that must coordinate with your marketing. As we mentioned in Section I, marketing and sales are distinct but tightly related functions of your business.

OBJECTIVES

The goal of this section is to give you a thorough understanding of advertising, public relations, and sales with respect to the home inspection profession. We will tell you what works and what doesn't, based on our experience, and the experience of many other home inspection companies.

There are many generic books that give you in-depth information about advertising, public relations, and sales techniques, but this course is specific to the home inspection industry.

By the end of Section II, you should have the tools to create effective advertising and public relations campaigns as well as a whole set of sales skills. You will learn

- how your marketing materials function as advertising tools,
- how to evaluate different advertising options and select the optimal ones for your business,
- the types of public relations methods that work well for home inspection businesses,
- how to target your sales efforts, and
- skills for closing sales and managing customer relationships.

INSTRUCTIONS

There are nine Study Sessions in Section II. Each Study Session should take 45 minutes to 90 minutes to complete. The entire Section, including the Quick Quizzes, Assignments, and Final Test should take 15 hours to 20 hours. It's all right if it takes more or less time than we've estimated. Don't rush and try to do more at one time than you can absorb.

1. Read each Study Session.

2. At the end of each Study Session, take the Quick Quiz to review what you have learned.

3. Do the Assignments to turn your learning into practice. The Assignments are important steps in growing your business. In other words, these are things you should do anyway; they are not just a learning exercise. We encourage you to take the time and spend the effort to complete these assignments to the best of your abilities.

4. Take the multiple-choice Final Test (available in a companion volume to this book or from your course instructor).

Here we go!

ADVERTISING THROUGH MARKETING MATERIALS

Study Session 1 deals with the advertising function of some of your marketing material. The concepts in this study session will help you create better advertising tools.

LEARNING OBJECTIVES

At the end of Study Session 1 you should be able to

- describe your target market;
- outline the principles of AIDA;
- write a sample advertisement using the principles of AIDA by choosing the right kind of ad format and writing compelling messages;
- describe one key element of effective design for any of your marketing material;
- list three key elements to writing compelling marketing material;
- put together an information package by listing the contents of an information package and justifying its marketing value;
- design a sample business card;
- outline the process of creating a Web site; and
- outline five key elements of an effective Web site.

Study Session 1 may take you roughly 90 minutes to complete.

This section looks at the different ways in which home inspectors advertise. We will discuss our experience with various methods and pass on some tips on how to make the most of your advertising.

We will start with some of the basic principles of any advertising effort, and then move into specific advertising activities. Some of the advertising activities are almost mandatory—there is an advertising/marketing component to your company name and business card for example. Some of the advertising opportunities are discretionary. We don't expect that you will pursue all of these.

We will present some advertising ideas that are targeted at homebuyers, and others that are targeted at real estate agents. Some of the ideas apply to both target groups. If you have decided to concentrate on one or the other of these groups, you may want to just skim the sections of less interest.

DEFINING ADVERTISING

Advertising is a subset of marketing. Advertising gets your marketing message out in a focused way. *The Portable MBA in Marketing* defines *advertising* as, "Any impersonal form of communication about ideas, goods, or services that is paid for by an identifiable sponsor" (Schewe & Hiam, 449). One key word here is "impersonal." While this sounds bad—you want your audience to feel personally connected to you—most advertising depends on impersonal communication.

Some definitions add the concept of "distribution by mass medium" to the definition. This would take direct mail out of advertising and put it into the broader definition of marketing. For our purposes, we will include "direct mail" under advertising. We will also talk a little bit about company name, logo, business cards, brochures, and Web sites under advertising, although these do not fit in the most narrow definitions of advertising. The definitions don't matter as much as the concepts that we hope will help you build a successful business. So, with apologies to the purists, here we go!

Advertising Is Beginning, Not End

Advertising does not stand alone. While people may be introduced to your service through an advertisement and may even call you as a result, there is typically a sales effort to be made when prospects call.

Target Your Advertising

Your advertising should be targeted to people looking for your service. The person who sees your ad should be someone looking for a home inspector. With this in mind, place your ad where those people are likely to look. A real estate magazine that highlights homes for sale is a logical spot, for example. A home decorating magazine is a less logical choice.

Professional home inspectors may target two very different groups in their advertising, public relations, and sales efforts. The first is the prospective client, someone who is looking to buy a home. This is the person who engages the home inspector and pays the bill. While this is a logical target group, and is the sole focus in many businesses, there are a couple of complicating factors in the home inspection business. The first is that homebuyers are a somewhat difficult group to identify and to direct the marketing and advertising energy toward.

The second and perhaps more important factor is the real estate agent, who often has tremendous influence over the homebuyer. The goals of the real estate agent are often not completely aligned with the homebuyer. The real estate agent is a businessperson who only gets paid when a home sells. The homebuyer is trying to make an informed decision on a large financial investment that will dramatically affect their lifestyle.

It is somewhat ironic that the real estate agent is much easier to target than prospective homebuyers and is more important to home inspectors than homebuyers in one critical way. The potential importance of the real estate agent to the home inspector becomes obvious when we look at the potential return on the marketing money and time invested in affecting the behavior of the two groups.

If we do a great job of reaching out to homebuyers, and persuade them to engage our company, we receive a reward of one inspection fee each (let's say $350). If we are lucky, we may get a referral or two, and several years later when the client buys another home, they may remember us and engage us again. Over a five-year period, we may see up to four or five inspection fees from the relationship ($350 × 5 = $1,750).

On the other hand, a real estate agent who recommends us to their homebuying clients may generate ten or more inspections, year after year. We have one agent who sends us more than 100 clients every year, for example. Over the same five-year period, we may see 50 inspections as a result of this relationship ($350 × 50 = $17,500). Figure 1.1 summarizes the relative value of these two relationships.

Real estate agents may drive considerably more revenue to your business, although they might never pay a single inspection fee. This creates a very interesting situation for the home inspector. Because the goal of the real estate agent is not always identical to the goal of the client who pays your bill, to whom do you owe your allegiance?

We have answered the question this way—"Our allegiance is to the house." This may sound strange, but our goal is to represent the condition of the house as accurately as possible. Any other approach seems to lead to business failure. We do not want to be pursued by clients who find out later that we made the house sound better than it really was. Nor do we want to have to answer to sellers or buyers if we make the house sound worse than it really is. It is clear to us; the only sensible strategy for long-term business survival is to tell it as we see it.

We spend a little time on this issue because some home inspectors refuse to have anything to do with real estate agents, and do not market or advertise to this group at all. We respect this position, but have not adopted it. We do market to the real estate community and are comfortable that we do not compromise ourselves in the process. That is why we include advertising and marketing approaches

F I G U R E   1.1   Growing Your Business Through Relationships

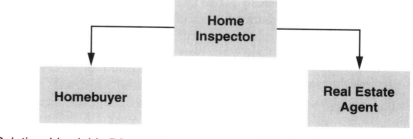

Relationship yields **5** inspections over five years.

Relationship yields **50** inspections over five years.

to the real estate community in this book. You will undoubtedly make your own judgment on this issue, and whatever you decide, we hope this book will be a useful tool in building your business.

For each of the specific initiatives we discuss, we will make it clear whether the program is directed to homebuyers or agents, or whether it is suitable for both.

Now, let's get to the nuts and bolts. We'll begin with a discussion of a basic advertising principle called AIDA. Then we'll discuss things like logo, business card, brochure, information package, and Web site, before moving to specific advertising programs. We will finish this section with a discussion of possible public relations initiatives.

AIDA

Make AIDA Your Mantra

AIDA is an acronym that helps people write material that will persuade readers to act in a certain way. Whether you are creating an advertisement, a brochure, a direct-mail piece (such as a postcard), or a newsletter to send to real estate agents, you should be thinking AIDA.

As summarized in Figure 1.2, **AIDA** stands for the following:

- **A**ttention
- **I**nterest
- **D**esire
- **A**ction

Let's look at each component of AIDA in detail. Whether you are thinking about homebuyers, real estate agents, or both, AIDA applies.

Attention

Create Attention-Grabbing Headline

Immediately grab the reader's **attention** with a headline and subhead. Because advertising fills our daily lives—ads cover almost every conceivable surface and fill the airwaves—most of us have become desensitized to them. We look but we don't see. Successful advertising finds a way to break through our desensitization. For instance, some have used shock tactics to get our attention. It doesn't matter if the shock tactic has nothing do to with the product or service. The goal is to jar us and create a memorable connection to the product or service. Humor is another tool of the advertising world. If the advertiser can make us laugh, we may remember the product or service with fondness. Another time-honored tactic is using sex to sell. Again, the goal is to make a connection in the consumer's mind between something pleasant and their product or service. Sex is used in lots of advertising, but we do not believe it works in home inspection advertising. We have seen shock value and humor both used effectively in home inspection advertising. An image, in addition to or instead of words, might also function to grab your audience's attention.

While this is not a college-level course in writing advertising copy, here are a few tips you can try.

Use Action Phrases

Keep the attention grabber short. For example, don't say, "Get a Home Inspection to Protect Your Investment." The "get a home inspection" part is not necessary

FIGURE 1.2 AIDA

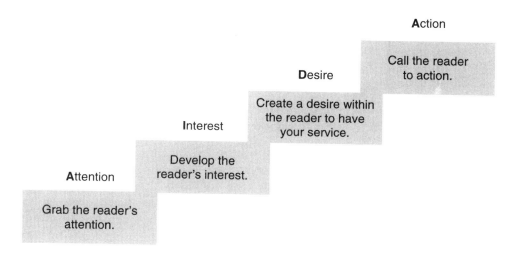

for a headline because the reader will realize they need a home inspection when they read the next lines of your ad. Some better headlines follow:

- How To Avoid a Money Pit
- Don't Gamble When Buying a Home
- Reduce the Risks In Buying a Home
- How To Avoid Buying a Lemon
- Will Your Dream Home Become Your Nightmare?
- Invest $350, Save Over $10,000!
- Knowledge Is Power—Let Us Empower You
- Protect Your Investment
- Make the Right Decision
- Don't Get Burned

You will notice that these titles create a problem and suggest there is a solution in a few words. The idea is to grab the reader's attention by telling them that buying a home can be a big financial risk, and that the home inspection dramatically reduces the risk.

Offer Something for Free

The word **Free** usually makes people look twice. If you can't incorporate the word in the headline or subhead, you should incorporate it in another key area of your ad. You would think that with so many companies offering things for free, readers would have become desensitized, but it hasn't happened. So what can be free about a $350 home inspection? You can offer the following:

- a FREE disposable camera to use during the inspection
- a FREE home encyclopedia for every client
- a FREE checklist for clients of things to look for in a home during the homebuying process
- FREE telephone consulting for as long as the client owns the home
- a FREE first-time buyers' seminar

Interest

Now that you have grabbed your reader's attention, you need to develop their **interest.** Present the most important and interesting aspect of your service up front. There should be a seamless flow from reading the headline to reading a very important and interesting piece of information. For example, ask: "Did you know that 40 percent of homes in the Chicago area have wet basement problems?"

Desire

After you have the reader's interest, you should increase the reader's **desire** for your product or service. State the benefits from the reader's perspective. For example, you could say: "You have enough tough decisions to make in buying your new home. Our professional evaluation of the home gives you one less thing to worry about." Remember, the benefits are more valuable than the features to your prospect.

Action

Finally, ask the reader to do something. This is called the **call to action.** Tell the reader what the next step is and invite him or her to take it. If you don't do this, your advertisement is empty. The reader thinks, great, this is good information and then forgets about it. Here are a few examples of how you might call the reader to action:

Again, use the word "Free." Here's an example: "Call now to receive a FREE Home Improvements Costs package."

The call to action can be as simple as, "Call now, at 555-1212, to book your inspection." It's good to include your phone number in the call to action, even if it appears somewhere else in the ad.

Create some sense of urgency. You might say, "Inspection time slots book up fast. Call now to reserve your preferred time." Home inspection is a time sensitive service. Because the odds of a reader needing a home inspection when reading an ad are low, you might make the call to action a limited-time offer for a discount coupon for a home inspection, or a free booklet that helps them screen homes, showing them a list of common problems to watch for.

Adding color photos of house defects makes this a dramatic and valuable piece. The problem list and photos heighten homebuyers' awareness of risk and give them a better appreciation for the value you provide. There may be a little shock value in the pictures.

The following example takes you through the AIDA process. This ad is mailed to past clients, offering an indoor air-quality inspection one year after the owners have bought the home.

Please note: This ad has no basis in fact. We're using it for illustrative purposes only. (As you go through this fictional ad, see if you can identify the features and benefits statements discussed in Section I of this book, which was all about marketing.)

Title

IS YOUR HOME KILLING YOU?

Attention

Interest

Is your health suffering? Do you or your family often feel ill in your home?

Many families spend their lives breathing contaminated air. They never make the connection between their poor health and the air in their own home.

Fact: One in ten people suffer from asthma.

Fact: While there are effective treatments for an asthma attack, the best solution is to remove the asthma triggers from your environment.

Fact: Allergies have a compounding effect, and most people with allergies are allergic to several things. If you are allergic to dust, pollen, and smoke, you may get rid of all your symptoms by reducing only one of the three allergens.

Fact: The air quality in nine out of ten homes can be improved by 75 percent at little or no cost to the homeowner.

Desire

Our indoor air-quality assessment can get you the answers you need. As a past client, you will receive our service at $245, rather than our normal fee of $300.

We will identify sources of indoor air contaminants and give you expert, unbiased advice on how to improve the quality of the air you breathe. We have no affiliation with any contractor or manufacturer, and we don't do repairs or sell products. We just give you the advice you need. Our recommendations can most often be implemented with little or no cost.

You and your family will enjoy a healthier existence and a better home life. Here is what some of our customers are saying:

> "Thanks so much. The solutions you gave us are worth their weight in gold. We never knew it was so easy to improve the quality of the air we breathe." D. Johnson, Washington, DC.

> "I can't thank you enough. Because you put the cover back on the furnace filter cabinet, my headaches have completely disappeared." Sincerely, J. Walsh, Chicago, IL.

Action

Call 555-1212 now to book an inspection time. Mention this letter and you will receive the inspection and the detailed report for $245 instead of our normal fee of $300.

PS: Make sure you book an appointment when you can spend time with our expert in your home. Our clients say the education they get during the inspection is as valuable as the inspection report itself.

Summary

This example concludes our discussion of AIDA, but we hope that you will refer to this section frequently as you develop your materials designed to persuade people to use your service. In the next section we will look at your logo, business card, brochure, information package, and Web site.

YOUR LOGO

If you are starting a new company, you will be making decisions about company name, logo, tag line, and so on. Once you have settled on a name, you may also want a logo. If you are creative, you may be able to design a logo yourself that works well. On the other hand, many large corporations pay up to $1 million for logo design. We suggest getting some professional help, and luckily, there is lots of help available well below the $1 million mark.

Another Option for Your Logo

Some online companies will design a logo for you fairly inexpensively. This is how it works: You go to the site and look at a sampling of logos posted on the Web site. You choose a design concept that appeals to you. You e-mail your information, and they respond with a logo design. Just type "logo design" into a Web search engine and you will find many companies offering this service, some for less than $100, and many from $200 to $600.

Color Considerations

If you are going to have a logo, it will probably be incorporated into your letterhead, business card, brochure, fax cover sheet, vehicle signs, newsletters, and Web site as well as any advertisements you create. Multiple color logos can be very attractive, but color will increase the cost of all of your printed materials.

YOUR BUSINESS CARD

One of the steps in starting a new business is get a **business card.** In Section I, on Marketing, we said that a business card would not transform your business, but you need to have one.

You Must Have a Business Card

A business card is almost essential in many business settings. You risk being perceived as unprofessional if you cannot produce a business card. Exchanging business cards is a very common business ritual.

It is standard for real estate agents showing a house to leave a business card in that house. This practice is a courtesy to the owner of the home, letting them know who has been through the house. It is also a form of advertising for the agent. Similarly, in the home inspection business, protocol dictates that you hand a business card to all parties present at the inspection, including the agents and your client. Leaving a card for the seller is a courtesy and advertising for you, since the seller is probably buying another home.

Business Cards Have Marketing Value

Although it's part of our culture to have a business card, we don't often spend time considering the card's inherent marketing value. Yes, you need a card. But the card should do its job well. If the card is shoddy, you will look unprofessional. A well-designed business card boosts your image.

Homemade or Professional Design?

Make It Look Professional

You will decide whether to make the card yourself or hire a designer. There are many ways to create a business card, but the goal is to project a professional image. Many homemade business cards look homemade and may suggest to agents and prospects that you are not fully committed to the inspection profession. Homemade cards may also suggest that you are inexperienced. *Inexperienced* means you don't have the technical competence to do the job. When you first start out, you *are* inexperienced, but you can't afford to appear that way. Whether you hire a designer, or make the card yourself, the following discussion will help you keep your card looking professional.

Homemade Cards Look Amateurish

Homemade cards often suggest poor service quality, even if your service is excellent. For example, in Section I, on marketing, we mentioned that printing business cards on laser printer perforated sheets looks unprofessional. The paper feels thin for a business card, and you can see the perforations once you tear the cards away from the sheet. But homemade does not have to mean home printed. You can create a simple layout on your computer and bring your design to a printer who can do a good printing job on high-quality stock with a nice finish.

There are companies that will design and print cards for you. There are also software programs that help you design your own business card.

If you are just starting out, and don't have money for a professionally designed card, making your own is probably a good, temporary solution. If you go this route, you should keep your design simple, with lots of white space. The more you put on the card, the more important it becomes to have a professional design.

Professional Design Worth the Money

A designer can develop your card on a number of different levels. For instance, a designer can lay out a simple business card for a few hundred dollars. It will look much more professional than anything most people can lay out themselves. It's well worth the investment.

The next level up from there is to have a designer create a logo, business card, letterhead, and envelopes for you. The design should be consistent with your company image. In fact, it may define your company image. At this level, you are getting a designer to brand your company. The designer creates a theme that ties all your marketing material together. This theme is made up of:

- logo design;
- company color, or colors;
- font choice (font means type or letter styles); and
- card, letterhead, and envelope layout.

These are just a few of the items you would tie together with a theme. Some companies use images as well. Others use colors targeted to a specific market segment. For your purposes, it's probably enough to try to make sure your fonts and logo are consistent on all your material. You can go further down this road, designing brochures, report formats, and so on. A consistent look throughout your organization (Did we mention your Web site too?) will reinforce your professional image.

Here are reasons why it might be worth your while to spend the money up front for a quality logo and design:

- A designer will be able to make a much nicer looking card than you can.
- You will likely use the logo for as long as you are in business.
- The logo is an important part of your brand.
- You will use your logo on your business cards, in reports, in brochures, in mailers to past clients or real estate agents, and on your Web site. You should be consistent from the start.
- Agents and clients will have a tough time evaluating your technical competency. They will therefore judge you on things they can evaluate. This happens in every business, and it is a good reason to present a high-quality professional image in everything you produce.

Cost Considerations

For the level of branding that a professional designer can help provide, the costs involved may be in the order of

- $1,000 to $3,000 for the logo, company colors, and business-card layout, plus
- an additional $1,000 to design letterhead and envelopes that tie in with your business cards.

Don't Forget Design and Print Costs

These costs are for basic design. Big companies spend much more to have a company image and brand designed.

Here are more factors to consider involving printing costs:

- The more colors you have, the more it costs for printing. If you have a color photograph on your business card, you have to print in four colors. Black text on white card stock is obviously the least expensive.
- Full bleed is more expensive. Full bleed means that the ink reaches the outer edge of the card rather than having a margin.
- Thicker paper is more expensive. There are many different types of paper qualities to choose from.
- Printing on both sides of the card is more expensive.
- Tent cards are more expensive. (These cards are twice as big as regular cards and typically fold in half.)

Design Approaches

There are many different philosophies around business-card design. We will present some of the common ones.

Simple-Card Approach

Many designers will advocate a simple design with lots of white space. The design might include

- a logo;
- company name (either incorporated in the logo or separate);
- your name, along with any certifications or licenses; and
- contact information.

The idea is to present a clear, professional image. Most home inspectors prefer simplicity for their business cards.

Tell-Your-Whole-Story Approach

Another approach is to treat your business card as a mini-brochure. This is more of a marketing concept than a design approach—you are marketing yourself. You may choose to use both sides of the card, putting your contact information and logo on the front and the benefits of hiring you on the back. Or you can dispense with the contact information on the front and go with two sides of marketing. You would, of course, use the AIDA approach we discussed earlier.

This whole-story approach may eliminate the need for a brochure. A business card holder is much easier to put on display in a real estate office than a brochure because it takes up less space. If the office will only let you leave a business card holder, it's a big benefit to have a marketing message on the card.

Tent-Card Business Card

As we mentioned, a tent card is twice the size of a standard business card but folds to form a self-standing tent. This type of card gives twice as much space for your message, and it stands on a table or counter. You can design the card to fold along the side or across the top.

A business card with useful information may give it more life. For example, the front of the card may have your contact information and the back of the card may have a calendar. The calendar is a basic example, but one you have no doubt seen before. There are many more interesting things that you can put on the back such as the following:

- Cost-to-repair data. List the 20 most common repairs and their costs. For example, to shingle a roof costs $X per square foot. Clients and real estate agents might keep this card as a handy reference when looking at houses.

- Ten most common problems with houses.

- Emergency contact phone numbers. It does not have to be relevant to home inspection to be useful to your customers.

- Ten questions to ask a home inspector before you hire one.

- A mortgage calculator that real estate agents and homebuyers can use.

Provide information that the agent and the client would use. If the information is only useful to the client, the marketing impact of your card is diminished.

Many real estate agents use this approach, but it's not common among home inspectors. The front of the card has all your contact information, while the back has a list of other professionals whom the client may wish to contact. For example, the back may list a moving company, a locksmith, a real estate lawyer, a mortgage broker, an alarm company, or any other vendor of product or service that comes after the home inspection. You, of course, would charge the companies a small fee for the placement.

The benefit of this concept is that you may break even, or make money, on your design and printing costs. There is little else to be gained, and perhaps something to lose. If real estate agents are the focus of your marketing activities, this approach might not be a good idea. Some agents like to recommend suppliers to their clients, and they may resent you doing it as well. Run it past some of the agents you know in your area to find out if they would have a concern with you producing your card this way. You may be able to choose products and services that do not threaten the agent's territory.

This discussion raises a small but important point. Agents consider the home-buyers to be their clients. You may be only one of several suppliers that the agent may have referred to the client. Agents value the relationship with the client, and many object to you or other suppliers trying to take over the relationship.

To summarize the card-that-pays-for-itself discussion, the effort involved in finding good suppliers who are willing to pay to be listed on your card, when compared against the return, may make this approach unappealing.

Many home inspectors include a photograph of themselves on their card. This can have a strong impact and help people remember you—something that is important in a relationship business.

If you are a professional engineer or an architect, and a member of a professional association, the association may have strict guidelines for the design of your business card. The organization may consider it unbecoming to have advertising and marketing on the business card. In addition, if you want to add the organization's logo, you may have to comply with their guidelines.

"Useful" Business Card

Business Card That "Pays For Itself"

Your Photo on Your Card

Business Card for Engineers and Architects

YOUR BROCHURE

Some inspection companies make up a **brochure** immediately after they get a business card. It seems like an obvious next step. But before you spend time and money on a brochure, consider whether it is necessary. Real estate agents will expect you to have a business card, but a brochure may not be a necessity in the early stages of a business, particularly if you are having success marketing. Brochures are **background marketing.** The brochures float in the background but don't by themselves convince homebuyers or agents to use your services. Brochures introduce people to your company and provide a little information.

Having said this, here are two reasons why you may want a brochure:

A Brochure Has Its Place

1. If you participate in buyer seminars, first-time buyer talks, trade shows or home shows, the attendees will expect to see a brochure in the handout package.

2. As your business grows, people will expect you to have a brochure. Clients and agents who refer others will want something to give to the prospects they refer to you.

Write from Client's Perspective

Regardless of your reasons for producing a brochure, if you decide you want one, we encourage you to do it right. Just like a business card, a brochure that doesn't look good could hurt your business rather than help it. When you create your brochure, don't forget the following fundamentals we have learned:

- Use AIDA as your guide for writing the text.
- Write the brochure from the client's perspective.
- Write about benefits to the client, not about features of your company.
- Less is more. Write about just a few compelling benefits rather than many mediocre benefits. And remember, most of us are discouraged by having to read lots of text.

Give the Reader Something

One of the reasons most brochures don't work well is that the focus is all on the company, not on the reader. A series of features that describe how great your company is does not hold a reader's interest as well as giving them something they can use. If you focus on their well-being with respect to home ownership, they may sense that you are a company that will take care of their interests.

People Work with People They Like

While your brochure will include your credentials, don't make those the focal point. Every consumer will assume you have the technical skills to perform an inspection. Consumers will not want to dwell on this issue because they will always feel inadequate and frustrated trying to evaluate technical competencies.

A medical analogy works well here. Most people cannot determine whether their family doctor is the best or worst in the field, but they can evaluate how they are treated. Does your doctor make you feel important or make you feel that you are just one more commitment in a busy day? Does he or she listen and take the time to find out what you are feeling? Does the doctor explain things to you in a way that makes sense, or does he or she use medical terms, speak quickly, and not invite questions? Does he or she keep you waiting and then seem distracted and distant? These are issues that consumers can measure, and that is how they choose their service professionals.

Customer Service in Your Brochure

Your brochure and your entire service should be built around doing these things well. Many home inspectors are fascinated by the technical side of inspec-

tions and pay little attention to the customer service side of the bu
be noticed in their brochures, on the phone, and in the field.

Everyone understands that customer service is common ser
require high-level training. Most people say they are customer s_
asked, but most pay far less attention to this than it deserves. Remember, you.
customer service is the only thing most people will use to judge you. We suggest
you make the first impressions and the relationship all about the customer.

Designing the Brochure

There are many ways to design a brochure. We think the following design works
well:

Choose a Theme

■ One common approach is a tri-fold brochure. This kind of brochure is relatively inexpensive because it can be printed on standard 8½ × 11 paper. It's
easy because even the simplest desktop publishing program and word proces-
sors have templates for creating a brochure like this. It also fits nicely into a
standard letter envelope.

Use Punchy Headlines

■ Put your headline on the front flap. The headline should present a compelling
reason to read further. For instance, it could say something like, "Want a
Smoother Real Estate Transaction?"

*Know Which Flap Is
Important*

■ When the brochure is opened up fully, the left-hand panel should have an
introductory paragraph, the middle panel should have the most important
benefits of your service, and the right-hand panel might describe why you
have a competitive edge in the business. This can be your unique selling
proposition (USP), the one thing that makes you different from everyone else
in the business.

*Subheads Tell the
Story*

■ Your inside panels should have subheads that play out the theme of your
headline. For instance, on the inner left-hand panel, above your introductory
paragraph, you could have a subhead that said something like, "We're in the
Business of Solving Problems." The subhead over the middle panel might say
something like, "Five Steps To a Smoother Real Estate Transaction." Here's
where you list benefits. And, for the right-hand subhead, you can say something like, "We Make It Simple." or "Every Home Has a Story, and We are
the Storyteller." On this panel you could put your USP and testimonials from
clients that prove you deliver it.

■ Turn the brochure over and spread it open again. The middle panel on the
back should have your company and contact information, including your
logo, telephone, fax numbers, and Web site address. The right side of the
back already has your headline on it. That leaves one flap empty, the left
flap. Why not put a relevant image on it, such as a picture of a fantastic
house or a disaster house? It's the least important flap. But it's a great place
for a compelling photo that speaks about your business. This is also a great
place to put something valuable for the reader. It might be ten tips for
spotting common house problems, a list of frequently seen defects in your
area, or an inexpensive solution to a problem common to many homes. It
could also be a list of great Web sites that are of interest to homebuyers and
owners. You might include a list of useful phone numbers for your area
including fire and police, building department, utility companies, and so on.

Some inspectors use this panel to offer home safety tips. Because all of these things are seen as valuable to readers, people might even keep your brochure because of this feature.

Keep Design Elements Consistent

■ Use lots of white space. If your brochure is packed with dense text, people are not likely to read it. Wide margins draw the reader's eye to the center of the page, where your text is. We are a generation of lazy readers. Make it easy for people.

■ Your fonts, margins, and all your other design elements should be consistent. A good graphic designer can help ensure stylistic consistency.

Design for Other Media

Good designers contemplate other uses for brochure text. You may be asked to fax your brochure to someone. The three-panel layout is not ideal for this. You may want to produce your brochure in a faxable format as well as the three-panel mailer. Similarly, you may want to e-mail your brochure and post it on your Web site. There are some layout issues to consider here as well. The more of this you do up front, the easier it is to maintain a consistent professional look for your company. The hard part is to do all of these things before you know whether your business will be successful.

Time and Cost Considerations

It takes time to get a brochure together, more time than you might think. The following is a rough estimate of the time it will take:

Estimate Time Realistically

■ Writing: two days to a week

■ Designer's time: one to two weeks

■ Printer: one to two weeks

■ Distribution: depends on how you intend to get your brochure to your target destination

In addition to the time you spend on the brochure, there are costs associated with designing, printing, and distributing it.

Consider Outsourcing Your Design

If you are not good at laying out a brochure, you should hire someone who is. A little money spent on a good design can make the difference between a professional image and one that screams "Amateur!" The cost can vary depending on whether you hire a home-based designer or a professional design company to come up with a company image. Most sole-proprietor home inspection companies go with the first option because a custom-design and company-image consultation is too expensive. A basic brochure layout might cost a few hundred dollars.

Research All Associated Costs

As seen below, printing costs vary dramatically depending on number of colors, format, paper quality, and volume:

■ A single color printed on your choice of standard photocopy paper may cost you 5¢ to 10¢ per page. Color printing may cost 25¢ to $1 per page, in small volumes.

■ If you print on glossy, heavy paper, your costs could double or triple.

■ Most home inspection companies print in small enough volumes that the only feasible way to print is with a photocopy process. The price per print is fairly stable regardless of volume with a photocopy process. The price may vary by 20 percent or 30 percent for larger volumes. Once you get to very large volumes, offset printing becomes feasible, and the costs do vary dramatically. Regardless of the volumes and type of printing method, it's always a good idea to ask what the price break points are. For example, if you ask for 500 copies, the shop may not tell you that if you get 1,000 copies, the price per copy drops by 40 percent. So ask.

The final cost involved in producing a brochure is distribution. If you plan to keep real estate offices stocked with brochures, you may want to buy acrylic brochure holders. These are available at most office supply stores. Don't forget to consider your time to keep the offices stocked with brochures. If you deal with 40 real estate offices and you want to drop in once a month to verify that the office is stocked, and chat with the broker or agents while you are there, it means you have to be in two offices every day! This is probably more time than you have.

Brochure Holder Tip

You should have your company name and logo on the front of the holder, so it does not get used for other people's brochures. On the face of the holder, print something like "Call 555-1212 for more free brochures." This message makes it more likely that someone will call you to bring more brochures.

If It's Worth Doing,
It's Worth Doing Well

A poorly designed or printed brochure can work against you rather than for you. Let's look at the medical analogy again. If you go into a doctor's office and the waiting room is filthy, would you wonder if the medical equipment is clean? Similarly, if you have trouble reading a home inspector's brochure, would you wonder whether the inspection report will be the same? In other words, if you can't afford a decent brochure, put your money into something that will give you greater payback and will not hurt your business.

YOUR INFORMATION PACKAGE

When you meet someone who may refer business to you, it's nice to have an **information package** you can give them. This package can include your brochure or even take the place of a brochure. An information package may include the following:

- Company prospectus. A *company prospectus* is a brief story about you and the company. It may include your certifications and professional memberships. It typically includes a description of the services you offer, and it may provide some background about the company and its owners.

- Benefits of using or referring your company. This is a marketing page. Explain the benefits of your company to the person you are leaving the package with.

- Sample newsletter or newspaper article. If you have a newsletter, or if you have submitted articles for publication in a newspaper, include them in the information package. If your article was published, make sure the copy you include looks like it was taken from the newspaper.

- A testimonial letter. Include one or two good testimonials.

- A few business cards.

- A brochure, if you have one.

- A sample inspection report.

- Useful tips or advice. Include answers to common questions or solutions to problems here.

- A handwritten cover note.

Benefits of an Information Package

An information package is a good way to go if you don't have lots of money because, even without a brochure, you can get professional results. You can write or assemble the relevant pieces and have the package printed and bound at a copy shop. You may also make up folders to contain the material. These cost a little to print up, but then you can assemble packages as you need them. It requires little upfront cost, and you can print small volumes as needed.

When you meet with a real estate agent, you are taking up valuable time. If you have something substantial to leave at the office, it makes a good impression and gives you a reason to follow-up after the fact. We often leave a sample of our reporting system and an information package after meeting with a real estate agent.

A Piece of Advice

Although a well-presented information package and brochure are effective tools when meeting with real estate agents or potential customers, it is your approach and presentation that will ultimately determine how effective you are at selling your service. Once you have built rapport with your customer and earned their trust, your marketing materials will be more effective in showing your customer how your service will solve a problem or satisfy a need. We will look more closely at sales strategies later in this Section.

Get a Testimonial Letter

Testimonials are a great way to influence a prospect, whether the prospect is a real estate agent or a homebuyer. Look for people who would write you a testimonial. If you do an inspection, and you find the homebuyer to be particularly grateful, or you have a real estate agent tell you that you did a great job on the inspection, ask for a testimonial letter. Sometimes it's more appropriate to phone the agent in the office if you don't want to ask while the client is standing by, but strike while the iron is hot.

Just Ask

The only downside to asking for a testimonial is, you guessed it, asking. It is an uncomfortable thing to do. Because it's so hard to do, not many inspectors do it. But if you ask, you will be ahead of the game because most of your competitors will not have testimonial letters.

A testimonial letter also helps to introduce you to a top real estate agent. Mail the agent a letter with the testimonial attached. Then call and ask if he or she would be willing to meet with you for five minutes.

Here are tips on the testimonial letter:

Write the Letter Yourself

- Most people are intimidated when it comes to writing something nice about someone else. One good way around this dilemma is for you to write the testimonial letter. All the other person has to do is read it over to make sure he or she agrees with what is written and then sign it.

Ask on Your Questionnaire

- Another vehicle for obtaining testimonials is through your client questionnaire. A well-designed questionnaire invites your client to say something positive. A simple but effective questionnaire may have only three questions:

  1. Was there anything about our service you particularly liked?

  2. Was there anything about our service you did not like?

  3. Do you have any suggestions for improving our service?

  The first question is the one that generates testimonials. Include a self-addressed, stamped envelope so the client can easily pop the questionnaire into the mail. E-mail and fax responses work well, too.

We often get questionnaires back with a long paragraph indicating how happy the client was with the inspection, and that they would be happy to be a reference. These are testimonial letters. Make sure you get permission to use the comments. One way you can do this is to add a request on a questionnaire. That way, the respondent simply checks the box, and you don't have to call to ask permission. The text beside the box may say, "May we use your comments on our promotional material?"

Paraphrase the Testimonial Letter

- Testimonials are great to have on file. Any marketing piece you write will benefit from a well-placed testimonial. For example, if you are targeting past clients to offer a follow-up or ancillary service, you may decide to launch a direct mail campaign. The mailer would indicate the benefits of the service. Throw in key statements from the testimonial letter with the name of the person who sent the testimonial and the city in which the client lives.

Include Names and Faces

- Readers often question the validity of testimonials. You can add believability to the testimonial by using the client's name and a photo of the client, with their permission. Testimonials that include only initials are less credible.

YOUR WEB SITE

A Modern-Day Necessity

These days, a Web site is just as important as a business card. A basic Web site is a location on the Internet (like a piece of real estate that you buy) on which you display information you wish to share. Web sites come in all shapes and forms and serve all kind of purposes. A Web site may serve as an online brochure, at least for home inspectors. It's where people might find you and learn about you.

Put Yourself on the Map

Like a business card or brochure, a Web site will not likely transform your business or change any agent's referral behavior by itself. So, why have one? Because *not* having one can be as much of a liability as not having a business card. The Web site is probably more important for attracting prospective clients than agents. Many people go online to research companies before making a selection. It's easier to go online and get information about a company than it is to make a phone call. People can do the research on their own time.

If you don't have a Web site, you simply don't exist for some prospective clients. Because a simple Web site is fairly inexpensive to build, you should have one. It raises your profile and gives you legitimacy. If your competitor has one and you don't, you give your competitor an advantage.

Unfortunately, setting up a Web site can be intimidating. There are lots of companies who can help you with this, but because many inspectors set up their own Web sites, we will outline the process briefly here.

There are four steps to getting yourself on the Web. In our opinion, the best order is the following:

1. Register a domain name.

2. Get your site built (you can do this at any stage after registering your domain name, but there's no point in paying for a hosting package if you don't have a site to host.)

3. Pay a company to host your site (Web-hosting package).

4. Pay an Internet service provider (ISP) to give you access to the Internet from your home or office.

We will look at steps 1, 3, and 4 in more detail in the following subsections. Step 2 is covered last because it is a big topic.

Some companies provide registering, hosting, Internet access, and Web site design all under one roof. Others provide only some or one of these services. You may decide to mix and match companies because each has its own strengths and weaknesses, as well as different pricing packages.

Register a Domain Name

Register Your Domain Name, NOW

Your most critical step is the first, **domain name registration.** A domain name is simply the name you give to your Web site. It might be *www.perfectinspection.com,* for example. Even if you don't plan to have a Web site now, register the name. You might change your mind later. You want to be sure the name is still available for you down the road.

Company Name and Domain Should Be Same

In Section I, on marketing, we urged you to register your domain name before you carve your company name in stone. Why? Because it's best to have a company name that is also your domain name. That way, people can find you on the Internet more easily.

It's important to research registrars because each offers different levels of service, and each answers to different laws, depending on the country they are in. Good resources for researching a registrar include the following:

- ICANN (Internet Corporation for Assigned Names and Numbers): *http://www.icann.org/new.html*
- InterNIC (Internet Network Information Center): *http://www.internic.net/*

At these sites you will find Frequently Asked Questions (FAQs) about registering domain names and lists of accredited registrars.

Finding a Registrar

The best place to find a registrar is online. If you type "domain name registrar" into a search engine (such as *Google.com* and *yahoo.com*), a number of pages will appear with links to various registrar Web sites. Take a look at a few before you decide which registrar to use.

Get More than One Extension

Your domain name will need an extension, such as .com, .org, .ca, .net, and so on. You can register with just one or try registering as many as you want. The more extensions you have, the easier it is for someone to find you on the Web. For instance, say your company name is *Inspectionarian.* You might register *www.inspectionarian.com* but not *www.inspectionarian.net.* Someone else might take *inspectionarian.net.* If someone looking for your Web site keys in .net instead of .com, they might find your competitor or someone else altogether. The most common extension, with the least restrictions, is still .com, but many of the names with .com extensions have been taken.

Registering a domain name costs money every year, and how much depends on the registrar. Some registrars will register your domain name for free if you agree to host with them.

Do an Internet Search for Your Name

How do you check if a domain name is taken? Enter your chosen name into a search engine and see what comes up. One search engine to try is *www.check-domain.com.* It will even give you contact information for the person who has that domain name.

Check with a Registrar

You can also go directly to a registrar to see if anyone has the name you want. Try your name with different extensions. You may find the .com extension is taken, but .net or some other extension is not. Once you've registered your name, your registrar sends it out to the networked computers all over the world, telling them that you are *www.myhomeinspections.com* and that no one else can use that name. But beware, when your registration expires, if you don't reregister in time, someone else can grab your domain name and register it for themselves. The people who take your domain name may offer it back to you for an exorbitant fee. They know you already have business cards, brochures, and so on printed with your Web site.

Find a Web Site Host

A **Web site host** is a company that owns large computers, called *servers*. Your Web site gets stored on the server. You pay a fee to have your Web site on that server. Why can't your Web site live on your computer at home? Theoretically it can. But in order to be available on the Internet all the time, your server would have to be hooked up to the Internet all the time, leaving your computer vulnerable to hackers. Web site hosts have equipment to store your Web site, to maintain the server so it doesn't crash, and to protect your Web site from hackers. It's more practical to host your site with a Web hosting company.

Your registrar may also be your Web site host, or you may choose a different company to host your site because the pricing is better. Again, the cost varies, and some places will host you for free. The cost of hosting typically varies with the size of the Web site. The larger the site, the higher the cost. But you often get what you pay for, so do the research. An Internet search is your easiest way of finding hosting companies.

Get an ISP

If you connect to the Internet from home or office, you already have an Internet service provider, or **ISP.** In simplest terms, the Internet is a worldwide system of interconnected computers that talk to each other. In order for you to jump in on the conversation, you need to pay a company to give you access to the system. Once you get access, generally speaking, your computer can access all the information that's available on the system (with some exceptions). But that does not mean information floats freely on the system all the time. Information is stored on specific servers, such as the one hosting your Web site, and these servers allow people access to the information stored on them through the Internet.

Most home inspectors have Internet access in their office or home. You need Internet access to surf the World Wide Web. The Web, as it is commonly called, is a part of the Internet that is a system of interconnected servers set up to transfer information. The Internet is also used for e-mail (electronic mail). E-mail has become such a standard form of communication that you can't really run your business without it. Almost everyone has an e-mail address on their business card.

High-Speed Means Easy Access

Getting online means you need to find an Internet service provider (ISP), a company that you pay to hook you up to the Internet. Most cities have more than one ISP, and each provider offers different packages to get online. The price for this service depends on how fast your connection is—regular dial up, high speed DSL, satellite, cable company high speed, and so on. Most high-speed packages have unlimited usage and are connected to the Internet all the time.

Wireless Access

Technology is always changing, and we are now starting to see more and more wireless ISPs. This technology allows data to be transferred using radio waves instead of wires. The service is not yet widely available across North America and is concentrated around busy public locations such as airports and hotels. But it is coming. This would allow inspectors to access e-mail and Web sites while traveling to and from inspections.

Dial-Up Service

For dial-up service, your price package depends on how much time you think you will spend online and how much space you want for your Web site (if your ISP provides Web-site hosting). Most dial-up packages offer you five to eight online hours a month, with five to ten megabytes (MB) of space for a basic Web site. (One megabyte is one million specific characters.) But be careful, the Web space that comes with your ISP means you don't get your own domain address. Your address will usually look something like *www.websitehosting.com/~inspectionarian,* instead of *www.inspectionarian.com.* Don't spend extra money for this Web space. You will get Web space with the Web site hosting package you buy anyway, and the space you get with the dial-up package will become redundant.

You probably don't know exactly how much time you need to spend online, so start with the least expensive package. If you find you are online for longer, move up to a package that allows you more time online. But be careful, if you spend more time than your package allows, you will get charged per minute or per hour at a higher rate for every minute over your package allotment. So, monitor your time and find an appropriate package.

Internet Access and Fees

Typical fees might range from $10 per month for a limited dial-up package, to $75 per month for a high-speed or wireless connection. The cost for ISP service depends on where you live. If you live in a city or town where you pay for each local phone call you make, dial-up access will cost you more than if you live in a place with flat-rate phone service. High-speed and wireless connections allow you to be online, even when you are on your phone, and you pay a flat rate.

Design Your Web Site

Find Design Software Online

Now that you know the basics of getting a Web site, the next step is to create the Web site. Like the brochure and business card, you have two choices: (1) to design it yourself or (2) to get someone else to do it for you.

Web site design can be simple once you know the coding language. There are many sites and software programs to help you create your own site. For instance, *www.webmonkey.com* gives you online tutorials for learning basic coding language and Web site design. If you want to purchase a piece of software to help you do the job, just type "Web site software" into a search engine to find a number of options for free, or for sale.

Getting someone else to design the site will cost you money but will likely save you time and headaches. The choice depends on what your own design background and computer skills are.

Outsourcing Makes It Happen Faster

Some people hire a student to do the work at a lower cost. Because your site will likely be simple, you don't need someone with fancy computer-design skills. You just need someone who can do a decent job and wants the experience. If you design your site yourself, there are few design tips to keep in mind.

*Easy Navigation
Is Key*

Unlike print brochures, Web sites are interactive. They allow you to move through Web site pages in more than just a chronological way. Hyperlinks, which are clickable icons, can jump you from page one to page five instantly.

A flashy, graphically intense site will not necessarily impress your clients. They may simply want to get in, get the information they need, and get out as quickly as possible. A Web site should deliver information in a simple, accessible way. If your Web site has more than one page, you will need a navigation bar that stays in one place on each page to help guide the reader through. A navigation bar (or menu bar) lists the topics on your site and takes you there if you click on the topic. Each page has a title. For instance, your navigation bar might have headings like: Who We Are, What a Home Inspection Is, When You Need a Home Inspection, Satisfied Customers, Contact Us, Home. This navigation bar should appear on every page of your site, and each heading should be clickable.

Keep It Simple

Like a brochure, the site design should be simple and uncluttered. Most Web sites are overcrowded with information and hyperlinks, making it almost impossible to know where to start. Because your service is straightforward, your site should be as well. Lead your viewers to the information they want and need. Don't make them work to get it.

You want to keep it simple for the following reasons:

- At the most basic level, your site is a brochure, so apply the same design rule you would to a brochure—simplicity.

- You are not trying to sell things. Complicated sites are designed to draw you deeper into the site. You don't want to draw your viewer in deeply. You want your audience to get the information almost immediately.

- For your purposes, it would be fine if the prospect only looked at the first page and then called you up to book an inspection.

- A simple site will cost less and take little time to set up, no more than a day or two.

- The site can evolve over time.

Because your first page is the most important, remember to

Use AIDA

- use AIDA to state the benefits of your service;

- have contact information easily available either on the menu bar, or on the first page (and subsequent pages), or both; and

- keep it uncomplicated: A well-executed one-page Web site is better than a site with 20 complicated, un-navigable pages.

Keep Fonts Consistent

Keep your fonts consistent. You don't want your viewer to pay more attention to the look of the letters instead of your message. Also, use lots of white space. We're using the term "white space" loosely here. You may color your white space, but leave a lot of room around your text. Remember, we are all lazy readers these days.

*Don't Make Viewers
Scroll*

Don't make your site too text heavy because people won't spend a lot of time reading on your site. Be sure all of your text appears on the screen. Most people will not scroll down to get information. Keep the information short, to the point, and available without scrolling. You may need a designer to help you figure out how to account for most browser sizes.

If you have some design know-how and are comfortable with design software, you are well on your way to creating your Web site. But you have another hurdle to jump before you get your Web site online. You have to code your design in

Web-friendly language. HTML is the name of the most basic Web language. HTML stands for hypertext markup language.

Hire a Programmer

Like anything else, you have to weigh the value of your time against the price you would pay someone else to design your site. Chances are, a professional would do a better job and in less time. If you keep your site simple, it shouldn't cost much to have a designer do it for you. But be vigilant. Some Web site designers want to apply all kinds of bells and whistles to Web sites just because they can. Don't get sucked into other people's design obsessions—fancy designs may clutter up a site and diminish its user-friendliness.

Ask for What You Want

Before you take your site to a designer, find a simple site on the Web and take it to your programmer/designer as an example of what you want. Don't forget, your programmer/designer might be an HTML expert, but you are a business and advertising expert. You have learned more in this course about selling your business than an HTML programmer may ever know. So, tell them what *you* want! The content of the Web site is your responsibility.

If you do decide to build you own Web site, you may want to read these two books: Jakob Neilsen's *Designing Web Usability: The Practice of Simplicity* (New Riders Publishing, Indianapolis, IN, 2000) and Lynda Weinman's *Designing Web Graphics 4* (New Riders Publishing, Indianapolis, IN, 2003). Neilson's book focuses on Web design philosophy while Weinman's book gives you the nuts and bolts of how to build it. Using both books in tandem is ideal. Also, check out Weinman's site at *www.lynda.com* for her tips and other Web design books.

Advertising Your Web Site

There are two things you may look at doing on your Web site. The first is finding ways to make your Web site come out of a search near the top of the list. The ways are not straightforward, but there are people who can help with this. You may consider getting help here because when someone types in "home inspection Detroit" into their browser, you want to be one of the inspection companies that appear on the first screen. This makes it much more likely that people will click through to your site.

The second thing to consider is buying advertising that will direct people to your site. You can purchase advertising on real estate and other sites that homebuyers may be looking at. You can also buy advertising from search engines that will have your company pop up beside the search results when people type "home inspection Detroit." You may want to look into the costs and benefits of these advertising tools. Their performance is typically very easy to measure.

Include Web Address on Everything

A good Web site is important, but it is no more important than letting people know it is there. Your Web site address should be on your business card, letterhead, inspection reports, mailers, flyers, etc. Make it easy for people to find you.

YOUR VEHICLE

Many home inspectors customize their vehicles to advertise their services. This is a common practice among many businesses, of course. The customization can range from magnetic signs to window decals to multicolored paint jobs. The effectiveness of this background advertising is difficult to measure, but because so many organizations do it, one might assume it does work.

The advantages of a customized vehicle are obvious, but there are a couple of things to be aware of. The vehicle itself should reflect the company's image. A modern, clean, well-maintained vehicle is probably necessary to create a positive impression. Your driving habits will also reflect on your company if your vehicle is identified. Vehicle signs may not be the best tool for you if you regularly experience bouts of road rage.

Summary

This concludes our discussion of logo, business card, brochure, information package, Web site, and vehicle. In the next section we will look at some advertising efforts you may consider.

KEY TERMS

AIDA	call to action	ISP
background marketing	domain name registration	Web site design
brochure	information package	Web site host
business card	interest	

STUDY SESSION 1 QUICK QUIZ

You should finish Study Session 1 before doing this Quiz. Write your answers in the spaces provided. Then, check your answers in Appendix A.

1. What does AIDA stand for?

   _____

   _____

2. If you want your ad to attract attention, do the following: (Circle one.)

   a. Take out an ad in a glossy fashion magazine.

   b. Include the word "free" somewhere in your ad if possible.

   c. Get an agent to sponsor your business card.

   d. Use sex to sell your service.

3. Describe two approaches to business cards.

   1. _____

   2. _____

4. A good business card or brochure will go a long way to convincing your prospects to buy your services. Circle one.

   a. True

   b. False

5. Some professional associations have strict guidelines for the design of your business card. Circle one.

   a. True

   b. False

6. What is the first, and most critical, thing you should do when naming your company and before you build a Web site?

   _____

   _____

7. A 1-page Web site can be as effective as a 20-page Web site if it's done well. Circle one.

   a. True

   b. False

8. Your information package should include all the following EXCEPT: (Circle one.)

   a. A newsletter sample

   b. A prospectus of your company

   c. Benefits of hiring you

   d. Information on how to advertise in your information package

If you had trouble with the Quiz, reread Study Session 1 and try the Quiz again. If you did well, it's time for Study Session 2.

S T U D Y   S E S S I O N

ADVERTISING STRATEGIES AND METHODS

Study Session 2 describes how to evaluate and handle the most common advertising requests. It also teaches you effective advertising strategies.

LEARNING OBJECTIVES

At the end of Study Session 2 you should be able to

- describe the pros and cons of the different advertising options in the Yellow Pages;

- prepare two responses to either decline to participate in, or to ask for more from, any kind of advertising request;

- list six elements of a successful direct-mail campaign;

- design a direct mail campaign;

- describe how to track your advertising campaigns; and

- describe the three-hit rule.

Study Session 2 may take you roughly 60 minutes to complete.

Now let's look at some conventional advertising activities. We will begin with an overview of advertising for home inspectors, and then drill down to specific programs you can consider.

PRINCIPLES OF DISCRETIONARY ADVERTISING

Where Do I Advertise?

There are many ways to spend money on advertising. Some are almost mandatory, and others are discretionary. We have discussed the nearly mandatory advertising that appears on your business cards, letterhead and envelopes, and brochures, for example. In this section we'll look at discretionary advertising.

Discretionary advertising includes things like print, radio, TV (cable), billboards, buses, bus shelters, benches, and the Internet. Print advertising may include ads in newspapers, magazines, newsletters, information folders, and so on.

Before we go too far, let's stop and focus on our targets again. Some advertising is primarily for homebuying consumers, and some is focused on real estate agents. Some can be effective with both groups, but never lose sight of your target group in any advertising.

Advertising to prospective homebuyers is expensive, so focus your efforts. Daily newspapers are costly because they reach so many people. Any advertising here will reach many people, but most of them will not be buying a home. Community newspapers, often published monthly, are less expensive and target neighborhoods rather than entire metropolitan centers. But these, too, touch many people who are not buying homes.

Radio, TV, and billboards have the same disadvantage. They are not targeted. While broadcast advertising to the public can be effective, it takes longer and costs more to achieve success.

So what other options are there? Let's think as a homebuyer. Where do people go when they are looking to buy a home? Real estate newspapers and magazines are a logical choice. Real estate Web sites are also logical. While we said that daily and community newspapers are not focused on your target market, many of these have real estate sections that are targeted to your market. They may not publish a real estate section in every edition. Many have a real estate section on Thursdays and Fridays, for example. These target the people you are trying to reach. Because they will also be read by real estate agents, make sure your message here will be suitable for the homebuyers you are concentrating on and the real estate agents who will happen to see your material.

How Much Do I Spend?

Many people use a percentage of sales as a yardstick for how much to spend on advertising. We often see numbers ranging from 3 percent to 12 percent. We think there is a better way to figure this out, but it takes a little work. We view advertising as an investment and like all investments, you should be looking for a return. If you find an advertising tool that provides a consistently positive return on the investment, you should borrow money and do all the advertising you can possibly do. The trick here is that you have to do some work and measure the performance of the advertisement. We'll talk more about measurement later on.

How Long Do I Have to Run An Ad?

Generally speaking, the longer you can run ads, the better. Many successful ad programs run continuously, although the ad itself changes. The logic is sound. If the ad is generating a good return on the investment, why would you stop doing it?

*The First Results Will
Take a While*

Many people run ads once or twice and, when they do not generate sales, drop them, concluding that advertising does not work. This does not make sense because ads must be repetitive to be effective. Very few people completely understand any message the first time they hear it. And fewer still retain the message for any time, even if they understood it. Ads have to be repeated several times so that people understand the message, and then repeated persistently to help them retain it.

Many professionals recommend a minimum of ten exposures for any print ad, for example, before trying to evaluate its effectiveness.

*How Often Do They
Have to Change?*

We just talked about repetition being necessary for ads to be effective. Why would we ever change them? While repetition is key, ads to the same target group do get stale after a while. Depending on the medium and the target audience, many suggest that ads should change after 35 to 50 exposures.

With home inspection ads, we suggest a different approach to ads that reach out to homebuyers than ads directed to real estate agents. We may not have to change the ads directed at homebuyers because people are only homebuyers for a few months at a time every five years or so, on average. The ads will not become stale to homebuyers because the target group changes every few months.

Real estate agents, however, stay in the market and are targeted over a longer period. Ads to this group should change from time to time. You can keep a consistent message about your home inspection service, but change the ads. Home inspection ads may include a dramatic house photo or illustration of a problem. It may be enough to change the photo or illustration periodically and leave the text unchanged.

Some parts of your ad will never change. Many inspection companies have taglines that are part of their image. Here are examples:

- ABC Inspections—The Standard of Excellence Since 1990
- XYZ Inspections—A Great Inspection Is Just the Beginning

If you have a tagline, you will probably include it in all of your ads.

*How Do I Know if
Ads Are Working?*

Measure everything! We will talk more about measuring results later, but the idea is to track where your business is coming from. This means asking prospects and clients how they heard about you. You are looking to see whether the ad increases your business over time.

Test Different Ads

If you find that an ad is working, you might try changing it and watching for a difference in the response. If it does not perform as well, go back to the original. If it performs better, use it and discard the original. Then start to design the next ad to be tested. Small changes in ads can have a dramatic effect on their effectiveness. Many experts recommend continuous testing of a new ad against the current ad. Keep it simple. Only test one ad against one other. If you always take the better one as your standard, you will refine your ad over time into the most effective possible tool. Keep the old ones though to avoid recycling ideas you tried two years ago.

ADVERTISING OPPORTUNITIES

So far we've looked at advertising methods that tap into your existing marketing tools. You can apply these methods in any ads. In this section, we'll look at some advertising opportunities that may not be as straightforward as they first seem.

A Real Estate Agent's Newsletter

*Beware Real Estate
Agent Newsletter*

Some real estate agents write their own newsletters to send to previous clients and prospects. As a way to defray the costs, some agents sell advertising spots to suppliers, like home inspectors.

*Do It if It Helps Your
Relationship*

In terms of an advertising opportunity, this is clearly focused on the real estate agent even though the ad is directed at the homebuyer. The opportunity to reach homebuyers is not great for a home inspector, but that may not be the point. If a real estate agent refers 20 or 30 clients per year, it's hard to say that you don't want to spend $100 every quarter to advertise in his or her newsletter. The money you spend is not really for advertising at all; it's for maintaining a relationship. We are often told that if we don't take the opportunity, another home inspector will.

If you have 50 agents who refer business to you, and all of them write a newsletter and tap you for advertising money, you may be in trouble. You will probably have to be selective if you do this kind of advertising.

You have some options for dealing with this kind of advertising: You may choose to stay out of it altogether, negotiate the deal, or ask for more benefits or opportunity. You may offer to submit a column that will make the newsletter even better. The same column, or series of columns, can be used for any agent. You don't have to write a custom column just for this agent. And the column doesn't have to be long. The agent would rather have your advertising dollars, but your article may be attractive as well. The article has the added benefit of putting you in the role of an expert rather than an advertiser. The column can also be used on your Web site and in your information packages.

*Ask for Something
in Return*

You may want to try to get more out of it for your money. Following are some things you can ask for:

- Ask for an exclusive. That means no other home inspectors will get their business card in the newsletter. Tell the real estate agent that it's not worth $100 if other inspectors buy ad space next to yours. In many cases this is easy to get. It may even be offered at the outset as an inducement.

- Ask the agent to refer you exclusively to their clients.

- Ask for an endorsement. Maybe just above your business-card-sized ad, the real estate agent can write an endorsement of your services or tell a testimonial story.

- Ask the agent to help you set up a presentation at his or her office. Clear the way through to the office manager or the broker.

- Ask for an introduction to other successful agents.

- Ask for a testimonial you can use in your other advertising.

- Ask for a link from the agent's Web site to yours.

*Beware Real Estate
Agent's Business Card*

Some real estate agents have a laminated business card. They may have advertising on the back to cover the cost, and they may come to you for advertising on that space. Once again, this may not be good advertising for you, but you may want to maintain a relationship. Remember to ask for something more.

Direct Mail

*Direct Your Efforts to
the End-User*

The official term for advertising to the end user is direct marketing. But because most direct marketing campaigns involve direct mail, especially in the home inspection business, we'll refer to this strategy as **direct mail.** Direct mail may be addressed to real estate agents or to consumers, but there would usually be a different piece for each group.

Direct mail looks for a response directly from the customer. But it has specific applications. For instance, contacting your past clients directly by mail is effective for offering an ancillary service. On the other hand, direct mail to the general public offering a home inspection may not make sense. To decide if a direct mail campaign is worth considering, it should have at least a few of the following features:

Identify a Target Market

■ An easily identifiable target market. For example, a company that washes cars by hand, including interior shampoo, might target owners of cars that park overnight in an outdoor parking lot in the winter. Such cars are likely to be filthy and in need of the company's service. The company might send people out to parking lots to put flyers under the windshield wipers of the cars.

An example from the world of home inspection is to mail to people who have a home for sale. There is a good chance they will be buying another home in the community and need your services.

Focus Your Efforts

■ Highly focused marketing material. For example, if your business is building decks, you need to reach homeowners who are likely to want a deck. If you send a mailer to a house that has no yard, or a house that already has a deck, you have wasted your money.

Use a Focused Delivery System

■ Mail is the usual route for such campaigns, but this is not always the best because it may be hard to focus your efforts. If you use your imagination, you may come up with a highly effective, and inexpensive, delivery mechanism. For example, a new restaurant might hire someone to stand on a street corner to give out two-for-one dinner coupons. But to focus things a little more, this person stands in an area where people tend to go out for dinner, and at a time when people are going out for dinner—Friday night between 6:00 P.M. and 8:00 P.M. Now you have focused your efforts on people that like to go out for dinner on Friday night. Our example of sending mailers to people who are selling their homes is a focused approach.

Know the Time Sensitivity

■ For home inspectors, the critical time to reach prospective homebuyers is right when they need your services, but the chances of your mailer reaching them within that narrow time frame are slim to none. Prepurchase home inspections are time sensitive, whereas indoor air-quality inspections for homeowners can be done anytime. Sending a mailer for indoor air-quality inspections to past clients might give the homeowner a sense of urgency about hiring you (because they are concerned about their health), but you are not under the gun to deliver the mailer at a critical time.

You want to offer a service that your prospect can make immediate use of, but your schedule for delivering the mailer is not critical. Another good example is a warranty inspection. If you are offering inspection services on new homes prior to the one-year warranty expiring, then the timing component becomes very important. They will need your services about a month before the warranty expires. This would be the best time to approach them because your reminder will create a sense of urgency.

Make It Easy to Explain

■ A direct mailer has to offer something people can grasp in a few lines.

Measure Response: Track and Test

■ Easy-to-measure response. Measurement is critical in this kind of campaign. When you are dealing with large numbers, you have a good opportunity to experiment. For example, you could do a mailer with a particular offer, then do another mailer to a similar area with a slightly different offer and compare the response rate. You may find that reducing your fee from $325 to $299 increases your response rate by five times. If that were the case, it would make sense to reduce your fee. We will talk more about testing later.

Here are two areas in the home inspection profession that respond well to direct marketing:

1. Inspection of new homes
2. Ancillary inspection services targeted to past clients

The main reasons for the successful response is that these two markets are easy to target and there is some time flexibility. They also meet the other criteria we have outlined above. You may come up with other things you can offer using direct mail.

A SAMPLE CAMPAIGN

Let's look at new home inspections as an example direct marketing campaign. In some areas, new home warranty programs are mandatory. All new homes may come with a warranty that the buyer has paid for directly or indirectly through the purchase price of the home. The warranty has three parts:

1. One-year warranty on workmanship and materials
2. Two-year warranty for water leakage through the exterior envelope including foundation, walls, and roofing
3. Seven-year warranty on major structural items

We saw a direct-mail opportunity—to offer an inspection on new homes with one-year warranties about to expire. Let's look at how this service satisfies all of the criteria listed previously, and where the campaign succeeded and failed.

Little Research Goes Long Way

A new residential development is an easily identifiable target. All of the houses in a given area are about the same age, making it easy to target them. Based on this information, we decided to hire a delivery person to stuff our advertising in the mailbox of each home, thinking it would be cheaper to pay the delivery person than to mail a flyer to each home.

But what seems to makes sense can sometimes backfire. It turns out that all of these developments have central postal boxes. We could not get the flyers into the boxes. Because the houses themselves don't have mailboxes, there was no place to leave the flyer, short of shoving it under the door. And with new, tightly weather-stripped doors, it's hard to get something under the door. This approach did not work.

Our next attempt worked much better. We bought a mailing list from a list broker. List brokers are people who maintain lists of things. Some specialize in a particular area, some don't. You would be surprised what mailing lists are available for purchase. If you want to mail letters to homeowners with three kids, a poodle and a BMW, a list of these people is available.

Our list broker specialized in creating and managing databases for real estate transactions. They were able to give us a list of all the houses in a particular area that were ten months old. We could also specify the price range for the houses. Every month, more addresses came to us that fell in the ten-month-old range. We chose 500 names to start. This knowledge allowed us to send a timely message and keep all of the inspections within a small geographic area. That minimized travel time for our inspectors.

Simple More Costly But More Effective

The mail delivery mechanism for this direct marketing campaign is as easy as it gets. It's not the least expensive when you consider the stamps, stationery, list broker, and fulfillment house, but we found that mail was the best way to get the information in the hands of these prospects.

Make Your Services Seem Critical

Our campaign had a critical timing component. Although the target does not have to get the inspection done within five days, once they get the flyer, they feel a sense of urgency to get the inspection done before the warranty expires. The combination of the pending warranty expiration and the timing of the flyer will help motivate the homeowner to use the services.

Explain It Clearly

The service offered in our campaign was easy to explain and was desirable. It's easy to explain to your prospect that they have a warranty about to expire. It's also pretty straightforward to explain that the owners are unlikely to recognize a problem on their own. You can increase their desire to hire you by explaining some of the problems you have identified in similar homes in the area.

Track the Response

Because we targeted a particular postal region, and we had a specific list in database form, tracking response to the campaign was a simple matter of verifying which mailer the caller was responding to.

TECHNIQUES FOR A GOOD MAILER

Let's look at a few techniques for making your direct mail campaign work. The first thing you should do is review the discussion about the AIDA technique:

Use AIDA

- *Attention:* Grab the reader's attention.
- *Interest:* Arouse the reader's interest so that he or she reads the rest of the page.
- *Desire:* Increase the reader's desire by telling him or her all the benefits of using your service.
- *Action:* Include a call for action, preferably with a compelling reason why the reader should act immediately.

A direct marketing campaign is the ideal place in which to use the AIDA technique because you have no space constraint. You can use the front and the back of a single sheet of paper, or as many pieces of paper as you need.

Make It Look Professional

Because you are offering a professional consulting service, your layout and language should be professional. Ideally, send out the appeal on your letterhead. If writing and laying out a mailer like this is not your strong suit, pay someone to do it for you.

Envelope and Its Contents

When you mail something like this to a prospect, the goal is to get the prospect to read it. We all know what we do with junk mail. It usually goes straight into the garbage. Make sure your mailer does not look like junk mail. Here are examples of things that look like junk mail and should be avoided:

Avoid the Junk Mail Look

- Junk mail packages. Avoid participating in a joint mailer with local businesses. You know the packages we're talking about because you've probably thrown lots of them into the garbage yourself. It's a bulk package that has a bunch of flyers inside.

■ An envelope without a stamp. This will indicate that it has been delivered by a local junk mail fulfillment shop.

■ Loose flyers. A loose sheet of paper delivered by a local service looks like junk and usually goes straight into the garbage.

Handwrite Parts of Your Mailer

We all know that anything that even remotely looks like junk mail goes into the garbage. Anything that looks like a bill gets tucked under the microwave. A handwritten envelope with a real stamp on it gets opened immediately. If you have the resources, a handwritten envelope with a stamp, rather than a postage meter imprint, is the way to go. In addition, a plain white envelope is preferable.

On the mailer itself, address the recipient by name rather than, "Dear Homeowner." And make sure it's handwritten. Personal touches go a long way to creating a more intimate connection between you and the recipient. The mailer feels like it's from a friend. Don't undo the goodwill you've created, and waste your efforts, by spelling their name wrong! Also, write a little message at the end of the letter, before you sign it. Depending on the mailer, your message might range from demonstrating that you remember the person as a past client, to saying you look forward to working with the person.

Postcards

Some inspectors use postcards for direct mail campaigns. Postcards send a different message than a letter in an envelope. They are less private and less personalized. They can also be less expensive to produce and to mail. You may want to experiment with these as an alternative to letters. One advantage to postcards is that people are more inclined to look at both sides of the card and see your message than to open an envelope from someone they don't recognize. If you have a short simple message, a postcard may be good. Postcards can also work as a stay in touch program with existing clients and customers because the message is often a quick reminder.

MULTIPLE MAILERS AND RESPONSE RATE

The goal is to get as many people as possible to use your service for as little cost as possible. You should think of the **multiple mailer** as a giant funnel, as follows:

■ You send out 500 letters—this is the top of the funnel.

■ Of the 500 you send out, 300 get opened and read.

■ Of the 300 that are read, 75 will call you for more information.

■ Of the 75 that call, 25 will book your service—this is the bottom of the funnel.

Response Rates

If your campaign pans out as described, you would be doing fairly well. This is a 5 percent **response rate.** What is a reasonable response rate? For an untargeted mailer, a 2 percent response rate is considered typical. You should do better than that because you have carefully selected the target. If you target a receptive market segment, such as previous clients, for an indoor air-quality inspection, you could get up to a 15 percent response rate.

The techniques discussed in the previous section will help you maximize the response rate to your direct marketing. Using the preceding example, we assumed that of 500 mailers, 300 would get opened. If you had sent your mailer out in a junk mail pack, you would likely have gotten less than 100 people even looking at your offer. How you send your mailer has a dramatic effect on your response rate.

The content of your marketing piece itself is critical because it gives you the biggest jump in the funnel. In our example, one in four (75 out of 300) called after reading the message. A better or worse message can change that response dramatically.

You can now analyze your campaign. If you got a 5 percent response rate, and each mailer cost $2 (including stamp, envelope, stationery, list broker, fulfillment house) and you were charging $299 for the inspection, you would have the following:

- Costs: $1,000 (500 mailers at $2 per mailer)
- Revenue: $7,475 (25 inspections at $299 per inspection)
- Net: $6,475

Your marketing cost or cost-of-acquisition of this business is 13.4 percent of sales ($1,000 ÷ $7,475). Evaluate the profitability of your inspection business to decide whether a 13.4 percent marketing cost is reasonable. If, for example, your profit is $50 per inspection, you make ($50 profit × 25 inspections) $1,250. Because the $1,000 cost of the program resulted in a profit of $1,250, it makes sense.

Here is another way to look at it: If you get a 5 percent response rate and your cost is $2 per mailer, the cost to acquire an inspection is $40. This isn't bad. It sounds like a lot, but it's realistic. A $40 cost to acquire an inspection with a $50 profit is all right. Is it the best place to spend the $40? Only good testing and tracking will tell.

Use Three-Hit Rule

Conventional wisdom suggests that multiple mailers are much more effective than a single mailer. The **three-hit rule** asserts that for a message to be effective, it has to be delivered three times in close succession. The problem is, the term "effective" is stated without regard to the cost of each mailer.

If we sent a multiple mailer, say three mailers, we may get a much higher net response rate. The only way to know whether this makes good business sense is to test and track it carefully. If you do three mailers to 500 people and it costs you $3,000, but you have a 20 percent response rate, you would be doing very well. You would get 100 inspections from the 500 people. The cost to acquire each inspection would be $30 ($3,000 in costs ÷ 100 inspections). It costs you more, but your costs to acquire each inspection are reduced. The 100 inspections represent $29,900 (100 × $299) in sales. Your marketing cost is now 10 percent of sales ($3,000 in costs ÷ $29,900 in sales). Looking at the profit side, your $3,000 cost results in ($50 profit × 100 inspections) $5,000 in profits. This is a pretty good return on investment.

There may be an additional benefit if there is an economy of scale. The houses may be close together and similar, allowing you to do the inspections more quickly and to do more each day. If your profit per inspection goes from $50 to $60, you are further ahead here too.

If, on the other hand, your three-part mailer only pulls twice as well as a single mailer, your cost to acquire has gone up to $60 ($3,000 in costs ÷ 50 inspections) per inspection. Your marketing cost is 20 percent of sales ($3,000 in costs ÷ $14,950 in sales). The $3,000 investment yields a profit of $2,500 ($50 profit × 50 inspections). This seems like a losing proposition.

The secret is to experiment and track. Don't be satisfied with something that is working well. Try something different. Refine your marketing piece—offer something for free, list more benefits in your ad, list fewer benefits but in a larger font, change the title of the ad, include a discount coupon, or use a different color envelope. There are many variables that may affect the response rate funnel. We have found that the title is the most important component, and changes to the title alone can have a significant effect on performance.

Resources

If you don't have time to print, assemble, and mail your own mailer, you can hire a **fulfillment house** to do it for you. They have tricks to get the mailing costs down, but the costs go up if you want a handwritten envelope and a real stamp.

List brokers will charge you more for a more specific list. The broker can combine two lists and get something more specific. For example, if there is a list of all BMW owners in your city and a list of all families with three children in your city, you can get a list of families with three children and a BMW. As you can imagine, the more specific the list, the more you pay. You should decide what search and sort criteria you require. It usually pays to have a more specific list. If half of the people in your mailer are irrelevant because you have not made the list specific enough, you will be wasting money on your $2 mailers.

Our direct mail program for new home inspections has been a success. We have complete control and can increase our efforts when prepurchase home inspections are slow and decrease them when prepurchase inspections are busy. It is a throttle we can use to control our business.

Fallout

You may get a homeowner who wants to know how you got their address. Think of it from their perspective. They have just moved into the house, and people are already contacting them to sell them something. Even worse, it appears that you know a lot about their home, that it's ten months old and that they have a home warranty about to expire. You might not be the only person who has thought to offer services to new homebuyers. Alarm companies, landscapers, furniture shops, and deck builders may have already contacted these people. Some people get upset because their home is supposed to be their sanctuary. We have minimized this problem by careful wording of the marketing piece. We tell them the following:

- We are contacting all of the people in the area who have purchased a new home.
- We are an independent inspection firm.
- We have no association with any builders or government agencies.
- We keep the results of the inspection confidential.
- We will not be passing your name on to anyone else.

Direct marketing is a lot of fun because you can easily and accurately measure the response to your efforts. The results tend to either happen immediately or not at all. The fun is in the testing and tracking, discussed later in this Study Session.

PRESENTATION FOLDERS

*Be Ready for Any
Sales Call*

A **presentation folder** is a simple folder with pockets on the inside of the front and back covers. Real estate agents put their clients' documents inside and give them the whole folder. The outside of the folder usually displays the real estate company logo and address. The inside usually has advertising. At some point, you will be asked to advertise in this space. We want to tell you the story so that you can make an informed decision about advertising in these folders.

A printing company usually spearheads the design and advertising sales of these folders. Whether the printing company calls the real estate office for the folders, or vice versa, the printing company offers some kind of deal on the folders in exchange for the real estate office's supplier list. In both cases, the printing company makes the sales calls to the suppliers, often intimating that the call is somehow coming from a real estate office. It's not. The following scenario may happen to you.

You get a call from a salesperson who introduces himself or herself as though calling from the real estate office. The sales pitch goes like this:

> "Hi, I'm John Smith from Top Producers Realty, and I want to let you know about our unique referral program in which the real estate agents in our office will refer home inspection business to you. Do you have ten minutes to meet with me to show you the program?"

Compelling, isn't it? You are likely to say "yes" to the sales professional, who is typically an outside consultant, not an employee of the real estate company. At the meeting, the salesperson brings a sample folder with your competitor's business-card-sized ad on the inside cover. The salesperson offers you a business-card-sized ad for only $300. Your ad will appear in every presentation folder for one year. They will be printing thousands of folders. It sounds like a great deal, doesn't it? But it's not. Here's why.

*This Ad Will Not
Get You Referrals*

The real estate agents in the office have not agreed to any kind of referral program. They will not refer business to you just because your ad is in the folder. Your ad may not change their referral behavior at all. Worse still, the agents may not even give these folders to their clients and prospects! They may be comfortable in their sales skills and confident that they don't need any corporate gimmicks.

So, who is the target group for this advertising? It's not as clear as some other cases. Because the folders are for prospective homebuyers, you may conclude the target group is the homebuyer. This is true, up to a point. However, you may find yourself advertising in these folders in order to maintain a relationship with a real estate office that refers many clients to you every year. This gets a little gray.

Your ad reaches only one real estate office. If you consider $300 for an ad that reaches only 30 or 40 real estate agents, the cost per agent is very high. You would be better to advertise in a real estate magazine that has a higher readership of real estate agents. Don't forget, this is just an ad, not a referral program.

While it is possible that you will get an inspection or two, it may not be the best investment of your limited marketing dollars. You might be better to spend the $300 directly on a few top agents in the office in some way, like lunch meetings, an office presentation or supplying donuts for an office meeting.

The salesperson may use the following tactics:

■ "If you don't advertise here, your competitor will." Who cares? If your competitor spends the $300, then that's good news for you because that means they have $300 less to spend on meaningful campaigns.

- "You only need to get one inspection to break even." First, as we know, a $300 inspection fee does not generate $300 in profit to offset the cost of the ad. Second, breaking even is not the goal. You want marketing campaigns to pay for themselves many times over.

- "The office manager is expecting your cooperation and will be very disappointed if you don't participate." The office manager or broker may not know you at all, and the sales representative has probably picked your name out of the Yellow Pages. Further, this information may not even make it back to the office manager or broker. Don't forget, the call is typically coming from an outside company, not the real estate office. If the sales representative says that the broker or manager is counting on your cooperation, call that person and talk to him and her about it. You may get an office presentation out of it. At the very least, you will find out how much the manager cares about the program.

While the manager can be an ally, it is important to understand that the goals of the manager, broker, or owner are not always the same as the goals of the salespeople. The salespeople live purely on their own commission income and are on the front lines. They operate with considerable independence and may or may not adopt corporate programs.

Be Demanding

Most home inspection companies that have participated in these presentation folders agree that there is little benefit. If you decide to participate as an experiment, or as way to get a foot in the door at a real estate office you're interested in, ask for

- a list of all of the real estate agents in the office;
- a meeting with the office manager or broker;
- an office presentation;
- copies of the folder with your ad in it;
- an advertisement on the company's Web site, with a link to your site; and
- whatever else seems reasonable.

YELLOW PAGES ADVERTISING

Most companies have a **Yellow Pages listing.** This advertising is directed at consumers. When you register your business, you may get a basic Yellow Pages listing for free. But this kind of advertising does not generate a lot of sales for many home inspectors.

The Yellow Pages has been the topic of discussion for home inspectors for many years. The consensus is as follows:

- Should you be listed in the Yellow Pages? Yes.
- Does it get you a lot of business? No.
- Should you pay for display advertising in the Yellow Pages? No.

We have tracked how much business we get from the Yellow Pages over the years and found we get less than 1 percent of our business through this source. We likely just break even on the advertising costs. We do not get the return we would like on our advertising investment. As a result, we have reduced our ad size to a single, boldface entry. We are the largest home inspection company in our city, yet we have the smallest size entry available in the Yellow Pages.

It is generally accepted in many mature home inspection communities that a Yellow Pages ad is not the best investment of marketing dollars. Remember, you have to invest your funds in the areas with the best returns. So even if we are wrong by 100 percent, or even 1,000 percent, it still may not be worth having a display ad in the Yellow Pages when you compare it with the payoff from other strategies.

Why are the Yellow Pages the first place almost every company advertises? In most cities, when you set up a business phone number, it's easy for the salespeople to try to sell you. The sales agent shows you how your competitor has a larger and more elegant ad than yours. According to the salesperson, your single-line entry makes you look unprofessional.

Not Ideal for Home Inspectors

So, is everyone who advertises in the Yellow Pages stupid? No. Yellow Pages advertising works for some businesses. For example, Yellow Pages may work very well for companies that advertise services someone might need in an emergency, like contractors who can stop a flooding basement.

Referrals Come from Agents, Not Yellow Pages

But home inspection may not be a service that benefits significantly from a Yellow Pages ad. Why? Because although a home inspection is something people need quickly, the prospect usually asks an agent or a friend for a referral. Here's the scenario: A homebuyer makes an offer on a home conditional on inspection and financing. When the offer is accepted, the homebuyer has to find a mortgage lender and an inspector immediately. Do you think the homebuyer will look in the Yellow Pages to find a home inspector and a bank? Probably not. The homebuyer turns to the agent and says, "Where can we get a good home inspector, and who is offering good mortgage rates these days?" Many homebuyers also rely on referrals for title insurance and moving companies, for example. A 2002 survey of homebuyers found that 70 percent of buyers relied on a referral to choose their home inspector. In a largely referral-based business, the Yellow Pages does not figure into the picture.

Most Callers Just Want a Price Check

Most home inspectors agree that when they do get calls from the Yellow Pages ad, the callers are often just checking your fees to make sure they are getting a reasonable price from the home inspector they have already booked. Although *you* know you can't compare services based on price, a caller who found you in the Yellow Pages is likely to be judging you on exactly that. The bottom line is, inspectors priced at the low end of the market are more likely to generate business from a Yellow Pages ad.

If you have not been involved in the Yellow Pages process before, this section will prepare you for what lies ahead. It's easy to underestimate the costs involved in a Yellow Pages ad. Following are a few things you should know before the sales agent calls.

Multiple Directories

In a large city, there may be more than one Yellow Pages book to cover the city. There will be an edition for central, east, west, and so on. You have to pay to be in each of the **multiple directories.**

Multiple Locations in the Directory

In the same way that there are different directories you can advertise in, there may be more than one location in any given directory in which to place your ad. For example, you may want to be located under, "Inspection," "Building Inspection," and "Home Inspection." Each is considered a separate ad. You pay for each, but you may get a discount for multiple locations. You can mix and match—you can put a display ad in the home inspection area and have a single-line entry in the other two or three locations. In some geographic areas, home inspectors have gotten together to petition the Yellow Pages people to consolidate the listings into a single "Home Inspection" category, with referrals from other headings to this area.

Single-Line Versus Display Ad

We have a **single-line entry ad** in the Yellow Pages of nine different directories that span our territory. An entry is just a single line placed in alphabetical order. An entry can be boldfaced, or it can be more than one line if you are willing to pay more.

Display Ads

A **display ad** is a box displaying your company name and can be any size you like. These ads don't appear alphabetically; you pay for a particular location. You can pay for more than one color if you like. In fact, you can have a full-color photograph in many books.

Distribution

Ask the sales agent about the circulation of the directory. If there are three directories that span your territory, you should find out how many books are distributed in that territory. The costs may vary with the number of people who receive the books. The cost-per-household is generally consistent within a market.

Ask about Demographics

There may be a demographic difference between the different directories, too. **Demographics** give you useful information about an area, such as average age, average household income, and consumer habits. Ask the sales agent if there are any identifiable demographics to a Yellow Page's territory. You may learn something about your city that will help you in your other marketing efforts.

Business and Consumers

Yellow Pages are distributed to companies as well as households. You may want to determine the ratio for each book, if you decide that households are your target.

The Web Site Entry

Many Yellow Pages directories are on the Web. You may want to check if a printed listing also includes an online listing. If it does not, you have to consider the value of being listed both in print and electronically because you may have to pay an additional fee to be included there. Multiple directories and locations in the directory are another consideration. Online listings usually have the option of including a link to your Web site at an additional cost.

If you are a new company, don't forget that the Yellow Pages ad will not even reach the public until the next issue is distributed. This is typically done once per year. So don't wait for the phone to start ringing after you sign the deal.

Experiment Cheaply

The sky is the limit when it comes to how much you can spend on a Yellow Pages ad. Our recommendation is to proceed cautiously. Start with a single-line entry, which allows a prospect to find you. If you want to experiment more aggressively, do it in one directory so you can compare the results. For example, if you want to try a display ad, don't enter it in three directories that span your area. Just try it in one location and then track its effectiveness compared to the entry in the other two directories.

Multiple Yellow Pages Directories

In some areas, there are several telephone companies, all of which issue directories. This complicates life even more.

TRACKING AND TESTING

Track All your Campaigns

Tracking helps you determine exactly how much business you gained from a particular strategy. *Testing* allows you to tweak a campaign to see if it brings in more or less business. Tracking and testing also give you an opportunity to modify any of your advertising campaigns. They help you realize that nothing is written in stone. They often help you save money, letting you know that you should stop doing what isn't working. Many companies continue with advertising strategies because they have always done their ads that way. You need to be critical about where you are spending your advertising dollars. Here's an example we gave you on page 93 in Section I, on Marketing, that applies particularly well here.

You decide to place a display ad in your local Yellow Pages. It costs you $500 per month. At the end of the year you have spent $6,000. The sales team from the Yellow Pages contacts you and asks if you would like to place a larger ad for the upcoming year. You, of course, have no idea whether your $6,000 has generated 1 or 150 inspections for you. How do you decide if you want a bigger ad, or whether you want to remove the display ad altogether? If you have not tracked the effectiveness of the ad, you are in no position to make a decision.

Ask, Ask, and Ask

How do you track the effectiveness of an advertising strategy? The tracking procedure has to be built into the design. One good way to track advertising is to ask every customer or client how he or she heard about you. You then need to keep track of this information. At the end of the month you can make a list of all of the ways you advertised and how your clients heard about you. You should also have a list of inquiries you got and cross reference the list with your client list. If you have a client list, you have a list of the actual inspections you got. For example, you may discover that the leads you get through the Yellow Pages are more price resistant—the callers are often price shopping. But the leads you get from the mortgage broker convert easily to deals. This is the kind of information you need to track.

Survey Clients

Another way to track your ads is to have a clipboard on the job site that has a simple survey form for the client to fill out. You need the client's name, address, and telephone number for many reasons, such as possible follow-up service calls (remember about ancillary services), so why not ask the client on the form how he or she heard about you?

If You Can't Track It, Don't Do It

Some advertising strategies just can't be tracked. How do you deal with such a strategy? You don't do it!

The Three T's

As far as testing goes, the best way to test a campaign is to Try it, Track it, and Tweak it. If your tracking indicates a campaign is working, try tweaking it to see if it still works. If it's better once you tweak it, throw out the old campaign and continue with the new one.

EVALUATING AN ADVERTISING OPPORTUNITY

By now you probably have gathered that we don't believe that all advertising lends itself well to the home inspection business. Our suggestion is to look at every advertising opportunity the following way:

Don't Be Pressured

Step 1: Determine if it's something you *have* to do. For example, if you don't do it, the business you will lose far outweighs the cost of participating. Be realistic about this. If you lose a relationship with a top agent because their demands are offsetting your profits too much, it's not the end of the world. There are other top agents. Consider whether the cost to maintain the demanding agent might be better spent building a relationship with another top agent.

Does Your Public Expect It of You?

Step 2: Determine if it's something the public *expects* of you. For example, everyone expects that you will have a business card. In addition, more and more people expect that you will have a Web site and that your e-mail address and Web site address will appear on your business card. But does the public expect you to advertise your services on someone else's card? Probably not.

Compare Strategies

Step 3: If you don't have to do it, or your public does not expect it, think long and hard whether it's the best approach. The key word is "best." Even if you determine that you will make money on the advertising strategy, compare it to a dozen other campaigns and see if you still think it's a good idea. The goal is to optimize the return on every dollar you invest, putting your resources where they will produce the greatest result.

Make Sure It's Trackable

Step 4: If you decide that the advertising strategy may be a good idea, see if it can be tracked. Sometimes a little imagination is required to come up with a tracking procedure that makes sense. Put the onus on the person offering you the advertising opportunity to help come up with a tracking procedure.

Tracking tools may include different prices for different offers; coupons that will tell you where the business came from; or an instruction in the ad for prospects to mention the ad when they call so they receive a reward. You should always be asking callers where they heard about you, and you should include a question in your client survey or questionnaire asking clients why they chose your firm.

Direct Mail Is One of Best Strategies

Direct mail advertising is often preferable to display advertising in the home inspection business. Consider the example of the direct mail campaign that offered indoor air-quality inspection to previous clients. Even though your cost to acquire an inspection with a direct mail campaign might be $30 or more, it may be better than display advertising. Direct mail advertising may be more effective because you can track it and you can turn it on and off quickly and inexpensively—a good fit with your home inspection business.

KEY TERMS

demographics	list brokers	response rate
direct mail	multiple directories	single-line entry ad
display ad	multiple mailer	three-hit rule
fulfillment house	presentation folder	Yellow Pages listing

STUDY SESSION 2 QUICK QUIZ

You should finish Study Session 2 before doing this Quiz. Write your answers in the spaces provided. Then, check your answers in Appendix A.

1. When a Yellow Pages salesperson offers you an ad, it usually goes into all the sister directories without extra cost. Circle one.

    a. True

    b. False

2. Renting billboard space will get your ad out to a wider audience. This is always a great way to spend your advertising dollars. Circle one.

    a. True

    b. False

3. The collective experience of the home inspection community suggests that the best use of your advertising dollars is to pay for which kind of Yellow Pages entry? Circle one.

    a. Single-line entry

    b. Display ad

4. Name three features of a good direct mail campaign.

    1. _____

    2. _____

    3. _____

5. You shouldn't worry if you lose referrals from top producing real estate agents because you refused to pay for advertising in their newsletter. Spend that money getting new agents. Circle one.

    a. True

    b. False

6. Give two examples of how you can ask for more when someone solicits your ad in a newsletter, business card, or presentation folder.

    1. _____

    2. _____

7. Printing companies speak for the real estate office when they call you with a referral program offer in exchange for your advertising. Circle one.

    a. True

    b. False

8. What's the simplest and the best way to track a campaign?

    _____

9. What is the "three-hit rule?"

    _____

    _____

If you had trouble with the Quiz, reread Study Session 2 and try the Quiz again. If you did well, it's time for Assignment 1.

ASSIGNMENT 1

RESEARCH AND CREATE ADVERTISING TOOLS

This assignment asks you to complete exercises that are useful to the development of your company. We are going to ask you to do some research and make a few phone calls.

You should allow yourself five hours to eight hours to complete this assignment.

1. Develop a single page "quick fax" document. The document is used to send to callers who don't have time to discuss your inspection service with you. They just want you to fax them some information. Use the AIDA formula to create a compelling document.

2. Assemble an information package that you can give to real estate agents or other interested parties. Include your single-page document that you wrote in Question 1 above, a company prospectus, a testimonial letter, if you have one, and a business card, if you have one.

3. Look in the Yellow Pages for your competition's ads. What do their ads look like? Are they a single-line entry, or do they have more elaborate ads? Call two of the inspectors and ask them if they track the business that the Yellow Pages ad brings them. If so, how much business do they get directly from the ad?

When you have finished Assignment 1, you're ready for Study Session 3.

3

PEOPLE-DRIVEN PUBLIC RELATIONS

Study Session 3 discusses how to plan and participate in a first-time buyers' seminar and how to give an office talk for real estate agents.

LEARNING OBJECTIVES

At the end of Study Session 3 you should be able to

■ write a proposal for a first-time buyers' seminar to give to an agent or a bank that

   ■ describes the goals of the seminar,

   ■ outlines the components of a compelling seminar program, and

   ■ describes the positive outcomes for the four key speakers;

■ list four topics likely to get you invited to speak at an office meeting; and

■ plan and execute a successful office talk.

Study Session 3 may take you roughly 60 minutes to complete.

In this section we will look at public relations approaches that involve direct contact with buyers and real estate agents. But before looking at specific tactics, let's get an overview of what public relations is.

THE MEANING OF PUBLIC RELATIONS

Get Your Name Out

Public relations (PR) refers to communication to a market with the goal of persuading them to use your service. It is a promotional activity that may be directed at consumers or a target group such as real estate agents. There may or may not be a fee paid by the company directly for public relations. The medium may be print (newspapers or magazines for instance), radio, television, or live events, for example. Public relations is actually a form of advertising.

Examples of public relations campaigns are

- speaking at a first-time buyers' seminar,
- sponsoring events at real estate offices or banks,
- writing newsletters,
- writing newspaper columns,
- sending press releases,
- speaking as a guest or host on a radio or TV show,
- sponsoring events, and
- exhibiting at home shows.

With some exceptions, most public relations campaigns don't cost you any money. Your cost is primarily your time. For a new business, this is ideal because many new business owners don't have much money but they do have lots of time.

Many people hire you because they heard about you from a number of sources. When people say, "I hear your name everywhere." you know your marketing is working, and it usually includes a public relations component.

Not Self-Promotion

Public relations often includes messages that are not advertising and do not follow the AIDA format. They more often position you as an expert or authoritative source on a topic. People assume you are competent and qualified because the media recognizes you. Because you often pay nothing for PR, it makes sense that people want something other than money. They may want to leverage your knowledge, expertise, brand, or personal reputation to enhance their publication, program, or project.

PR Puts You on Map

In our experience, PR is a good way to get your name out, but it may not result directly in referral business. Most agents have inspectors they refer business to regularly. An agent is not likely to dump his or her favorite inspector and give a referral to you just because you gave away a television at a golf tournament. In fact, we have found that our public relations activities do not change the behavior of the agents at all. Here is an example: We did a series of office presentations at a particular office over a period of about ten months. We were in the office about once every six weeks. We tracked the referral behavior of this real estate office. The net result was that for our efforts to increase our business with that office was 0 percent. So why bother with public relations?

Do PR Before Asking for Business

Public relations is the first step in a two-step process. The public relations event introduces you to your industry, but the next step is the follow-up phone call where you ask for the business.

With real estate agents, step one is the pubic relations event. Step two is a phone call to top agents to ask if you can meet them for lunch, or meet with them in their office for five minutes.

With homebuyers, step one is the public relations event. Step two may be a homebuyer choosing you instead of another home inspector because he and she has seen you speak. Step two may also be a follow-up offer to the attendees of a seminar, for example.

As you can see, the public relations event alone does not drive business to you, it's just a piece in a puzzle. The problem is that most home inspectors and home inspection companies get so involved with the first step, they fail to follow through on the second. If you do not follow up, PR is just background marketing, and very few businesses will thrive with background marketing as their sole marketing tool. Step two is the critical, and more difficult, part of the process.

PR Bolsters Sales Effort

Most home inspectors don't like making the sales call. They don't like confronting an agent they don't know, and they don't like the uncomfortable question, "Will you refer business to me?" The answer, for most people, is to choose marketing campaigns that are less personal, like writing a newsletter. If you ask a home inspector to list all of the marketing campaigns he or she does in a year, inevitably the campaigns will include "comfortable" events, like newsletters. While there's nothing wrong with a newsletter, it's just not effective on its own.

Most people do not like to make sales calls. But if you can learn to do them well, you will be one in a thousand people able to accomplish this task. Your business will thrive. And while sales calls are difficult, they are easier if they follow up an advertising or PR effort. The introduction is always simplified if the target has heard of your company.

The rest of Study Session 3 and Study Session 4 describe PR activities that have been successful for us over the years, but don't limit yourself to our experience. Use your imagination to come up with events that involve the real estate community, whether that means agents, lawyers, lenders, title companies, or homebuyers. Some of our peers host parties for agents, take agents to sporting events, participate actively in real estate boards, offer continuing education seminars for agents, and so on.

FIRST-TIME BUYERS' SEMINAR

Connect To Clients and Industry Contacts

The **first-time buyers' seminar** is a powerful way to acquire new clients and, more importantly, to create working relationships with real estate agents, bankers, mortgage brokers, title companies, and real estate lawyers. Again, when we look at the target group, it is homebuyers on the surface, but the real estate agent and allied professionals are below the surface.

Offer Unbiased Service Information

The seminar speakers are all of the professionals involved in the real estate transaction. Each gives a brief overview of what they do, some practical advice, and the cost of their service. While the seminar is obviously a business development opportunity for the service providers, it is also an opportunity for homebuyers to learn a great deal very quickly. Each of the professionals who presents should give advice on the service without promoting themselves directly. There is no need to promote your company during your talk. Your participation as the guest expert is enough for the attendees to pick you for their inspection. You gain credibility by position and association.

Usually, a real estate agent or a bank hosts the first-time buyers' seminar. The bank and the real estate agent are in the best position to find participants, and they have more to gain financially from the event than other service providers. The bank can put up a sign or poster in the bank advertising a free seminar designed to help homebuyers survive the real estate transaction. Agents often advertise seminars in magazines or newsletters that list homes for sale. Agents often have a database of people interested in purchasing a house.

The seminar participants may include a

- bank mortgage specialist or bank manager;
- mortgage broker, rather than a bank;
- real estate agent;
- home inspector; and
- real estate lawyer or title company representative.

Who Pays for the Event?

There are costs involved in putting on this event. Usually the bank will offer its space for the seminar at no charge. Other costs include advertising, answering consumer questions, registering attendees, providing snacks, assembling handout material, renting audiovisual equipment, and so on.

Don't Offer a Financial Contribution

Before you agree to split the costs equally, consider this: The home inspector has the least to gain from each prospect. If the agent acquires two or three clients who end up buying houses, he or she will gain thousands of dollars in commissions. The bank may write a million dollars in mortgages. Even the lawyer may make three times what the home inspector will make. The home inspector makes less on every real estate transaction than the other parties.

Offer to Speak

We have participated in first-time buyers' seminars for years and don't pay anything. Instead, because we have developed a reputation as great guest speakers, our contribution is our presentation. The very nature of our business ensures a compelling presentation because people learn something new about the systems of a house. If you have visuals—an example of a bad renovation, scary wiring, a leaning house—your presentation will be entertaining, valuable, and memorable. It's easy to capture attention with a few well-chosen pictures.

Presentation Formats

There are two basic formats for this presentation: either with or without visuals. We present many seminars in each format, and each has its place.

Visual Presentations Pack a Punch

If you choose to have a **presentation with visuals,** you need an overhead projector or a media projector, a screen, and portable computer. The other presenters may have visual presentations as well, which may make things easier. This format provides a great opportunity to show interesting pictures of house system performance (or nonperformance!). The goal is not to put on a horror show, but to pose problems and then solve them.

Nonvisual Presentations Are Portable

If you choose to have a **nonvisual presentation,** your presentation is less exciting but more portable. In fact, most of the first-time buyers' seminars we do are in this format. Most seminars have only 10 to 30 attendees, and the speakers present from the head of a table rather than in a large space. This nonvisual format is most appropriate for a quick presentation.

Long Seminars Bore Attendees

When using visuals, speakers often find themselves doing too much. The lender makes a slide for every possible mortgage option, the agent projects a copy of an offer to purchase and goes through each detail, and the lawyer puts up a list of conditions that should be added to the offer to purchase. This level of detail is unnecessary.

Most first-time buyers don't want to commit to an entire evening of presentations. They would prefer a quick informative session. Be informative, be dramatic, and be brief. Your audience will love you.

Elements of a Successful Seminar

This section outlines the features of a first-time buyers' seminar that increase the chances of success. Whether you are invited as a guest speaker, are involved in the planning stage, or decide to organize the players yourself, keep these points in mind.

Create Relationship with Other Presenters

If you have any input, make sure all your seminar speakers think in terms of goals. Each presenter's goal is to be recognized as an expert or leader in his or her field. Recognition is an important goal for the home inspector, but it's not the only goal.

The other goal is to create a relationship with the other presenters. In the long run, their referrals may be worth more than the attendees' inspection business.

Know Attendees' Goals

The main goal of the attendee is to get some advice that will help them avoid a costly mistake. They also want to walk away with something. Your promotional material and a piece of educational material may be ideal. These allow the attendees, and the other presenters, to absorb your message. The material also makes it easy for the attendees to contact you.

Overall Seminar Outline

Golden Rule: Keep It Short

Everyone's goals are best served by a short presentation followed by a question and answer period.

After participating in many first-time buyers' seminars, we have consolidated our experiences and put together the following seven-step winning outline:

1. Introductions (five minutes): Bank manager introduces all of the guest speakers and gives an overview of topics.

2. Bank mortgage specialist (ten minutes): He or she gives an overview of the preapproval process, why preapproval is preferable to applying after finding the house, and what information the bank needs to approve someone.

3. Real estate agent (ten minutes): Who pays the real estate agent? What the agent does for you. Who the agent is representing, how you choose an agent, and, finally, a few tips on house hunting.

4. Home inspector (ten minutes): What is a home inspection? How much does it cost? When is the inspection performed? How you find a good home inspector? What questions should a homebuyer ask a home inspector?

5. Real estate lawyer or title company (ten minutes): When does the lawyer enter the picture? How much does it cost? What is title insurance? A few tips for your offer to purchase.

6. Question and answer period (fifteen minutes) Attendees are invited to ask questions. If the answer is too long and complicated, the subject expert offers to discuss it with the attendee afterwards.

7. Snacks and discussion.

The entire first-time buyers' seminar is one hour plus any discussion after the seminar over coffee.

Know How To Run a Good Seminar

Presenters have a tendency to think their topic is so important that they will talk for 20 minutes rather than 10. Now you have a first-time buyers' seminar that is an hour and 40 minutes—far too long to keep people interested. To compensate, you move the break to the middle and you end up with people trapped for over two hours. This time commitment is usually not worth it for anyone. Try to become part of the seminar planning team and make suggestions to keep it short.

THE HOME INSPECTOR PRESENTATION

Now that you know the general principles of the seminar, let's look at the particulars of your **home inspector presentation.**

So what do you say at a first-time buyers' seminar? Here is a script you can consider. We modify it, depending on how much time we are expected to speak, and whether there are visuals. You may also have to modify things to accommodate your local conditions.

My name is John Smith from ABC Inspection Company
I will cover three points in the next ten minutes. They are

List Topics You Will Cover

1. What is a home inspection?

2. How much does it cost?

3. How do you find a good home inspector?

Explain a Home Inspection

1. What is a home inspection?

A home inspection determines the condition of the home you are about to buy. This is key: You get an inspection of the home you are *about to buy*. In other words, you don't inspect every house you are interested in. While it would be great for our business, it's costly to you.

You have already been preapproved by a bank. Jill from XYZ Real Estate will have already helped you find the perfect home, and you will have made an offer conditional on the results of a home inspection. That's where we come in. The best way to explain our service is to walk you through a typical home inspection.

We would meet at the home. Jill would likely be there to assist us. By the way, this is not the time to show your relatives through the house. All of your attention should be focused on the inspection. You should follow the home inspector through the inspection and ask questions as you go. Take notes if you like, but the information will be compiled for you in a comprehensive report at the end of the inspection.

Go Through Each House System

The first thing we will do is look at the roof. Now, I did say that you should follow the inspector. The roof inspection is an exception. I see a few people breathing a sigh of relief. We have found that getting up onto a roof is much easier than getting back down. Being rescued from the roof by the fire department is not an ideal way to introduce yourself to your new neighbors. When we are on the roof, we look for the following things:

- Is the system doing its job?
- Is the system near the end of its life?

The roof is doing its job if water is not getting through, but it still may be very old. An asphalt shingle roof lasts about 15 years. If yours were 14 years old, it would be nice to know that it was on its last legs.

The next thing we look at is the structure. We step back from the house to take in the big picture. Here is a tip. Many major structural problems are quite evident, even to the untrained eye, if you step back far enough. When you look at houses, take a moment to step across the street. If the house is leaning, you have a problem. You don't need us to tell you that. We then look more closely.

The next thing we do is look for evidence of water seepage into the basement. If it seems like my presentation is out of order because I am still outside the house but talking about the basement, let me assure you that we are OK. Most basement dampness problems are the result of surface water in the form of rain or melting snow from the roof or from the ground around the house. As a result, we pay close attention to the gutters and downspouts and to the grading around the house. It's interesting to note that damp basements are the number one problem with houses in this area, whether brand new or 100 years old.

Now let's head into the house. We begin in the basement. This is where we look at the systems of the house, such as the electrical, heating, plumbing, and so on. For each system, we determine whether it's performing its intended function, and we determine if the system is near the end of its life.

Once we finish with the heart of each system, we trace it up through the house. We do this because the newest part of these systems is usually in the basement. In older homes, the systems get older as you go up through the house. Take the plumbing system for example. You may have new copper pipes in the basement, but there may be old galvanized steel pipes on the second or third floor. It's easy to run pipes through the basement or first floor, but it is much more difficult to get new pipes up to a second or third floor.

We finish the inspection in the attic, where we look for appropriate insulation and ventilation and evidence of water leakage.

We are finished with the inspection, but we are not finished with the job. At the end of the inspection, we document all of the conditions that we identify in a comprehensive inspection report that we provide to you on-site.

2. How much does a home inspection cost?

The inspection fee for a typical home will vary from one company to another, but fees will generally range between $300 and $500. Our inspection fee, for example, is $425 for a typical home.

3. How do you find a good home inspector?

I'd like to say that the only way to find a good home inspector is to hire me, but there are many excellent home inspectors in our area. There are also many that are not so good. Your real estate agent is a good referral source. He or she will likely know the home inspectors in your area. Ask friends and relatives that have recently purchased a home. Most importantly, ask some questions when you call the home inspection company. In addition to the questions about their background and experience, you should ask the following questions:

- "How long does the inspection take?" Depending on the area and on the type of home, the inspection may take one-and-a-half to three hours. For example, in our area most homes take about two-and-a-half hours. If the inspector says that the inspection takes half an hour, you should wonder about the quality of the inspection.
- "What kind of report do I get and when do I get it?"
- "Are you licensed or a member of any professional association?"

When we get to the question and answer period, I would be happy to answer any questions you may have.

Thank you.

Following Up

We use the **three-hit rule** as a follow-up technique for most of our campaigns, including seminar presentations. Here is how you might apply this rule to the first-time buyer seminar. We may not apply it to the attendees, but we do use it with the other presenters.

Follow Up with Real Estate Agents

The first hit is to call the real estate agent, the mortgage specialist, and the lawyer or title company representative. You will presumably have met and interacted with these people. You should be able to determine whether they are in a position to refer business to you. You may also consider whether there is any way you can help them. Offering to do presentations for their organization or prospects is one way. Offering to contribute technical articles to their newsletters is another. In many respects the best way to get something from people is to give them something.

What do you say when you call? It can be as simple as asking if you can send them some information or if they would meet you for lunch. Ask questions about how they build their business. You may get ideas for your business and may see an obvious way you can help them. The next two hits could be sending marketing material and then following up on that.

You probably have a relationship with one of these three already because you were invited to be a presenter. Focus on the two you did not know before the seminar.

Follow Up with Attendees

Ask for a list of attendees with contact information. You will have to decide to what degree you will follow up with attendees. If your main goal is to meet the agent and banker, you may choose to spend your time and energy on them instead. Which investment in follow-up is likely to yield the greatest return? If you do decide to follow up with attendees, you might send a brochure, call to verify that they've received it, and then offer to send an interesting report that presents a solution to a problem with houses. You might offer to add them to your mailing list for your newsletter, if you have one.

Real Estate Investment Clubs

This is a twist on the first-time buyers' seminar. It is an interesting one because each attendee may buy many homes, not just one. This audience is looking at homes as a business and in many ways is easier to deal with than homebuyers because investors are less emotional. The presentation can be similar, but again, think about what your audience wants. Because a real estate investor may be interested in the lowest maintenance and highest durability, your presentation may focus on bulletproof homes.

You may search out local investment clubs and offer to make a presentation at one of their regular meetings.

Getting Invited as a Presenter

Create Your Own Opportunity

The best way to find an opportunity is to create one. Suggest a first-time buyers' seminar to an agent or mortgage lender who has never heard about this concept. Make sure your offer is from their perspective and clearly show them the benefits they will receive.

Or, mention in your agent newsletter that you are willing to participate in first-time buyers' seminars. Then proceed to outline how the first-time buyers' seminar works. You may be enlightening the agents. Do the same for the banks. Follow the letter up with a phone call.

THE OFFICE TALK

Deliver a Weekly Talk

A great way to get in front of agents is to become a guest speaker at a real estate office meeting. Learn to deliver what's called an **office talk.** This public relations effort is clearly focused on the real estate agent.

Many real estate offices have a weekly meeting where they discuss new listings, who sold what, for how much, and so on. This meeting keeps all of the agents up-to-date on what is out there. The office manager or the broker will often have a guest speaker at the beginning or the end. If you are invited to one of these meetings, a room full of real estate agents will hear you.

Know Your Audience

How do you get invited to a real estate agent's office? It's not easy. But good strategy and persistence will pay off.

Offering What the Agents Want

Many home inspectors fail to get into real estate offices to speak because they are not offering anything of interest to the agents. You are not the only home inspector who has asked to speak at these meetings. The broker or office manager gets such requests every day. Moving companies, painters, renovators, lawyers, and home inspectors are all looking for the same thing: to earn some referral business from real estate agents.

Don't Put Your Newness Front and Center

Here is a classic scenario: A new home inspector calls up a real estate office and says, "I have just gotten into the home inspection business, and I would like to introduce myself to your agents. Could I come in for five minutes to tell everybody who I am and what I do?" The answer is, you guessed it, "No!" The inspector has little chance of success unless the broker or office manager is a relative or friend.

The home inspector in the above example made the following mistakes: Agents are not as excited about your new business as you are. In fact, they don't care at all about your new business. Agents already know what a home inspector does. The last thing an agent wants is a new home inspector. A home inspector who has just gotten into the business may be a big liability to an agent. Your newness should not be front and center in your offer to speak at the meeting. This home inspector did not think from the agent's perspective. What is in it for the agent in this case? Nothing. You can't ask for something until you give something.

These guest-speaking spots are hard to land unless you have something of value to offer the agent. We have had success getting into the offices by offering a **technical office talk** on topics of specific interest to real estate agents.

A Technical Presentation Is Not Enough

Armed with this information, you may be tempted to call up a real estate office and excitedly offer a series of winning ten-minute technical presentations. They might be something like the following:

- The Hazards of an Undersized Electrical Service
- Damp Basements
- Foundation Problems

You may even have a great **PowerPoint presentation** for each topic, with cool photographs showing the deficiencies close up. Furthermore, because you know lots about these topics, you can answer questions and demonstrate your expertise firsthand.

Sound like a winning pitch? Then you're in for as surprise when the answer is, again, No!

You made the following mistakes: Sure these are interesting technical topics, but they are not interesting to a real estate agent. What's in it for the real estate agent? Nothing. These presentations just confirm what an agent already knows about home inspectors and home inspections—you are there to find problems.

Demonstrate How the Agent Directly Benefits

What you need is a series of topics of specific interest to the agent. What interests an agent is a topic that can solve a problem, close a deal faster, make more money, or save time. Following are some examples of office talk offerings that are more likely to get attention:

- *Solving Insurance Hassles.* Insurance companies are getting fussier about what they will insure. Here is a common scenario: A homebuyer finds out that they can't get fire insurance because the house they want to buy has some knob and tube wiring. No fire insurance, no mortgage. No mortgage, no sale. This ten-minute presentation gives you an overview of the issues that insurance companies are picking up on, and it provides some easy ways around the problems.

- *Five Tips to Quickly Recognize Serious Structural Problems.* Your time is money. Don't waste your time listing a home with a major structural problem, only to discover the problem during the inspection. Any house can be sold, but if it has a major problem, you need to know about it upfront. This ten-minute presentation will teach you five secrets to noticing structural deficiencies.

- *Get More Listings.* In today's competitive market, a prelisting inspection is a great way to get more listings and avoid having to sell the house twice. This new program has been a real hit with buyers and real estate agents. This ten-minute presentation will focus on how a prelisting inspection can help you get more listings, sell homes faster, and earn more money.

- *How to Avoid Having the Home Inspector Kill the Deal.* Many real estate transactions are delayed or fall apart needlessly due to bad home inspections. Let us show you how to keep the inspection from ruining the sale in less than ten minutes.

What's good about these presentations? They offer information that will save time, make money, or solve a problem. These are much more likely to get you in the door.

Turn What You Know into Benefit for Agent

Many technical topics can be reworked to be valuable to a real estate agent. Start with what you know a lot about. If you are an electrician just getting into the home inspection business, do a talk on solving a critical electrical problem. Your pitch may be, "Don't let a deal fall through because the electrical system is old. Here are five tricks to make an old electrical system function safely without expensive upgrading." If you do some brainstorming, you will probably come up with several topics that could solve a problem or make more money for a real estate agent.

Your goal is to become the solutions person, not just the technical expert. You can differentiate yourself in the market by helping to make problems go away, rather than adding new problems. What's really great is that's what homeowners want too.

Tips for an Effective Presentation

Keep the Presentation Short

This is definitely a case of "less is more." Even if your topic has many points, limit yourself to a few key points. Many presenters have a hard time paring down. You may think you are doing the agent a favor by making the presentation comprehensive, but the agents will not retain an overload of information. In the end, your presentation will be boring, long-winded, and will not make a good impression on the agents.

Omit Key Information

We took the less-is-more approach to an interesting level that works well for office talks. We discovered that omitting key information generates further contact with the agents. For example, one of our office talks deal with "hot spots" for termite infestation. It's a short talk that shows areas of the city particularly prone to termite infestations. We hand out a map of a small area of the city of about 20 blocks wide and 20 blocks long, and we highlight the streets that have termite activity. This helps the agents know when to recommend a termite inspection. They can then arrange to have the termite inspector on site at the same time as the home inspector.

During the talk, we knew that the agents in this office covered a much larger territory than the map covered. At the end of the presentation the agents said, "This is great, but what about the next map zone over?" Our response was, "Give me your business card, and I will send you the maps that cover those areas." We created opportunity to contact the agent one-on-one through a personal letter with the requested valuable information. You might deliver the information personally to the agent. So, if possible, build in a reason for further contact into the presentation.

Contact Target Three Times in a Row

The three-hit rule applies here too. You might do the talk, send the follow-up information as requested, and then send a separate thank-you letter to each attendee. The thank-you letter would invite the agents to call you any time if they need a problem solved. Invite them to refer inspection business to your firm. Invite them to your Web site.

Many experts assert that if you can't come up with a three-hit process for a particular campaign, you shouldn't bother doing it at all! Many successful companies have a 12-hit rule. A credit card company may send you a letter asking if you would like to apply for a card. When you get this letter, expect another 11 letters over the next year or two.

Design Creative Strategies

Here is a way to get all of the real estate agents' business cards. We always bring a prize to give away at the end of our presentations. The prize might be movie tickets, a restaurant coupon, or a bottle of wine. At the end of the presentation, ask the agents to drop their business card into a basket for the broker or office manager to draw a name. The name is drawn and the prize goes out.

Luggage Tags

We take the business cards back to the office and enter the names into a database. Then the business cards get run through a laminating machine to create plasticized luggage tags that we mail back to the agents with a thank-you letter. The laminator costs about $50 and the luggage tag pouches and bands are about 25¢ each.

Ask for a Referral

Before you leave the office, ask the broker or manager if there are any other real estate offices they think would enjoy this presentation. You can now leave the office with the name of another office and the name of the broker. You've eliminated a cold call—"Hello Mr. Jones, Jane Doe from the RE/MAX office on Elm St. suggested I contact you."

Offer Other Topics for Follow-Up Presentations

Don't leave the office without offering to come back to present another topic that you conveniently have up your sleeve.

Don't Bad-Mouth Another Inspector

Here's a final tip that is important for all aspects of your business, not just presentations to agents: Do not ever criticize another firm, inspector, or inspection reports. It's not uncommon for an agent to comment on what another inspector did that killed her and his deal. It is tempting to say, "Yeah, that was a stupid thing for that inspector to do and I would do better." That inspector may be a friend of an agent in the office. Don't forget, you aren't hearing the whole story. More importantly, it looks unprofessional if you disparage another inspector or company.

The Managers' Meeting

Real estate companies with multiple offices sometimes have meetings for the managers. This is a great opportunity to build relationships with the team leaders for several real estate offices. These people are not the ones out in the field selling homes, but they are opinion leaders and a resource for the salespeople.

Ask if the managers meet and offer to put on a presentation that will help solve problems for them.

The Real Estate Board Meeting

Here is another twist on the real estate office talk. Local real estate boards often host continuing education sessions for agents. You may look at becoming a regular presenter or instructor for your real estate board. This is particularly valuable for agents with mandatory continuing education requirements. Almost every state has requirements for agents to get 4 to 15 hours of continuing education a year, on average.

In some cases you may also be able to get approved to teach real estate licensing courses. You can combine relationship building with agents with revenue generation if you teach continuing education or licensing courses because you get paid to do these! This is the best of both worlds.

KEY TERMS

first-time buyers' seminar	nonvisual presentation	presentation with visuals
home inspector presentation	office talk	technical office talk
	PowerPoint presentation	three-hit rule

STUDY SESSION 3 QUICK QUIZ

You should finish Study Session 3 before doing this Quiz. Write your answers in the spaces provided. Then, check your answers in Appendix A.

1. Public-relations events dramatically change the behavior of agents. Circle one.

   a. True

   b. False

2. What is the main purpose of participating in a first-time buyers' seminar?

   _____

   _____

3. Who typically puts on the first-time buyers' seminar?

   _____

   _____

4. Who are the four key speakers at a first-time buyers' seminar?

   1. _____
   2. _____
   3. _____
   4. _____

5. Why should you avoid splitting the costs of the first-time buyers' seminar with the agent?

   _____

   _____

   _____

6. Everybody's goals are best served with a longer and more detailed seminar. Circle one.

   a. True

   b. False

7. What is an office talk and why would you want to do one?

   _____

   _____

   _____

8. When you call a broker or office manager, it should be easy to convince them to invite you to speak because it is a novelty for them to have a guest speaker. Circle one.

   a. True

   b. False

9. List two topics likely to interest real estate agents.

   1. _____
   2. _____

10. A good technique to use for an office talk is to purposely omit discussing a piece of information that the real estate agent would be interested in having. Circle one.

    a. True

    b. False

If you had trouble with the Quiz, reread Study Session 3 and try the Quiz again. If you did well, it's time for Study Session 4.

MEDIA-RELATED PUBLIC RELATIONS

Study Session 4 deals with writing newspaper columns, press releases, and newsletters. It will also walk you through how to get on radio and television shows. These useful public relations tools are either free or inexpensive.

LEARNING OBJECTIVES

At the end of Study Session 4 you should be able to

▪ write a newspaper column on a topic about which you have technical expertise;

▪ describe the process of getting a regular newspaper column;

▪ write a press release;

▪ list five places you could send your press release;

▪ write a proposal to a radio or television producer for a series of shows; and

▪ outline four ways to maximize your exposure.

Study Session 4 may take you roughly 60 minutes to complete.

So far, our look at public relations has focused on direct interactions with clients and agents. In this section, we'll look at public relations opportunities that involve using various media to put your company in the public's mind.

NEWSPAPER COLUMNS

Writing a newspaper column is a great way to get your name out into the world. It doesn't cost you anything (except time), and the payback is high in terms of exposure. The goal is to find a newspaper interested in having you write a **regular column.** In this sense the target group is the homebuyer. A monthly real estate paper or magazine is ideal because you directly reach your two main target audiences—real estate agents and homebuyers.

Do You Like To Write?

Before we go further, you should decide whether writing is a joy or a curse. If you hate writing, this strategy is not for you.

Expert Status

Even if you do enjoy writing, don't jump into writing a column without first considering the pitfalls. For instance, a regular column is time-consuming and may not directly result in referral business, so don't expect this strategy to transform your business. Why do it, then? **Exposure.** This is background marketing. The more people read your name, the more familiar you become. And print has this funny way of conferring status. People think that if you are in print, you must be an expert. It's not enough to drive business to you by itself, but it is one of the tools in your bag.

Understand the Time Commitment

Writing a newspaper column takes a lot more time than most people think. Research, writing, editing, and proofing a small column of 200 words to 500 words takes at least a day (eight to ten hours). This is a big commitment for a weekly newspaper. You will spend 20 percent of your time doing work for which you will never get paid. A monthly paper or magazine is more than enough. If eight to ten hours once a month feels like an arduous task, then this is not for you. It is much better not to do it, than to do it poorly. A badly written column can hurt your reputation and your business.

Tips for Effective Newspaper Articles

Let's look at some best practices—both stylistic and mechanical—for writing effective newspaper articles.

Put Most Important Information First

What you learned in school about writing doesn't apply to a newspaper column. Most of us write in essay format—first we introduce the topic, then provide background, then build to some sort of climax, and, finally, write a conclusion. This format is not flexible—the sense of your story is lost if an editor chops off the end to fit the article into available space.

A newspaper column has to survive the editor's scissors. Put the most important information up front. Each subsequent paragraph is an elaboration on the first, reinforcing, giving examples, and providing more background. This way, if one of your later paragraphs gets chopped, the message remains intact.

Read the Professionals

Next time you pick up a newspaper, see for yourself how the stories survive the editor. Everything you need to know is in the first paragraph. In fact, if you want to save yourself time reading the newspaper, just read the first paragraph or two of each article and you'll be on top of current events.

Magazines Are Different

Keep in mind that we are talking about newspapers here. Magazine articles are different. They can be written in more of an essay style. People take more time to read magazine articles.

Activate Your Headline

Don't submit an article without a headline. The **editor** should not have to supply one for you. Although some editors will replace your headline with one of their own, provide a good, catchy headline for the editor's consideration. The headline should be attention-grabbing and should drive the reader to your article.

A headline is not a title. For instance, this section is entitled, "Tips for Effective Newspaper Articles." A title is descriptive. A headline is active. If we wanted to turn that title into a headline, it should be something like, "Sentences Die on the Block!" You could then use the title as a descriptive subheading:

Sentences Die on the Block!
How to write an effective newspaper column

Keep Your Paragraphs Short

Another device journalists often use is the shortened paragraph. Throw out the old rules about a topic sentence, explanatory sentences, and concluding sentences. Any paragraph over three sentences long should be broken up into new paragraphs.

Use Only Necessary Words

Cut out any unnecessary word or syllable. For instance, the following sentence is too wordy, "This sentence is the one that is too important to chop." Take out "is the one that is" and you have cleaner sentence: "This sentence is too important to chop."

Get Dictionary and Style Guide

Get a good dictionary and a style guide. Style guides give you basic grammatical rules. *The Chicago Manual of Style* (The University of Chicago Press) is the editorial industry standard, but other style guides are also fine.

Write in Active Voice

The active voice puts the subject in the driver's seat. The passive voice puts the subject in the passenger seat. You want the subject at the wheel.

Here is an example: "Sally was seen by the intruder" is passive. Why? Because the subject is *not* Sally, it's "the intruder." But this sentence construction buries the subject. It puts Sally up front when, in fact, it's "the intruder" who does the action. Sally is acted upon. The sentence should read, "The intruder saw Sally." The meaning has not changed, but the voice is now active. The active voice is direct, clear, and more concise.

Help from Software

Most word processing software automatically suggests the active voice when you type in the passive voice. You may have to turn this option on. If you are not sure the option is already on, try typing, "He was seen by us." Your word processor should highlight the sentence and suggest, "We saw him."

Clues to Watch For

If your word processing program does not have this function, here are some telltale signs of the passive voice to watch out for:

■ The preposition "by" usually signals the passive voice. For instance, "The ball was chewed by Rufus" should be "Rufus chewed the ball."

■ Look out for compound verbs in the past or future tenses, such as "is done," "was heard," "will be seen," and so on. "The stars *were seen* by the campers" should be "The campers saw the stars."

Beware of "That"

Your writing may be clearer if you minimize the use of the work "that." For example, which sentence is easier to understand?

■ You need to find an angle for your story that is newsworthy.

■ You need to find a newsworthy angle for your story.

We think the second sentence is better.

Make Sure Language Is Inclusive

Certain language usages make readers feel excluded. For instance, the pronoun "he" in your examples, tends to exclude your female audience. If you think home-related issues only interest men, think again. Assume your audience is everyone and use gender-neutral, socially sensitive words and phrases. Here are examples:

- Technician *not* serviceman
- Mail carrier *not* mailman
- Fire fighter *not* fireman
- Barrier-free access *not* handicapped accessible

Get Someone Else to Edit

Getting an outside editor is critical. You can't edit and proofread your own work. Why? Because after eight hours of writing, you are no longer objective. Your eyes gloss over mistakes because your brain fills in the gaps; it's a common phenomenon. Another person's eyes provide a fresh perspective on typos, spelling errors, and grammar mistakes. Your story makes sense to you because you know what you are talking about. But another person can test the clarity of your story.

Getting Published

Now that you know how to write effectively, how do you get a newspaper editor to let you write a column at all?

Have Writing Samples Ready

If a newspaper publishes articles related to your profession, and nobody currently writes an industry-related column for that paper, getting a column should be easy. Before you approach the editor, assemble some writing samples. Most editors won't consider even an article unless they have proof of your writing ability. An editor will often start you off with a special feature. It gives you a chance to prove yourself to the editor and to your public.

A Year at a Time!

Once you have written a few of these articles, the next step is to convince the editor to let you provide a regular column. An editor will be more inclined to commit if you can provide a year's worth of articles. This eliminates the risk for the editor—he or she won't have to chase you for articles.

Brainstorm a list of possible topics before you start writing in earnest. Here are just a few ideas to get you started:

- Preparing Your House for Winter [Spring, Summer, Fall]
- Home Maintenance Tips
- Tips to Avoid Costly Repairs
- Explaining How a [Home System] Functions

PRESS RELEASES

Try for Free Publicity

A **press release** is a kind of newspaper column. The main focus is the homebuying public. The rules we have discussed so far apply to a press release as well as a newspaper article. The press release, however, has a different focus.

A press release is a broadly distributed article designed to get publicity for your company. You should write it as an article that highlights interesting and valuable news about your company. The most common press release announces to the public that you have just formed a company with unique features, or you have developed a new product or service. Press releases should provide useful information to the reader, delivered in an interesting package. A good rule is to start with the benefit for the reader and then explain how you can deliver the benefit with the new feature.

A press release should highlight something newsworthy. While it may be exciting for you that you have launched your company, the general public may not see what the fuss is about. New companies form every day. You need to find a newsworthy angle. Remember, it's not about you; it's about the reader. For instance, if you are an expert in Victorian homes, push that angle in your release. Here's an example:

FOR IMMEDIATE RELEASE

Home Inspector Can Authenticate the Victorian-ness of Your Home

December 8, 2001, Boston—Pat Goodbar, a professional engineer, and a ten-year veteran of the Victorian Society of America, has launched Victorian House, the first home inspection company to specialize in the authentication of Victorian homes.

Goodbar began the venture in response to the recent wave of homebuyers looking for Victorian homes. Goodbar also responds to homeowners looking to restore their home to its original Victorian style.

According to Goodbar, most homes listed for sale as "Victorian" do not have all the original detail. "Most older homes have undergone years of renovation, often losing many of the original features," says Goodbar. "I can tell buyers what to look for in a Victorian home."

As a home inspector, Goodbar's expertise in home systems ensures buyers are not getting an aging money pit instead of their Victorian dream. "I help people maintain their homes, ensuring that any upgrades respect the Victorian details of the house," explains Goodbar, "but the house needs a sound structure and good systems in place first."

Does the Victorian home inspection take longer? "Yes!" says Goodbar emphatically. "Once we've made sure the house systems are performing properly, we spend time poring over the craftsmanship and detail that a Victorian home should offer. My clients love that part of the inspection."

For the person who already owns a Victorian home, Goodbar provides a detailed audit of the home's Victorian features, explaining which are original and describing those that have been lost over the years.

Bringing expert historical knowledge to every inspection, Victorian House offers homebuyers and owners a unique approach to their Victorian home.

For further information, please contact Pat Goodbar at 1.111.222.3333 or via e-mail at *pat@victorianhome.net.*

Put Most Important Information First

Other Topics

Notice in the sample press release that we have the most important information up front. The press release could be chopped anywhere after the first paragraph.

A press release does not have to be about a new company. It can feature the start of a new division, the hire of a new employee, or the development of a new inspection technique. Have a look through a local newspaper or magazine to see if you can identify which columns are actually press releases.

Distribute It Widely

Once you have written your release, and had someone else look over it, submit it for publication to all industry-related journals, magazines, and newspapers as well as community newspapers. You never know when an editor may have a small space to fill. The editor might just choose you!

There are also companies that will distribute your article to many editors for you. They will bundle your article with other articles. This saves you lots of time researching publications and the right person to contact, but there is a cost for this service, of course.

Understand Your Audience

Editors are receptive to pieces that meet their needs. Let's look at those needs. For most publications, it comes down to money. Most publications make their money from advertisers who pay to put their messages in the publications. The advertisers try to reach the biggest group possible. Advertisers pay more to be in the publications that are widely read by a well-defined group. Publications want content that interests their target market. The content is the publisher's tool to build readership. More readers mean more advertising revenue for the publisher.

Attract and Keep Readers

Your goal as a writer is to help the publication attract and keep readers by providing interesting and useful information.

Publishing Press Releases

Target Key Publications

How do you get your press release published? The first step is to identify some target publications in your area. Consider whom you want to read your press release. If you want real estate agents to read it, choose a publication that targets them. If you want homebuyers to read it, send it to a publication targeting home-buyers. Check the Internet. Type related key words into a search engine.

Once you have a list of publications, contact each one. Large publications may have more than one editor. The real estate or homes editor is your target in that case. Send them your press release either by mail or e-mail. An e-mail address is a good start. People tend to respond to e-mail because it's less demanding than returning a phone call. But get a phone number, too. Follow up the e-mail with a phone call. A phone call gives the editor a sense of you from the sound of your voice. The closer you can get to human contact, the less likely you'll get rejected.

Put Together a Press Kit

If you have not yet sent the press release, ask the editor if you can send it. Better yet, ask if you can send a **press kit.** What's a press kit? It's a collection of short documents about who you are and what you do. Your press release is one of those documents. A press kit might also include a short biography about you and another piece about your company. The best way to get published is to include a document the editor can publish, such as a fact sheet of interesting technical tips. For instance, your fact sheet can give four quick tips to help a homebuyer determine the age of a house.

The press release gives the publication a short clip they can squeeze some-where to make the layout of the page look better. As long as something from your press kit is newsworthy, an editor might publish it. The editor may not use it when you expect. In fact, the publication may never use it. But that's the price you pay for free advertising.

Beware of Advertising

The advertising person for the publication may notice that you have sent in a press kit, making you a good target to buy advertising space. While free advertising is always worth every penny, paid advertising is a very different issue. Don't confuse the two.

Here is how the advertising agent may try to convince you:

- Advertising in their publication will give you exposure to many homebuyers and/or real estate agents.

- The cost per person you reach is very low. When you consider the enormous circulation of this publication, your cost per person is less than two cents!

- Your cost is only $250. You will recoup this in a few inspections. Don't you think you will get a few inspections as a result of this ad?

The best answer is to say that while you would appreciate the opportunity to share an important message with their audience, you simply don't have room in your budget. There is no point offending the person or publication by saying that paid advertising does not make sense or is a bad idea.

Writing a regular newspaper article will increase your exposure and confer expert status on you. Over time, it will ensure your name is on a few people's lips. Writing a press release may not give you the same exposure because you can't be sure anyone will publish it. But it still may be worth doing, just in case.

Keep Your Copyright

It is important that people who publish your article or column understand that you own the material. Unless this is made clear from the outset, the publication may take ownership, preventing you from using the material elsewhere. The next section discusses ways to leverage your copyrighted material.

Maximizing your Exposure

Now that you have spent time writing a newspaper column or a press release, you should maximize your exposure.

If your article or press release gets published, ask the publisher for several copies. Make more copies. Never cut out your article from the rest of the publication. Always be sure the publication information is visible, as well as all the stories that surround your article. Why? Because you want to show that your copies are authentic. Laminate a copy or preserve it in a plastic slipcover to go in your portfolio. Use your portfolio to show your work to other publishers or magazines. Maybe another magazine will want to print this article or some other article at a later date. Either way, it's a good idea to have a copy of your work in a presentable format to show editors. Send copies to key real estate offices. For example, send a copy of the article to a top producing real estate office with a handwritten note to the broker or manager. "Here is an article I wrote that your agents may find interesting. Please post in the coffee room. Sincerely, Jane the home inspector."

Send copies to key real estate agents that you do business with. Include a handwritten note, "Dear John, here is an article I wrote that may interest you. Have a great day. Sincerely, Mike."

Invite real estate agents to reprint this article in their own newsletters to their clients. Put your columns and press releases on your Web site and include them in your information packages, after they have been published. All of this enhances your credibility as an authority.

NEWSLETTERS

*Use Newspaper
Column Techniques*

Writing a **newsletter** uses all of the techniques you've learned about so far. The format follows newspaper style, with the content arranged in columns. The content begins with the most interesting stuff in the first paragraph. Write it from the client's perspective. Keep it to the point—delete any unnecessary words. Use AIDA as your model. Grab the reader's attention, create interest, evoke desire, and call the reader to action.

Newsletters are a good way to keep in touch. Who are you keeping in touch with? Most home inspectors who write a newsletter are targeting real estate agents. If your newsletter is well-written and has general appeal, it may be broadly circulated. While we target agents in our newsletters, we make sure they are suitable for consumers as well.

Many of our newsletters have become standard inserts in the information package the real estate agent gives to the client. Agents and brokers often call to ask if they can reproduce our newsletter in one of their own, or post it to their Web site. We agree as long as we are given credit.

Newsletters Targeting Agents

Your newsletter must contain information of interest to real estate agents. If an agent takes the time to read your newsletter because it's so compelling, your newsletter may do you some good.

The newsletter has two general messages:

1. I want to help you. I provide useful information.

2. You will look good to your clients by referring me.

Let's look at the first message type—useful information for the real estate agent.

*Write From Real Estate
Agent's Perspective*

Offer something that is useful from the agent's perspective, something that helps them to

- save time,
- bypass problems in the real estate transaction,
- save money,
- look good to their clients, and
- prevent the home inspection from killing the deal.

Agents do not care that your moisture meter can identify wet and rotted material behind tiles in the shower. They are not interested in inspection horror stories. But they may be interested in how a first-time buyer can avoid spending money upgrading the electrical service by installing a gas dryer instead of an electric dryer.

If you write with the real estate agent's perspective in mind, you will be ahead of the game. Most home inspector newsletters focus on the inspector's technical knowledge and reinforce what a pain an inspector can be to an agent. That's not the message you want to send. You want the agent to see you as an ally, someone who can solve problems, not create them.

Let's look at the second message—the part where you sell yourself.

*Mix Marketing Message
with Content*

The trick is to get a marketing message across without making your newsletter look like a marketing piece. You will have to decide what tolerance your audience has for marketing content. Some home inspection companies put "in-your-face" marketing messages in their newsletters. These messages range from sidebars that include the company taglines, to open company plugs within the stories themselves. Other home inspection companies have no marketing content at all, aside from company name and contact information. Our choice is a sidebar in our newsletters that describes the benefits of working with our firm. It does not distract the reader from the article but provides an introduction to the company for someone who does not know us.

You can select the approach you are most comfortable with. The key is balance. If your content is not relevant to the reader and is too heavy on marketing, your newsletter is more likely to get thrown out, and, more importantly, your credibility will be reduced.

An Example

For many years, Carson Dunlop produced high-quality quarterly newsletters. They were printed on a single sheet of 8½ × 11 glossy paper. A professional designer laid out the two-color piece. We mailed 23,000 newsletters in batches to real estate offices. The content provided information that the real estate agents wanted to hang onto and pass on to their clients. For example, every year, we published the "Renovation And Repair Costs" newsletter. Agents looked forward to getting this information because it was helpful on a day-to-day basis.

A banner down the right side of the back of the newsletter clearly identified our value proposition. Real estate agents were gently reminded of the benefits of choosing us over the competition, but the focus of the text was always on giving agents something that would help them be more successful. The newsletters became more popular, and we sent them to real estate boards, newspaper columnists, real estate newsletters, and relocation companies. The printing and distribution costs grew to about $24,000 per year.

In an effort to reduce costs, we decided to try e-mail delivery. We saved money but lost touch with a number of agents who did not have e-mail accounts or did not check them regularly. We also lost contact with some agents by failing to collect their e-mail addresses. Although we announced the change in two printed newsletters prior to making the transition, we also got many calls from agents complaining about not receiving the printed newsletter anymore.

But what was really eye opening was that we got calls from some agents who had stopped referring us years ago, yet still read our newsletter, and they were disappointed that they didn't get it anymore. In other words, we were paying to deliver information to agents who were not referring clients to us. While this might be okay if you are using electronic delivery, you may reserve the printed newsletters for real estate agents who work with you. We have continued with electronic delivery; however, our most commonly requested newsletter is also available in print. If an agent asks for the newsletter but has never used us before, we at least have an opportunity to sell them on the benefits of using our service.

Bump Up Marketing Message

If you are spending time and money on your newsletter but not getting any referrals, the newsletter is not necessarily a flop. Newsletters are background marketing, and while they will raise awareness of your firm, they will not change agent behavior on their own. Newsletters do open doors and make it easier to make contact with top agents and real estate offices.

Levels of Marketing

We will look at three levels of marketing in your newsletter; each has its own level of marketing presence:

1. There is no actual marketing message at all. Your marketing is in the fact that you are providing useful information to the reader.

2. The marketing message is subtly contained in the information you are providing to the reader.

3. The marketing message is contained in a clearly delineated part of the newsletter.

You can decide, based on your company image, what level of presence you want. You may choose a different level for different newsletters, or you may use a combination of the different levels within a given newsletter. Let's look at each of the three levels:

Be Sure Content Is Relevant

No marketing message.   At this level, there is no *explicit* marketing message, but the marketing value comes from two areas.

Carefully choose topics that will interest real estate agents. Good topics are useful enough that agents also incorporate them into a newsletter of their own, or pass the information on to their clients.

Here are newsletter articles that we have produced:

- *Urea Formaldehyde Foam Insulation—Much Ado About Nothing.* This article discusses how the "problem" with UFFI is actually not a problem. This newsletter has been one of the most popular and most requested newsletters we have written. Agents will include copies with the listing for any house that has, or has had, UFFI.

- *Home Improvement Costs.* Real estate agents wait for the update every year. They give it to clients, and they include it with client packages. This is a very popular newsletter that we continue to print in addition to making it available electronically. (A copy of this newsletter is included on the resource CD that accompanies this book.)

- *In Search of the Perfect House.* This article is also very popular. This is the newsletter that is most often reprinted in real estate newspapers, Web sites, and office newsletters.

Let Them Know You Can Do Job

Marketing message contained in the text.   While offering useful information to real estate agents, subtly comment about how your home inspection company does things better. For instance, if you write an article on a particular house problem, show that as long as the issue is handled properly, there is no reason for it to be an expensive problem, *and* your inspection company knows just how to handle it.

Clearly Market Yourself

Marketing message clearly delineated.   This kind of marketing message involves formatting. The marketing messages appear as separate articles, or, more commonly, in caption boxes around the article. You could have little captions, such as "Our home inspection includes a free Home Reference Book, a $95 value," or "We specialize in helping first-time buyers."

Add Shelf Life To Newsletter

Make sure the topics will be of long-lasting interest, giving your newsletter a longer shelf life. If your newsletter has a long shelf life, it will stay on the real estate agent's desk and it may get copied and passed around. It will end up in the hands of prospective clients as well. The articles themselves may end up in real estate agents' newsletters and on their Web sites.

Newsletter Costs

Know Cost of a Newsletter

The three significant costs involving your newsletter are as follows:

1. **Design and production.** If you are not good with graphics, consider having a designer do the layout for you. You will be charged a fee to set up your newsletter's look and feel or template. You will also be charged a fee to insert the text and graphics for each issue. Once you have a template you are happy with, you don't pay this fee again. There is a large range in the cost of this service. If you find someone who works from home and can use prepackaged templates, your costs could be as little as $200 per issue. You may opt for a professional designer who makes a custom template keyed to your company image and colors. This could cost up to $2,000 for the initial design and a small amount per issue.

2. **Printing costs.** The printing costs can vary between 10¢ per copy to more than $1 for a single sheet, depending on the quality of the paper, the volume you print, and the number of colors.

3. **Postage costs.** You can deliver your newsletter by
   - mailing the newsletters individually to real estate agents—this is expensive;
   - mailing batches of newsletters to real estate offices—this saves on postage but is less personal;
   - delivering the newsletters by hand to the office—this may give you the opportunity to talk to the broker and agents, but it is time-consuming;
   - e-mailing it; and
   - posting it on a Web site and e-mail a link.

Should You Write Your Newsletter?

So far we have looked at how to write a newsletter and how a newsletter may help to build your business. Before you launch into it though, step back and decide if writing one is the best idea for you.

Buy Your Newsletter

You don't have to be a good writer to use a newsletter. You can hire a third party company to write it for you. You can also buy newsletters from companies that create them for home inspectors. This newsletter can be customized, adding your logo and contact information, or it can have space for you to over-print your contact information and personal message.

The hard costs are higher than if you write your own, but if you can use your time to help build your business another way, it may be cost effective to use a purchased newsletter.

Is a Newsletter Enough?

We have found that sending newsletters, much like doing office presentations, will not change a real estate agent's behavior when it comes to referring home inspectors. You need to do more. The newsletter is a preliminary communication to give you the opportunity to contact the agent in person.

For real estate agents who are already referring business to you, the newsletter will continually remind them of you and will help maintain the relationship. In other words, the newsletter may keep you from losing business and market share, but it's unlikely to build your business unless you follow it up with direct contact with your target, real estate agents. This background marketing is one tool in your bag, not a stand-alone marketing solution.

Re-Purpose

Writing newsletters is a lot of work. Try to find other uses for them. They might be handouts at home shows, features on Web sites (yours and others), materials provided at first-time buyers' seminars, press releases to community newspapers and magazines, and so on. Once you have done the work, maximize the return on your investment by making the newsletter work hard for you.

RADIO AND TELEVISION

Get Maximum Exposure

Many home inspectors have used radio and television as part of their public relations strategies. These two formats have the advantage of getting your name out to a very large number of consumers, including prospective homebuyers. They also provide an opportunity to convey a snippet of your personality—people can see or hear what you are like. It is often not targeted, but if there is no cost, it is still valuable background marketing.

You may be invited as a special guest or you may host a regular program on either radio or television.

If You Have Only One Shot, Give It Your All

As a special guest, you have one shot to make an impression. You are probably there to speak about a specific issue, or to be part of a special topic show. For example, the producer of a **radio talk show** might do a special on buying a home. The host may have invited a group of experts to talk about the homebuying process. Your role is to speak about your part in the process. Once you have established yourself as the "expert" in your part of the process, the producers may turn to you for information in the future.

Ask Whether Your Company Name Will Show

While it's great to be recognized on television by your family and friends, it's much more valuable if other viewers see who you are and how to get in touch. When you are going to be on television or radio, ask whether your company name and phone number will be included. The company name is probably more important than your name because people will be able to look up your company in a phone book or on a Web site more easily than your name. It's amazing how many experts appear on radio and television that you could never reach because their contact information is never mentioned or shown on screen.

Pitch a Regular Talk Show

As a talk show host, you have many opportunities to reach the public. What kind of talk shows could you do? Anything you can think of, related to your business, of course. What about a show in which you invite people to call in and "ask the expert" questions related to the house? If you are a good speaker and quick on your feet, hosting a show might be just the thing for you.

Pitch a Topic You Know

How do you get invited to speak as a guest on radio or television? Just to give you an idea, following are three steps for pitching a certain kind of show, but you can come up with a list of steps for any kind of show you want to offer:

1. Identify an appropriate show to be invited to. For example, a small, local talk show station that does shows on similar topics. Assemble a group of experts. For example, assemble a top real estate agent, a top real estate lawyer or title company, and a mortgage lender. Approach the station as a group and suggest that you could do a show on the homebuying process. Your group would give people valuable tips on buying a house.

2. You may also be invited as a guest on your own, if you can convince the producer that you are an expert, and that your expertise is interesting enough to warrant an interview. If you formed your company with a focused market segment in mind, you will have an easier time pitching your expertise because you will not just be a generic inspector. For example, if your position in the market is "the expert in older homes" or "the first-time buyer specialist" or "an expert in Victorian homes," you will have a much easier time getting invited onto the show. It's just more interesting for a producer to introduce you as an expert on a specific topic rather than as an ex-contractor who now inspects houses.

Market Yourself to Producer

3. If you have connections at the radio or television station, use them. If you don't, you will have to market yourself to the producer of the show. Send a resume outlining your expertise, including a description of what you do and why the listening or viewing public would be interested in you. List other PR experience, such as newspaper articles you have published. It helps to suggest topics that you could speak on. Here are examples:

   ■ The American Society of Home Inspectors (ASHI®), and your chapter in particular. This topic is good because it is not self-promotion. You are now a consumer advocate telling people about a professional association. This helps the homebuyer identify qualified inspectors.

   ■ The implications of state regulation of home inspection, if relevant in your state.

   ■ The top ten problems home inspectors find when inspecting a house.

   ■ How to select a home inspector. Include checklist questions for the homebuyer, such as asking how long the inspector spends in the home, what kind of report the client gets, what credentials the inspector should have, etc.

   ■ What to do when something goes wrong with your house.

   ■ How to select a contractor. Include things like insurance, experience, what to look for in a quote, negotiating points, and so on.

   ■ Seasonal maintenance: in the spring, speak about drainage and wet basement issues; in the summer, speak about air conditioning, and so on.

   ■ Controlling termites.

   ■ Solving home insurance problems.

   ■ Hurricane-proof your home.

   ■ Ten home safety hazards and how to avoid them.

Calling up your local radio or television stations is probably still the most efficient way to make contact and get the most accurate information. Find out who is responsible for the show you are interested in and how to get on the speaker's list. It's best to be familiar with the show of course, so you know the players and how things work. You may be able to get the producer's name from the credits and contact the producer directly. If not, the station will tell you what you need to know. There are a number of specialty stations and call-in shows that might fit your agenda.

KEY TERMS

editor	press kit	radio talk show
exposure	press release	regular column
newsletter		

STUDY SESSION 4 QUICK QUIZ

You should finish Study Session 4 before doing this Quiz. Write your answers in the spaces provided. Then, check your answers in Appendix A.

1. A newsletter should only be sent to agents, never to clients. Circle one.
   a. True
   b. False

2. A newsletter's general message should be: (Circle one.)
   a. I am on call 24-hours a day, 7 days a week.
   b. I want to show you how knowledgeable I am about all house systems.
   c. I make promises to your clients that make them happy.
   d. I want to help you; I provide useful information.

3. Who do you approach to write a newspaper column?
   _____

4. Writing a weekly column is the best use of your time. Circle one.
   a. True
   b. False

5. When you construct your article, you put all your important information in which paragraph, first or last, and why?
   _____
   _____

6. Submit your newspaper article and/or press release to any kind of publication in order to get your name out there. Circle one.
   a. True
   b. False

7. List three documents that might go into a press kit.
   1. _____
   2. _____
   3. _____

8. Writing a newsletter, newspaper column, or press release will not directly result in referral business. Circle one.
   a. True
   b. False

9. List three topics you could present in a newsletter, column, or on a radio show or TV spot.
   1. _____
   2. _____
   3. _____

If you had trouble with the Quiz, reread Study Session 4 and try the Quiz again. If you did well, it's time for Assignment 2.

ASSIGNMENT 2

RESEARCH AND CREATE PUBLIC RELATIONS TOOLS

This assignment includes exercises that will help you develop your company. We are going to ask you to do some research and make a few phone calls.

You should allow yourself three hours to five hours to complete this assignment.

1. Write a script for a first-time buyers' seminar. Include exactly what you would say. Feel free to borrow from our script, but add your own flavor to it.

2. Make a list of the topics that you know enough about to write a newspaper column on.

3. Write a press release for your company. If you are just starting in business, the press release will introduce your company and your unique selling proposition (USP). If you are an established inspector, the press release will introduce something new about your company, such as a new area of specialization.

4. Add an advertising and promotion section to your marketing plan. Fill in the content as you did the rest of your marketing plan.

When you are finished with Assignment 2, you're ready for Study Session 5.

EVENT-DRIVEN PUBLIC RELATIONS

Study Session 5 deals with sponsoring an event and doing home shows. This session will help you decide if sponsorships are a good idea for you and how to handle home shows.

LEARNING OBJECTIVES

At the end of Study Session 5 you should be able to

- list three reasons for sponsoring a real estate company's golf tournament;
- outline the pros and cons of one kind of event sponsorship;
- evaluate most sponsorship "opportunities" to see if they would benefit you;
- design a home show booth around a single topic;
- develop three open-ended questions to determine if the prospect is qualified; and

Study Session 5 may take you roughly 60 minutes to complete.

This section looks at public relations efforts that use events and home shows to get your company and services noticed.

EVENT SPONSORSHIP

Use It to Your Advantage

Sponsorship of a real estate event helps your company get some visibility within the real estate community. At first glance, sponsoring an event seems like a great opportunity, but you need to take advantage of this. If you are the type of person who can circulate in a large group, **approach guests,** make contacts, and establish relationships, this may be a wonderful opportunity. If this is not your style, you may want to focus elsewhere. Remember in Section I, on marketing, we talked about evaluating a marketing opportunity? We said that a marketing strategy can't just be a good idea; it has to be the best idea. You have a fixed marketing budget, right? Is a sponsorship the best place to spend your money? In our experience, sponsorships are expensive and time-consuming and the payoff is marginal, unless you are a natural at building relationships in group situations.

Sponsorship Does Not Guarantee Good Exposure

The benefits of sponsoring an event are variable. The organizer may give you lots of press or may bury your name in a list. The event itself may or may not be a success.

Compare Sponsorship to Other Strategies

There may be more effective and less costly ways to get in front of real estate agents. For example, is it better to spend $500 sponsoring a golf tournament, in which your name appears on a sign located at the third hole, or delivering a large box of muffins to five real estate offices at their weekly meetings for a month? Or maybe you would do better taking one agent per week out for lunch for three months.

You may want to sponsor an event for two other reasons:

1. You are having a hard time getting a meeting with real estate agents, you need something to break the ice.

2. A valuable agent calls and asks you to sponsor an event and you can't turn him or her down without hurting your relationship. Agents know your position on the food chain, and any golf tournament organizer knows that the first place you look for sponsorships is to the people who rely on you for business.

Turn Sponsorship to Your Advantage

If, for whatever reason, you end up involved in a sponsorship situation, the key is to make the most of it. We have provided you with a number of strategies for turning a sponsorship to your advantage. Because one common type of sponsorship is the real estate office golf tournament, we'll use it as a context for all the sponsorship tips that follow.

Ask for Something in Return

Tip 1: Be demanding.   The event organizer has asked you to sponsor an event. They are asking for a favor by asking you to make a commitment. It is reasonable for you to ask for a commitment in return.

Here is what we mean: The organizer may want you to contribute $200 to the event in exchange for having your name appear in the list of sponsors prominently displayed on each dinner table at the banquet. Can you ask for the following in addition?

■ Ask for a list of attendees and a list of prizewinners or award winners. You could then send a congratulatory letter to the winners.

■ Ask the organizer to help you arrange to do an office presentation. If you don't have a contact at an office, this could be valuable.

■ Ask if you can attend the banquet if you are good at "working the crowd." If you are not good at mingling and getting business cards, then attending the banquet is just another expense.

You may want to play golf. The organizers will certainly want you to play. This is a commitment of several hours to three people. You may ask to be grouped with agents you know, so you can reinforce your relationship. You may or may not want to play with agents you don't know. You probably don't want to be paired with nonagents unless there is a business opportunity. This is a big time commitment and may be a gamble. If you love golf and people, it may be an enjoyable day with some business possibilities.

Make a Counteroffer

Tip 2: Don't always give them what they ask for. If you say yes to a sponsorship, you may want to offer something that is more palatable to you. You will still be saying yes, but with a slight variation.

Here is an example: Say the organizer of a golf tournament asks for $400 in exchange for your name on a sign located at the third hole. You could say that you will donate a free home inspection for an agent to give to their client. It still represents a $300 or $400 value, but more importantly, the prizewinner may be a good prospect.

Offer High Visibility Prize

Tip 3: If possible, go with a high-visibility prize instead of cash. Most organizers are looking for two things, money and/or prizes. The money is harder for them to get, so that is likely the first thing they will ask for. They will want money in exchange for your company name listed in a high-profile location. The more money you spend, the higher profile the location. This kind of sponsorship is not memorable. In our experience, if you are going to contribute a prize, a **high-visibility prize** packs more bang for the buck, and the cost is not as much as you think. A 20-inch color television set has a larger impact as a prize than a table sponsorship, for example, and it doesn't cost as much as some other commitments. The organizers usually see this as a significant prize. Its impact is far greater than the dollar value. Our preference would still be to contribute something that is more likely to result in a sales opportunity later on. Giving away an inspection, for example, will certainly result in someone contacting you to use it. If they have never used you before, this is your chance to impress a new real estate agent.

Give It Away Yourself

As part of our sponsorship, a representative from our company presents the prize to the lucky winner at the banquet. Some years, we have given other prizes that have less grandeur but create a big stir nonetheless. We donated two remote-control cars. While it was not a grand prize, it worked well. We put our logo on the cars, charged the batteries, and put them on the prize table ready to roll. Needless to say, it didn't take long before agents were racing our cars around the room and on the green during the putting contest. Two extra precharged batteries ensured that the fun continued. Unfortunately, the problem with these types of prizes is that everyone, including the winner of the prize, will forget who donated it. You want your public relations campaign to create awareness in targeted areas that will not be forgotten. While this is a challenge, it is important to your marketing and sales efforts.

The lesson: If you don't have much to spend, get some visibility by being creative.

Work the Room

Tip 4: The beginning of the banquet is prime time, so get to work!   We usually go to the **banquet** only. The banquet is usually in the evening so it does not conflict with your work schedule. And it provides more of an opportunity to chat or buy someone a drink. If you attend the banquet, the socializing *before* the meal is the best time to make contacts. For the meal, you are stuck at a table with about seven other people and, because of the loud chatter, you often can't talk to the person across the table. You will likely only speak to the people on either side of you. If you have a basement contractor on your left, and an accountant on your right, you might as well sit back and enjoy the meal. But eat quickly so you can get up and socialize. Standing near the bar is often a good strategy.

Stay Home if You Don't Socialize

If you are not a natural socializer, this part of the banquet can be an awkward time. If you can't make the best of this time, don't bother going to the banquet. It's not uncommon to see a group of home inspectors clustered together chatting at banquets. They may feel comfortable and secure together, and they all have something in common, but they are wasting their time and money.

After dinner, awards and prizes are given out. This part of the evening is the hardest time to engage anyone in discussion. And after the prizes, people are tired, ready to go home, and less receptive to chatting.

Don't Overdo It

It may be easy to get carried away buying and consuming drinks. You are working with business associates, not drinking with friends. Retain control of your faculties.

HOME SHOWS

Every major city has shows targeting homeowners and would-be homeowners. In our city, we have several major **home shows** every year. If you participate in these, you are reaching out to homebuyers. Renovation companies and home improvement supply companies tend to do well at these shows.

To determine whether you want to participate in a show like this, you should know the following fact about them: Most people don't buy anything at home shows. There are some exceptions, but the main goal of the exhibitors is to get leads for future contact. If your product or service is not the type that fits this scheme, it's not worth your time to participate.

Home inspections are a time-sensitive service. You need to be in touch with the prospect during the short homebuying process. The chances of getting any leads at a home show are minimal. We have participated in home shows as an experiment, assuming a large number of people attending would be planning to buy a home in the near future. The result each time was exactly zero business for our time and money.

Offer Ancillary Services

You may benefit from a home show if you offer a service for homeowners. Services such as lead, asbestos, carbon monoxide testing, energy audits, and indoor air-quality testing lend themselves well to home shows. A compelling display generates discussion that leads to contacts for post-show **follow up.**

We have assembled a few pointers based on our past home show experience. The overriding theme of all these strategies is to focus on getting leads.

Generating Leads

Design Display
Around One Goal

Design your booth strategy around one well thought-out goal. Some goals are better than others. Possible goals include: to sell something, to introduce your service to the public, to create a public relations opportunity, or to get leads to follow up with later. The only real contender from the list above is to generate **leads.**

If your booth is set up to sell an indoor air quality-testing service, you may be tempted to try to book people on the spot. In fact, it is better to get leads than to make a sale at the show. Here's why.

Don't Try to Sell
at Your Booth

There are many attendees at the show. Perhaps thousands of people will walk past your booth over a weekend. You are only there for a few hours for a day or two. That leaves you very little time to speak to people. You will only reach a very small percentage of the attendees. If you try to sell people on the spot, you will dramatically reduce the number of people that you reach. It takes very little time to talk to a person and find out if they would be interested in learning more, but it takes a very long time to make a sale. While you are making the sale, prospects are slipping through your fingers.

Another Reason
Not to Sell

People don't come to these shows to buy; they come to get ideas and browse. Most don't want to talk with you for 15 minutes. Those who want to chat for 15 minutes may be people who like to talk. They will take up your valuable time.

Demonstrate a
Concrete Benefit

Have something interesting at the booth to draw people in. It might be a product you can show or a service you can demonstrate. Termites are a good example. You might offer termite inspections. A well-established termite colony in a thin transparent display case worked well for us. Samples of hazardous molds in tightly sealed containers may be interesting. A strong visual that does not look like a sales gimmick is usually successful. High-quality photos may work if they are poster size, and very clear.

Don't Trap People
in Your Booth

Set up your booth space so that attendees can stop and look at your display without feeling trapped. For example, if people have to walk around a front table to come into your booth to see your display, they may choose not to come in. If you have an eight-foot long table as your main display bench, and your booth space is 10 feet × 10 feet, move the table well into your booth area so that people can get out of the traffic to look at your display, but can still be on the outside of your display. This is a nonthreatening layout.

Approach Those
Who Show Interest

Anyone who shows some interest by looking at your display or demonstration should be approached. Approaching **prospects** is better than letting them just look at your stuff. Some exhibitors don't like to speak to a prospect because they feel that nobody likes to be approached. While this is true in some cases, there is good reason to talk with them. If you approach a prospect and they say they are just browsing, they are probably not a good prospect anyway, and it's best to have them move on to make room for a good prospect.

How do you approach a prospect who has stopped to look at your display? Here are some tips:

- Don't ask them about an irrelevant topic like, "Nice day today, isn't it?"

- Don't ask if you can help them. If you ask people, "Can I help you?" most will respond, "No, I'm just looking." Most of us turn off when sales staff approach us with this line in every store we ever go into.

- Ask about something in the client's life. It's all about them, not about you or your product at this point.

*Ask Open-Ended
Questions*

■ Ask questions that can't be answered with just a yes or no or with a single word. **Open-ended questions** engage people in discussion. If you can't think of an effective open-ended question that works for your service, ask a closed-ended question but think of a follow-up response for each possible answer you may get. For example, if you are testing indoor air quality, you may ask, "Do you get sick more often in the winter?" This is a closed-ended question that can be followed up with another leading question or an interesting fact, depending on the yes or no response you get.

*Make the Question
General*

■ Specific questions restrict the answer. A better question than the one above is, "Does anyone in your family get sick more often in the winter?"

■ Ask a direct question that starts the qualification process immediately like, "Do you ever worry about the health impact on your family from a moldy, musty basement?" Maybe the person doesn't own a home, or doesn't have a basement or crawlspace, or doesn't have a family. When you ask this question, you find out a great deal about the "qualification" of the prospect from his or her answer.

*Determine if a Prospect
Is Qualified*

The goal of your questions is to qualify the prospect. What do we mean by a **qualified prospect?** It simply means that there is a chance that this person could benefit from your service. This is one of the main points of being at the home show. If you just want a list of people who live in a particular area, you can do that much more easily by purchasing a list from a list broker. You want to connect with people face-to-face, but only with those who need your service. The list you take away from the home show should only include people who are likely to hire you.

You find out if prospects are qualified by asking them about themselves. For example, you need to find out if they own a home, or are planning to buy one. If you test for health-related issues, find out if the prospect has children. People love to talk about their children. And parents will spend money on things that may have a positive impact on their children's health or safety.

If you are promoting your home inspection business, you may open by asking them how much they know about home inspections. This open-ended question may get people talking about whether they own a home or are looking to buy one; important information for your screening process.

*Offer Your Service
as the Prize*

The strategy in which people drop their business cards in a bowl for a **booth prize** draw at the end of the show is tried and true, but it has also been done to death. Yes, you end up with a list of leads. But most other booths at these shows have a draw, too. People walk through the exhibit hall and drop a business card into every bowl in sight. If you don't have a business card, some booths have a piece of paper for attendees to fill out and drop in the bowl. We have even seen exhibitors put out a bowl and not offer a prize at all, yet their bowls still fill up with business cards. Why? Habit. People now drop business cards in these bowls or fill out forms as a matter of course. They don't pay particular attention to who you are and what you're offering. They likely have no interest in your service. These leads are not qualified. Calling them for follow-up is only as good as making random calls from the phone book.

One way to make the draw more effective is to offer your service as the prize. This way, with any luck, only people who might be interested in your service will enter. The bottom line is: It may seem like a good idea to have a big prize at your booth to draw people in, but in our experience it's just a liability. You will get distracted speaking with people who will have little interest in your service. In addition, the big prize is usually costly.

Sometimes you can have a little fun with a contest that engages people and flushes out leads. You may ask them to match photos of three houses with the names of three architectural styles, for example. Make it reasonably easy; people don't like to look foolish. This kind of contest works better in shows with light traffic, because people need to spend a couple of minutes at your booth working on the contest. It can be a good conversation starter, which is great if you have enough time and people at the booth to explore the leads. We have found that many real estate agents like this kind of contest.

Getting the Information

You want to contact the good prospects after the show. Many people create a reason for the prospect to provide their contact information. It may be a prize or a discount on the product or service. Some people set up meetings with prospects for the week after the show.

Keeping Attendees Moving

You need a strategy for keeping traffic flowing through your display space. There are two categories of people you want to move along:

1. Someone who is not a prospect. You need a polite way to move these people along.

2. Prospects from whom you have already recorded information for the follow-up call. This is more difficult because you don't want to let them know you are moving them along.

Be Polite but Keep Them Moving

For the first category, a good way to move them along politely is to say, "Thanks for dropping in, and enjoy the show!" Alternatively you could say, "It has been great talking with you. Be sure to take a brochure."

Goodbye, with a Follow-Up

For the second category, you have to be very careful. One strategy is to have something you can give to this prospect, such as a pen with your logo and phone number on it, as you get them moving along. You can use the same lines as you used above, but with a gift. So your line would be more like, "Thanks for dropping in; it has been interesting talking with you. I have something for you. Here's a measuring tape." This is also an opportunity to say, "We will be in touch next week to discuss your needs in more detail."

There are lots of sources of help for shows. You can attend shows and collect ideas. Talk to some of the participants to learn about their experiences. Have they been successful in the past? Observe the kinds of strategies the participants use with the attendees. Could you do the same? Do you have it in you to talk a good game? If the whole idea gives you hives, don't do it. Your time could be better spent having one-on-one lunches with agents. No strategy will ever be successful if your heart is not in it.

KEY TERMS

approach guests

banquet

booth prize

follow-up

high-visibility prize

home shows

leads

open-ended questions

prospects

qualified prospect

real estate office golf tournament

sponsorship

STUDY SESSION 5 QUICK QUIZ

You should finish Study Session 5 before doing this Quiz. Write your answers in the spaces provided. Then, check your answers in Appendix A.

1. Golf tournaments are always a good investment of marketing dollars. Circle one.

    a. True

    b. False

2. Say a golf tournament organizer calls and asks you to contribute $200 toward a golf tournament. In exchange, you will get a listing in the banquet program. List two things you could ask for in addition to the listing.

    1. _____

    2. _____

3. What is a high-visibility prize? Give two examples.

    1. _____

    2. _____

4. For a golf tournament banquet, what is the best time to network with the attendees?

    _____

    _____

    _____

5. The most effective booth strategy at a show is to have many goals rather than being single-minded. It's best to be flexible. Circle one.

    a. True

    b. False

6. What is the goal of promoting a professional service at a home show?

    _____

    _____

7. A home show is a good spot to generate home inspection business. Circle one.

    a. True

    b. False

8. Give one good way to end a conversation with someone who is not a good prospect.

    _____

    _____

9. Explain why having a draw for a prize at your home show booth may be a liability.

    _____

    _____

    _____

10. What is the difference between an open-ended question and a close-ended question?

_____

_____

_____

If you had trouble with the Quiz, reread Study Session 5 and try the Quiz again. If you did well, it's time for Study Session 6.

STUDY SESSION

FUNDAMENTALS OF SALES AND SELLING

Study Session 6 will provide you with tips to help you get into a sales frame of mind and become a good salesperson.

LEARNING OBJECTIVES
At the end of Study Session 6 you should be able to

- design a short, educational sales presentation to deliver to an agent;
- describe one way to elicit a soft rejection over a hard rejection;
- list two ways to remove your sales fears; and
- list 18 questions that you can ask to learn more about your customers' needs.

  Study Session 6 may take you roughly 30 minutes to complete.

The goal of this section is to make you a better salesperson. We will begin by looking at some basic definitions and concepts.

WHAT IS SALES?

Let's be sure we are clear about sales and salespeople. We talked earlier about marketing being the precursor to sales. Marketing is responsible for making the phone ring, but *sales* answers the phone and is responsible for helping the prospect make a firm commitment to using your product or service. A good salesperson is not someone who makes you buy what you don't want. Sales should not be high-pressure fast talk with little substance. A good *salesperson* is an educator who tells you how the right product or service can create a benefit or solve a problem for you. The sales process should explore your needs and then fulfill them.

Sales Is Communication

Sales is more than just learning about the clients' circumstances and offering an appropriate match. Good salespeople must be excellent communicators, much like good home inspectors. They must know how to approach people, how to be empathetic, how to listen and identify customer concerns, and how to present logical solutions to their problems. This may seem like a daunting task, but you probably already do all these things during the home inspection process. Like home inspectors, the best salespeople see themselves as consultants. They are knowledgeable in their field and know how to give good advice after asking lots of well thought out questions and listening carefully to the answers. Only then do they show the customer how the service fits their situation.

An Easy Sell

We are fortunate because our service, home inspection, is a good match for almost everyone buying a home. We add real value that is regularly worth 10 or 20 times the inspection fee, and sometimes considerably more. Clients sell themselves on home inspection as soon as they understand it.

Follow-Up Is Critical

You may have noticed a common theme throughout this course: We keep saying, "This is a good marketing opportunity but it's worthless unless you follow up." That advice comes from our experience. Most marketing, public relations, and advertising campaigns are a good way to introduce your company to your prospects. They don't usually result in sales unless there is **follow up.** We have proven more times than we'd like to admit that most of these strategies do little to change the behavior of real estate professionals. Unfortunately, most of us spend all our efforts on these campaigns and forget about the follow-up. We "forget" about it because we don't like doing it, and we are afraid of rejection. Fear is the biggest obstacle to sales success. To overcome the fear, we must take charge, be persistent, and follow through on our activities.

Use the Two-Step Process

Let's look a little more closely at how to grow your business through sales. There are two sources of leads for your inspection company—soliciting business directly from the client (the homebuyer), or soliciting referrals from real estate professionals. In any business, if you solicit business from the end user, advertising, public relations, and marketing campaigns are the key to success. But if you solicit referrals from real estate professionals, the advertising, public relations, and marketing campaigns are only the first step of a **two-step process.** The two steps are as follows:

1. Get your name front and center (marketing, public relations, and advertising).
2. Make them lifelong customers by building long-term relationships.

Solicit Referrals

Step One is not very effective without Step Two, and Step Two is much more difficult (but not impossible) without Step One. If you must eliminate one of the two steps, you would be better to eliminate Step One than Step Two.

Many people believe that the quickest way to success in the home inspection business is to solicit referrals rather than soliciting business from the end user. The reason is that a real estate professional is in a position to refer you to more people than a homebuyer. That means you have to follow the two-step process. We believe that the key to success is to choose only a few well thought-out marketing, advertising, and public relations campaigns in order to get people's attention, and spend the rest of your time on sales.

Be One of the Few Who Can Sell

Most people are not good at sales. Furthermore, most people have an aversion to sales. But there is a bright side to all of this. Because most people have an aversion to sales, you will be able to capture market share by just doing a small amount of sales-related work a little bit better than everyone else. By learning and practicing these techniques, you will launch yourself into the top 20 percent of the home inspection companies that do 80 percent of the home inspection business.

GETTING INTO A SALES FRAME OF MIND

Forget the Salesperson Stereotype

The best way to grow your business, whether you are just starting out or you are a veteran inspector, is to learn some sales techniques. Few people like to think of themselves in the role of a salesperson. Why? Because salespeople have a reputation for being loud, pushy individuals, with no listening skills. But this reputation is built largely on myth and stereotype, based on a few bad apples. Sure, some salespeople are brash and pushy, but so are many people in other professions. These personality traits are not inherent to a salesperson. In fact, they are probably the worst, most self-defeating traits for a salesperson to have.

If you want to succeed, sales skills are a necessity. So, how can you embrace sales as a positive part of your business? By educating yourself about the value of sales, and about effective sales strategies that can help you achieve your goals. If you are committed to learning and practicing sales, you will quickly develop an edge over your competition. Begin by deciding to be among the best in your industry by becoming a little better at everything you do.

INTERPERSONAL AND COMMUNICATION SKILLS

People Skills Are Essential

You probably chose to become a home inspector not only because you know houses, but also because you enjoy working with people. Chances are, you already have the interpersonal skills necessary to be a good salesperson. That's great because technical expertise alone doesn't sell. **People skills** are also essential. You may know everything there is to know about houses, but if you can't communicate effectively, you won't have any clients to pass your knowledge on to.

Sales depends on your ability to effectively communicate information about yourself, and your services to a prospect, while listening to your prospects and understanding what they need. Ultimately, sales relies on ⅓ personality, ⅓ skill, and ⅓ hard work. Top sales people are ambitious, honest, empathetic, responsible, caring, and are excellent at building and maintaining relationships and servicing customers. This is also the foundation of a successful home inspection business!

Great Talkers Are
Great Listeners

Have you ever come away from a discussion and said to yourself, "That person is a really good conversationalist." If you could play the conversation back, you might find that you did most of the talking, and that the other person simply asked questions that allowed you to keep talking about something you are interested in. You can be a really good conversationalist too, and you don't have to say much. Just show that you are interested in the other person, and ask enough questions to encourage them to talk about what matters to them.

Handling Rejection

Grow a Thick Skin

If you are just starting out, remember that real estate agents likely already have established relationships with other inspectors. You will have a few conversations like this:

> *You:* "Good morning, I'm calling to ask you to recommend my services as a home inspector."
>
> *The agent:* "Look, I'm very busy. And I've been working with the same home inspector for ten years and am very satisfied. He's never lost me a deal. Please don't call again."

This kind of rejection might feel like failure. And you may wonder how you will ever break into the market if most agents already have home inspectors they refer.

Don't underestimate the difficulty of the sales process. You are soliciting business from people who don't think they need what you have to offer. Being told, "No, don't bother me!" is something you have to learn to live with. But here's another way to look at it. If you don't hear "No" from time to time, perhaps you are not knocking on enough doors. Each time you hear "No," it is bringing you a step closer to hearing "Yes." A "No" most likely means the benefits of your service are not clear. Treat this response as an opportunity to request more information. The rejection will help you better prepare for the next prospect. If you don't like being rejected, then congratulations, you're normal! It's important to know, however, that rejection is a part of sales and that successful salespeople know how to confront the fear of rejection. This fear is the main reason why home inspectors don't like prospecting new agents. The number and frequency of your sales calls will determine the quality and volume of your sales results. There's an old saying among sales people, "If someone just comes up to you and buys your product, then that's a purchase, not a sale. And you must sell if you want to increase results!"

Aim for a Soft Rejection

Flat out rejection is hard on the ego, but there is another reason to reduce your rejection rate. You want to avoid the word "Never." It's one thing to be told that a real estate agent doesn't want your services at the moment, but it's another thing when an agent says not to call them ever again. If an agent says "Not now," you may have struck out for the moment, but the door may open later. If the agent says, "Don't call again," the door has been shut and locked. Although you can't do much about rejection, you can increase your chances of a **soft rejection** by improving your sales technique. A soft rejection means the prospect said "No" but not, "Never." You can still try again with this prospect at a later date. How can you reduce flat out rejection?

Buyer Psychology

It is understandable that if you call out of the blue top agents who have never used you before, and ask for their business, you are likely to get rejected. Top agents are used to being inundated with sales calls from inspectors and others. Top agents understand sales techniques and are sensitive to being manipulated. Top agents are also the busiest in their profession. If your call gives an agent a reason to try your service, you will be far more successful in getting appointments. Let them know you understand their problems and their world. Perhaps the agent had a bad experience with a previous inspector, or they anticipate how they will feel once they have tried your service. Maybe your service offers more convenience or will make the agent look better in the eyes of their client.

Everything you say or do must accomplish one of two things. First of all, you must be able to solve a problem or satisfy a need, and secondly, you must answer a key question that will help them make the decision to try you out. By uncovering the problems that agents are faced with, you will be in a better position to present solutions that will motivate agents to make a decision about you.

Scripts Are Critical

Good professionals in any field rarely give impromptu presentations. They script every conversation to some degree, from an initial phone call, to formal presentations. Even your doctor has a series of questions to ask you when you feel sick. The questions are somewhat preset, but they also respond to the specifics of your problem. A script can help you stay relaxed and focused because you have something to fall back on.

You will give the impression of an experienced professional when you approach a prospect, provided that you are listening and adapting your script for the situation.

The other benefit of a scripted presentation is that you will never be surprised. In preparing your script, anticipate everything a real estate agent might say to you so that you can touch on the most common objections up front and get them out of the way. At the very least, your preparation will help ensure that even if you don't get the answer you are looking for, you are more likely to get a "Soft no" instead of a flat-out "No."

Setting Goals

Goal setting is vital to succeeding in sales. Because rejection is part of the process, you need the goals to turn the process into a positive experience. What are some realistic goals? Let's look at the math.

Start with Reasonable Expectations

Be reasonable about what your business will look like when you succeed and then aim for it. You can only inspect three houses per day. In a 20-day month, that's 60 inspections per month. If your fee is $300 per inspection, you'll earn $18,000 per month or $216,000 per year! Sounds good, doesn't it? Most inspectors do not average three inspections per day. Once you are busy, a more realistic number is 2.0 to 2.5 per day. Let's use 2.2 inspections per day or 42 inspections per month (19 days per month) or 501 inspections per year. An inspector who does 500 inspections per year is very successful, with a gross income of $150,000 (500 inspections × $300 per inspection). Let's use that number for our example. There are other variables you need to consider as well.

Agent Referrals— How Many Do You Need

Let's consider how much business we can solicit from real estate agents only. If you solicit agents at random, the numbers look very dismal. On average, agents sell only two homes per year! This means you would need 250 agents referring business to you in order to get 500 inspections in a year. If you factor in a success rate of 1 in 20, you would actually need to solicit 5,000 agents. (This success ratio is arbitrary—we chose to use a low success rate to show you a worst-case scenario. If you are a good salesperson, your success rate will be higher.) To build your business to full capacity in one year would mean making almost 20 calls per day and meeting with five to ten agents! Not only is this unrealistic, it raises another question. When are you going to find the time to do any inspections? This is a problem.

The solution is to solicit only top agents and to maximize your success rate through solid sales techniques.

How many inspections per year can you get from a top real estate agent? Our biggest agent refers over 100 inspections per year to us. Many agents refer five to ten inspections per year. A reasonable number of inspections from a top agent might be 20 inspections in a year.

What does the math look like now?

You need 25 top agents referring business to you. With a success rate of 1 in 20, you would have to solicit 500 agents. To build your business to full capacity in one year, you would have to make 1.9 calls per day and meet with two agents to three agents per week.

These numbers are starting to look more reasonable. And don't forget that this model grows our business to full capacity in one year. Full capacity in two years would be better than average.

Remember, too, that if you are doing your job well, you will get referrals from satisfied clients. Your marketing, advertising, and public relations campaigns will also generate prospects that will turn into satisfied clients.

You Are Now a Salesperson

Here's a reasonable goal for an established inspector: On an ongoing basis, call one top agent every day and meet with one agent per week. When you first start, however, you should be much more aggressive. Contact five top agents per day and try to meet with one agent per day. Once you start getting business, taper your efforts to one call per day and one meeting per week. If you can do this, you will have growth that is well above average, with a solid business in a year, and an exceptional business within two years.

TWO SALES PHILOSOPHIES

Sales techniques generally fall into two distinct camps:

1. Manipulative sales
2. Educational sales

Avoid Manipulative Sales Techniques

Manipulative sales involve tricks to maneuver your target into agreeing to buy your product or use your service. Most of us have had this experience: You spend time negotiating a car salesperson down to a price you're comfortable with. The salesperson says, "I'm fine with it, but I'll have to check with my manager, who has to approve it." The salesperson disappears into the manager's office and comes out shaking his or her head saying, "No, my manager will not approve the deal. We just need $500 more." If you're already in the mindset that the car will cost $30,000, the extra $500 won't seem like such a big deal to you.

But let's step back for a minute here. How do you really think the conversation went in the manager's office? They probably talked a bit about the weather, a game they saw last night, what they ate for lunch. But they probably didn't talk about the price of the car you are trying to buy. That's right. Talking to the manager is a sales tactic, a trick. It allows the salesperson to look innocent when he or she has to deliver the message that the price is $500 more than you bargained for. The manipulative approach to sales is considered old-style. This example may remind you how unpleasant it is to be manipulated.

Better sales techniques aim to educate instead. The **educational sales** process involves a two-part dialogue:

1. Your prospects educate you about their needs.

2. You educate your prospects about how your product or services will satisfy their needs.

The sales process is a dialogue. Asking the right questions and listening carefully to the answers is the best way to learn what the person wants. Knowing this gives you an opportunity to show them how you can meet their needs. You have to get prospects to talk about themselves. Telling is not selling. Everything you say should be in the form of a question. Asking questions rather than talking is the key to becoming a great communicator because it holds the attention of the listener. For example, ask an agent if their current home inspector can complete an inspection within 24 hours of your call. If fast turnaround is important to the real estate agent, you'll hear about it. You are then in a position to explain that you guarantee 24-hour turnaround time. This might be your unique selling proposition (USP).

Following are more questions that might lead to your USP, and, then to a commitment:

- Do all your clients get an inspection?
- How do they find an inspector?
- Do you recommend an inspector?
- Who do you recommend?
- How did you choose that inspector?
- Are you satisfied?
- Are your clients satisfied?
- Are they always available?
- Do they have geographical limitations?
- Do they have insurance?
- Do they offer free telephone support for your clients?
- Are they specialists in any area?
- Do they offer termite inspections?
- Is bedside manner important?
- Are you concerned about liability when referring an inspector? (Explain how your insurance policy covers agents, too.)
- Are you concerned that your client would sue you if a problem cropped up with the house at a later date? (You could explain how the liability is transferred to the well-insured home inspector.)
- Do you ever need to book an inspection in the evening?
- Is there anything you wish your inspector(s) would do differently?

Some of these questions are open-ended and cannot be answered with "Yes" or "No". Here is an example, "What could I do to help your sales go more smoothly?" This question encourages dialogue. Others are close-ended questions that yield a simple "Yes" or "No" response. "Do you appreciate a home inspector who is sensitive to clients?" You are likely to get a response like, "Yes." That's nice, but you don't have enough information to offer a list of benefits to the prospect. You can also ask a hypothetical question, such as "What if I promised to make myself available to do inspections on the weekend?" These types of questions open up the discussion and help deal with objections. We will look more closely at how to use these questions in the sales process in later Study Sessions.

Networking

Once you've engaged an agent by listening to their answers and addressing their needs, why stop there? Here's an example of how to network, using the educational technique. If you are meeting with a top agent, ask the agent what she needs from the home inspector for her to run a better business. Listen carefully to what she says and then show her how your services can meet those needs. If the agent is happy with what you say, ask if she can recommend you to another top agent that could benefit from hearing your message. If she says "Yes," then ask if you can use her name when you contact the new agent. If she says "Yes," you have permission to contact someone new, and you have the added bonus of being referred. When you phone the new agent, you can say something like, "Sally Smith suggested I call you." You have not tricked anyone. Sally said you could use her name as a reference, and she gave you the new agent's name. You asked for permission to make the call.

Keep in mind, the goal here is not to relieve someone of their money. What you are doing is educating the agent about your services and showing how those services can meet the agent's needs. What you are hoping for in return is a referral.

As you get yourself comfortable with the education mindset, here's another concept we want you to consider. It's called the "sales funnel."

Leads Eventually Yield Sales

The **sales funnel** acknowledges that your home inspection service is not for everyone. Imagine a large funnel. At the top of the funnel you have 100 real estate agents. If you phone all of them, 25 of them may say they are not interested in talking to you at all. Another 25 may tell you to send them information, but they don't have time for you now. Ultimately, you may end up with 25 agents that agree to meet with you. You meet the 25 agents and find that only five of them agree to refer an inspection to you on a trial basis. The sales funnel means you will reach 5 of 100 agents, or have a 20 to 1 funnel. Put another way, 20 "leads" yield one "sale."

Improving the Sales Funnel

The goal is to improve the sales funnel. If you try to convince agents to meet with you, you may end up with a 20 to 1 funnel. Sales training helps you "change the shape of the funnel" or improve your success rate. If your success rate improves to ten to one, you will grow your business twice as fast! Remember that small changes in ability can lead to dramatic changes in results.

Rejection Is Part of Success

But even with sales training, you will still get nine rejections before you get one "sale." Successful salespeople recognize that a certain number of people will say no before you get one yes. Here is how people successful in sales handle the rejections:

- Determine, on average, how many times you have to hear "No" before you hear a "Yes." You'll know through experience, over a period of time. With this knowledge in hand, you are now prepared for rejection. If you expect it, you won't be disappointed. Rejection becomes part of the process. You must have courage and must not let fear hold you back.

- If you expect rejection, you can measure success just by the phone calls you make. In other words, you are succeeding even when you hear "No" because you know that it's part of the process to hearing a "Yes." It means you are on the phone making a call. If you determine that your success rate is one in ten, when you make a call on Monday morning and the real estate agent says he has no interest in meeting with you, you can now say, "One down, nine to go until I hear a 'Yes.'"

This mindset helps you focus on success rather than rejection.

KEY TERMS

educational sales	people skills	soft rejection
follow-up	sales funnel	two-step process

STUDY SESSION 6 QUICK QUIZ

You should finish Study Session 6 before doing this Quiz. Write your answers in the spaces provided. Then, check your answers in Appendix A.

1. Sales people are much like home inspectors in that they view themselves as consultants. Why is it better to be viewed as a consultant than a salesperson?

    _____

    _____

2. What is the biggest obstacle to sales success?

    _____

    _____

3. What are the two steps you need to take in the marketing and sales process?
    1. _____
    2. _____

4. Name two things you must accomplish if you want to be successful in selling?
    1. _____
    2. _____

5. Describe one technique you can use to reduce rejection.

    _____

    _____

6. Which of the following is a realistic sales goal for an established inspector on an ongoing basis. Circle one.
    a. Call one real estate agent per day.
    b. Call five real estate agents per day.
    c. Call one real estate agent per week.
    d. Call one real estate agent per month.

7. Which sales technique engages the customer in dialogue? Circle one.
    a. Manipulative sales
    b. Educational sales

8. What is the best way to learn what your prospect really wants?

    _____

    _____

9. Which type of question is more effective at encouraging dialogue? Circle one.
    a. Open-ended question
    b. Close-ended question

If you had trouble with the Quiz, reread Study Session 6 and try the Quiz again. If you did well, it's time for Study Session 7.

TARGETING YOUR SALES EFFORTS

Study Session 7 will furnish you with concrete sales skills for each of the most common sales opportunities you will likely encounter.

LEARNING OBJECTIVES

At the end of Study Session 7 you should be able to

- design an approach, in one paragraph, that describes how to get a meeting with a real estate broker;

- design an approach, in one paragraph, that describes how to get a meeting with a real estate agent; and

- list multiple needs that real estate agents, brokers, and homebuyers have, respectively, that might be met by your service.

Study Session 7 may take you roughly 60 minutes to complete.

This section looks at the three distinct groups on which you probably want to target your sales efforts. It also covers the concrete sales skills for each of the most common sales opportunities you will likely encounter.

THREE DISTINCT GROUPS

We have said that many home inspectors feel that targeting real estate agents gives the biggest return on investment. This section explores that concept in more detail. Even if you target real estate agents, you will likely have three distinct groups to sell to in order to make the final sale. We are making the distinction here because the sales strategies are different for each of the three groups.

The three groups that you may sell to are as follows:

1.   The real estate agent. You may contact a real estate agent in hopes of building a new relationship.

2.   The real estate broker. You may solicit an agent office talk from a real estate broker, or you may ask to drop by a real estate office to meet with the broker.

3.   The homebuyer. Even if homebuyers are not a target, you will have to sell to the homebuyer when they call to ask you about your service. If they just call to book an inspection, you don't have a sales component. Many homebuyers will call several inspectors before deciding whom to use, even if an agent has referred them. By the way, many agents will refer three inspection firms to reduce their liability. While the agent referral helps, you will still have to show the client why you are the best one to meet their needs

Know the Prospect's Needs

Each of these three groups has different needs and, therefore, requires different sales strategies. The first stage of any selling process is to understand your prospect's needs. Remember that your prospects buy for *their* reasons, not for *your* reasons. It is your job to uncover the most important needs of your audience. This is the key to success in home inspection—recognize what people are looking for and find ways to deliver it better than anyone else.

The following lists are a starting point to identifying those needs. You will probably think of many more.

What does the real estate agent need? The agents need to

- sell more properties,
- list more properties,
- sell the property for a higher value,
- sell the property faster,
- remove obstacles to the sale,
- find tools that help with closing the deal,
- find more time in their day,
- develop a loyal clientele—better long-term relationships with satisfied clients and more referrals, and
- have home inspectors not kill their deals over trivial issues.

What does the broker/manager of a real estate office need? Brokers/managers need

- real estate agents to sell more properties for more money,
- real estate agents to sell properties more quickly,
- real estate agents to list more properties,
- fewer delays in transactions,
- better control of the sales transaction,
- more time in their day,
- support for their agents,
- to attract more agents to the firm, and
- elimination of complaints from unhappy homebuyers.

What does the homebuyer need? Homebuyers need to

- be sure they have made a good decision buying the house,
- be assured they are not purchasing a money pit,
- buy the right property for the best price possible,
- understand how to look after the home and protect their investment, and
- be sure they got a good value from their home inspection company.

So far we have identified the three groups we have to sell to and have identified some of their needs based on our experience. We will now look at the sales process. After that, we will discuss how you can satisfy the needs listed above.

THE SALES PROCESS

The sales process has five components:

1. Prospecting
2. The Approach
3. The Presentation
4. The Close
5. Customer Management

Prospecting ensures that the sales funnel is kept full with people who need a home inspector.

The **approach** is where you ask your targets' permission to sell to them. For instance, the approach happens when you call an agent to ask if you can meet him or her.

The **presentation** is your discussion of the benefits of your service relative to the prospect's needs. You must first uncover the needs or problems of your prospect by asking questions. Showing your prospect how your service is ideal for their situation involves handling objections. This relies on your ability to anticipate objections and overcome them with well-thought-out questions and responses. Create a list of all the reasons an agent may not want to refer their clients to you, and prepare your best response in advance.

The **close** is where you get the agent to agree to refer you on his or her next inspection.

Customer management involves organizing yourself so that you have time to build and maintain your relationships. This means that your customers use you over and over again.

In the following sections we'll look at applying the sales process to each of the three target groups.

THE REAL ESTATE AGENT

The Agent Is a Hard Sell

Let's look at how we would step through the process with a real estate agent. We have prospecting, the approach, the presentation, the close, and customer management. Because the needs of the agent are similar to the needs of the broker/manager, the phases of the sales process are similar. The main difference is the stakes are much higher for the real estate agent, so the close is more difficult. For the broker/manager, it's important to do everything he or she can to increase the sales volume for the office, but no single deal is critical. For the real estate agent, on the other hand, every single deal is important. If you do an inspection for one of the agent's clients, and the deal falls apart, the agent loses a lot of money.

The bottom line is, if you do a poor office presentation, there is no financial harm done to the real estate office, but if you mess up an inspection, it's money out of somebody's pocket. This is why changing a real estate agent's behavior is so difficult. If the agent has an inspector who is working out, why would he or she risk giving you a chance?

Prospecting for Agents

We discussed prospecting earlier with respect to brokers/managers. Again, we suggest checking with your local real estate board to find out who the top agents are. You may also find top agents identified in newspaper advertisements and real estate Web sites. This knowledge will allow you to focus on agents with the highest "life value."

Approaching the Agent

The approach to a real estate agent is difficult if he or she has never heard of you. You make the approach over the phone, asking the real estate agent to spend five minutes with you. There are three things you can do to make this easier:

1. Make sure the agent has heard of you. One of the most effective ways to make sure the real estate agent has heard of you is to do a real estate agent presentation. Although, in our experience, these talks do not change the referral behavior of real estate agents, as soon as you pick up the phone to make your first call to an agent, you will know why real estate agent talks are a good idea. The agent will already know who you are and may also see you as an expert.

2. Make sure someone the real estate agent knows has referred you. How can you get referrals? Every time you meet with a real estate agent, ask him or her to refer you to another real estate agent. For example, you have just met

with a real estate agent from the local RE/MAX office. The presentation goes well. Before you leave, you say something like, "My goal is to meet with top producing agents like you. Who else in your office is a top producer?" After taking the names the agent gives to you, then say, "Do you mind if I mention your name when I call them?" If you get a "Yes," it makes your job much easier because your opening line to the next real estate agent will be, "So-and-so from your office suggested that I give you a call . . ."

3. The third thing you can do is talk to the other agent attending your inspection. For instance, you are doing an inspection with a buyer's agent but the selling agent may be at the inspection. Talk to the selling agent.

These strategies will help make the approach easier and increase the probability that you will get a "Yes" when you ask the real estate agent for a five-minute meeting. But don't forget to offer a trade during the approach. If you ask for five minutes, it's not a fair trade. Even if it is unspoken, the question the real estate agent is asking is, "What do I get out of it?" You should have an irresistible offer. Here are some effective tools for generating interest:

Offer a Good Trade

■   Have something of value that you can give to the real estate agent for free. A popular book or a subscription to a high quality magazine related to real estate may be of interest, for example. If you have any material that is valuable to the agent, you can offer this. If it has been published, this also builds your credibility.

■   Speak to the ego. You can tell an agent that you are trying to improve the quality of your inspection service and you would like his or her advice. Could you drop in for five minutes? In return you will give the agent a gift certificate for a free lunch or tickets to a movie. You may even offer to pay a top agent for some of their time. A one-hour consulting fee may be fair.

There is one caution here. If you do ask the real estate agent's advice, you may hear something you are not prepared to, or cannot, do. For example, at a meeting with an agent, we asked what we could do to improve our service. The agent said that we should be available to do an inspection on 30 minutes' notice, 365 days a year. Needless to say, we could not make that promise. It made it difficult to follow up with that agent, although we pointed out that no one could live up to that commitment.

Solve a Problem

■   If you have an offer that will help the agent do more business, solve a current problem, or help the transaction go more smoothly, you may be welcome. For example, you call and say, "I have developed a system for home inspections that makes the deal more likely to go through with fewer stumbling blocks. This system will help you make more money. Can I drop in for five minutes to show you?" One inspection company uses a team of inspectors at every house, so the inspection takes about an hour. Agents like to get in and out quickly, and appreciate this shortened time commitment to the inspection.

Perhaps there are circumstances that make it difficult for prospective purchasers to get house insurance and you have found a way to solve the insurance issue. (We accomplished this by building a relationship with an insurer who recognizes our inspection reports and offers insurance to our clients when others will not.) This makes the transaction easier on the agent. There is a cost to the agent associated with anything that may interfere with the transaction. If you can eliminate just one of those frustrations, where others cannot, then you are in a better position to present your service as the best choice.

Presenting to the Agent

The presentation is the meeting with the real estate agent. Props can help with this. Some people like visuals, and a small flip chart or laptop PowerPoint presentation may be helpful. If you prefer to just have a discussion, that's okay, too, but if you have built up the agent's expectations by offering to show him or her a system that will sell houses faster and for more money, it's best to have some kind of physical presentation prepared. You can give agents a CD with your presentation so they may review it at their leisure.

Another presentation technique is to take the agent out for lunch or breakfast. The format of this presentation depends on how well the agent knows you, or on how good the referral was. For example, if the agent is your sister's friend, you may be able to take this agent out for lunch and make a less formal presentation. Good presentations are more like conversations in any case.

During the presentation, you should remember to

- consider everything from the customer's perspective; it's about them, not you;
- describe the benefits, not just features;
- select only a few of the best benefits because the more you say, the less they hear; and
- keep it short.

Closing the Agent

Once again, we have come to the part that distinguishes a successful home inspector from the average home inspector. You have finished your presentation and impressed the real estate agent. You now have two choices:

1. You can thank them for their time and say, "If you are ever in need of an inspector, please give me a call."

2. You can **ask for the order.** Asking for the order is sales terminology for obtaining a commitment from the prospect.

If you use method one, you've just wasted your time. If you have earned the right to ask for the order, then you must do it. Here are lines that some home inspectors use:

- "Can I ask you to add my name to your referral list?"
- "Can I count on you to give me a try?"
- "Will you refer me on your next inspection?"

These are very difficult things to say because you may get a "No." It also feels aggressive. However, because people make decisions based on emotion, if you feel like you have left a good impression, now is the best time to ask for the order. Here are three reasons you owe it to yourself to ask for the close:

Be a Little Aggressive

1. You are trying to get an agent to refer you instead of someone else. You will not get the referral unless you ask. You have to be a little aggressive. One thing we can be sure of, at the end of the presentation, the real estate agent will not make "the close" for you. If you are imagining an agent saying, "That's a great system you have, would you mind if I refer you on my next inspection?" then you must be asleep, because this only happens in dreams.

2. Most real estate agents will not say "No" to your face. If they reject you, you are more likely to get a soft rejection that leaves the door open for the future. For example, the agent is more likely to say, "We'll see, maybe I will give you a try when my regular inspector is unavailable," or, "I need to digest what you have been telling me; I cannot commit to you right now." If this happens, you should reply by saying, "I understand and realize this is an important decision." This will also give you an opportunity to ask what it is they need to consider. "You must have a good reason for wanting to digest the information; may I ask what it is? Or "Are there any questions or concerns that I have not addressed that will help make your decision easier?" Either way, you can still congratulate yourself because at least you had the nerve to meet the agent in person and ask for the close. If you had delivered your presentation over the phone, it would have been easier for the agent to flat out reject you.

3. When the real estate agent says "No," remember rejection is part of the sales funnel. You can't expect a "Yes" from 100 percent of the agents you meet. So relax and let them reject you. It's just business. Remember one other thing: "No" means *not now.* It does not mean *never.* And besides, if you suspect they are not interested in what you have to say, this is a perfect opportunity to practice your sales pitch and closing techniques.

Customer Management of Agents

A fundamental part of sales is your ability to keep good track of your contacts. If you don't have some kind of system to keep track of the real estate agents that you have spoken to and do business with, you will not be able to effectively grow your business and evaluate your marketing campaigns. We will discuss some strategies later on for tracking campaigns and managing your customers.

Leverage the Relationship

If you have built a high-quality relationship with a real estate agent and have earned high levels of trust through favors and gestures of kindness on an ongoing basis, then don't be afraid to ask for a favor in return. When you do something really nice for someone or extend a favor, they will want to reciprocate by doing something nice in return. For example, let's say you are having a really difficult time getting into a particular real estate office to do a presentation but you happen to have a great working relationship with a particular agent in that office. The very best approach is to have the agent refer you to the broker or person responsible for scheduling meetings. If the agent has something nice to say about you, it will be much easier to get a "Yes."

THE REAL ESTATE BROKER/MANAGER

If you want to introduce yourself to real estate offices, you will have to persuade the brokers that this is good for them. Before you proceed, you need to know who is in charge of the offices and what you want from them. Let's assume you want to speak at an office meeting and the office manager is in charge of guest speakers.

Prospecting for Office Managers and Brokers

Knowing how many real estate offices are in your operating area and how successful they are will allow you to focus on the most productive offices with the most successful agents. Your local real estate association should have statistics on which offices sell the most homes in your area. Because larger offices may have several brokers or office managers, you want to make sure you speak to the right person. When you call and speak to the receptionist, ask, "Who is responsible for scheduling office meetings?" Be friendly, polite, smile into the phone, and people will be far more receptive to helping you get the information you are looking for. The first step is making sure you have reached the right person.

Approaching the Office Manager or Broker

Let's look at how you might go through the process with an office manager or broker. Let's assume you would like to come into the office and speak to the agents at an office meeting. There are two ways to do this:

1. Do the approach, presentation, and close over the phone.
2. Make the approach over the phone and make the presentation and close in person.

The second has a greater chance for success. But time and distance constraints may make the second approach impractical; you may end up having to do it all on the phone.

Offer a Trade

If you plan to meet the office manager to make the presentation, one approach is to call the manager, introduce yourself and your company, and ask if he or she would meet with you for five minutes. It may seem like very little to ask—a five-minute meeting—but you are not offering a fair trade. The manager is offering you some of his or her valuable time, but you have not offered enough in return.

It would be better if, during your approach, you could address the broker/manager's list of needs. For example, you know that the manager wants fewer problems with transactions. You could say that you'd like to show the manager how your services can help the agents get through transactions painlessly. Here's a sample script: "My name is John Smith from A to Z Home Inspection Company. Do you have a moment to talk? I have noticed that real estate transactions often run into trouble when the buyers have a hard time getting fire insurance. Could I drop in for five minutes to tell you how these transactions can be salvaged?" Now you have offered a trade. The manager gives you five minutes, and you will tell him or her how to solve a problem the agents are having.

Here is another example. "This is John Smith from A to Z Home Inspections. A recent study done by the real estate board indicates that people under the age of 30 are 50 percent less likely to proceed with purchasing a house because they discover that the costs of homeownership are beyond their means. Would you be interested in hearing about a method to increase the success rate with this age group? Could I drop in for five minutes to tell you about this?"

Ask "Yes" Questions

A technique that may work for you is one of the oldest sales strategies in the book. Ask a few questions that you know you will get a "Yes" response to. For example, you might ask if they would like to see fewer deals falling through, or if they would like to see their real estate agents selling more and selling faster.

Of course, you have to have something to deliver after asking. Then you ask if you can drop in for five minutes to show them how.

Encyclopedia salespeople developed this strategy. The salesperson would ask about five or ten questions that they know you answer "Yes" to. It goes like this:

- Do you live here? (even though they know you live there)
- Do you have children? (even though there are kids' bicycles on the front porch)
- Do you believe that educating your child is important?

You can see where this is going.

One thing to keep in mind is that some of the sales strategies we present will seem unappealing to you. Maybe you don't want to use an old encyclopedia salesperson's strategy on the manager of a real estate office. That's fine. The fact is, some people can do this successfully and some can't. Take the idea, change it around, and make it your own. Furthermore, rest assured that there are many strategies to choose from to make your sales technique better. Good salespeople are always well-prepared, and having a large pool of questions to draw from makes it easier when you are calling to request an appointment. You should also understand that because people are different, a strategy that works on one person won't necessarily work on another. That is why there are different types of questions that you should learn and use at various stages in the sales process.

Aim for the Meeting   Here is another tip: Do everything you can to get the manager to meet with you. The manager may immediately say, "What do you have for me?" or "Tell me over the phone." Try not to give all of your message away over the phone. The face-to-face meeting is very important. How can you avoid having to explain over the phone? Try to form your introduction with a question that informs the broker that you want to come in for five minutes to show, not tell, what you have to offer. Don't forget that once the manager says "No" to you, it's very hard to call back and ask again another time. If you are face to face with the manager, it is much harder for him or her to give you a flat out "No". The worst that will likely happen is you get a "soft no." A "soft no" means the door is still open to try again down the road.

If they insist that you send them something to review, do so. But do it very quickly and make it memorable. Most importantly, follow up promptly. By sending the material soon after it is requested, and calling to follow up, you will make a positive impression. Then you have lived up to your end of the bargain and are more likely to get a better reception on the next call.

Keep It Short   Here is one more tip: Promise to keep it short. Don't forget how busy these people are. Five minutes is enough, ten minutes might be acceptable, but asking for 15 minutes is too much. If they are at all interested in what you have to offer, you will likely be there for 15 minutes anyway.

With any luck, and a bit of practice, we are now on our way to meet with the office manager or broker.

Presenting To the Broker or Office Manager

Now that you have promised the world to the office manager, you had better deliver. You should have a short, polished presentation ready. We are calling it a presentation but it should feel more like a conversation.

Plan with Care

Here are some tips for when you first meet with the broker or office manager. Begin by restating the problem that you have already discussed in order to get the meeting. "I mentioned on the phone that there is a way to salvage some of the transactions that fall through as a result of clients not being able to get home insurance. I think you are really going to like what I have to show you." You can proceed to show them how your service will solve their problem and how they are going to benefit from it. Get the manager involved in the presentation by asking questions and waiting for responses. Ask them what they think about your proposal or whether they have any questions.

Use Props

One effective strategy that we have touched on is to use props. Props also reinforce your reason to meet in person. A prop is a visual, something to show while you are giving your presentation. For instance, say you are presenting on how to sell homes to people under the age of 30. Your talk is about finishing basements with a new floor product that maintains virtually all the headroom in the basement. The props include an outline of your presentation printed in color and mounted on $8\frac{1}{2} \times 11$ cardboard, a color photograph of a finished basement mounted on cardboard, a list of benefits, and a sample of the flooring product. Props that people can keep are more powerful—samples, handouts, specialty items, gifts, and so on.

Props help arouse interest and create desire. If you have something to show, you will be much more effective.

Closing the Office Manager or Broker

Closing is the part that everybody hates. We get to the end of the presentation and say, "If you are interested, give me a call. Here's my card." You've come too far to chicken out now. If you have successfully earned their trust and the person needs what you have to offer, then you should have enough confidence to ask for the close. At the end of your presentation to the broker or office manager, you have to ask when you can present to the agents. Here are lines you can use for the close:

■ "When can I come and pass on this information to your office?"

■ "Do you have weekly office meetings? Is Monday the 28th good for you?"

■ "I am available on the first Monday in February. Does that work for you, or is there another date that makes more sense?"

Notice that we have not asked a question that they can just say "No" to. They can still turn you down, but it takes more work for them to do it. If you can, try to set a time now in person. You can always reschedule it later. If the broker says to call back next week to arrange an appointment, you are more likely to get rejected over the phone because he or she will have forgotten much of the conversation.

Customer Management of Office Managers and Brokers

Managing your customers involves building long-term relationships. You haven't worked this hard to have the broker or office manager let you into their office this one time only to have you go through the entire process again six months later when you have a new message to deliver. If you are successful in earning their trust and providing value to them, the next step is to maintain that trust so that you have an open door into their office whenever you have a new message that can help them. Getting in the office for the first time is the hardest and most expensive task. If you provide benefits, solve problems, and continue to pay attention to your customers, they will become your customers for life and your business will flourish.

THE HOMEBUYER

Let's look at prospecting, the approach, the presentation and the close with a homebuyer.

Prospecting the Homebuyer

This procedure is different from the process for real estate professionals and brokers because there isn't any easy way to keep the sales funnel full of prospective homebuyers interested in home inspection services. This forces you to be more reactive than proactive with respect to prospecting. Remember the following with a homebuyer:

- The transaction is done over the phone, usually in a single conversation that takes place when the homebuyer calls you.
- The homebuyer is a highly qualified lead. You know the person is looking for a home inspection because they have called you. Because 90 percent of the work is done, all you need to do is take them on the last 10 percent of their journey.
- This lead feels like they made a choice about you because they either picked you out of a list the agent supplied, picked your name out of the phone book, or saw your name in an ad, article, Web site, or press release. They may, however, be calling several home inspection companies. You should always assume these people are speaking to several inspectors, unless you know otherwise.
- The homebuyer's needs are different than the real estate professional's needs.

The homebuyer may just be calling to book the inspection; the sales process has been done for you by the real estate professional, or a previous satisfied client. You are now an order taker, not a salesperson.

Approaching the Homebuyer

Most often there is no approach: The homebuyer calls and initiates the presentation. For example, they call and say, "I need to have a home inspection. Can you tell me about your company and what I get with my inspection?" They have just done the approach for you.

Sometimes an approach is necessary as in the following cases:

- The agent may ask you to call the client to set up an inspection. This does happen occasionally. In this case, you would say something like, "My name is Bob Green of Green Inspection Services. June Smith asked me to call you to set up an inspection at 23 Brown St. May I get some details from you?" This approach assumes a close and generally gets one.

- The client calls you but in an adversarial way. For example, "My agent asked me to call you but your prices are $75 more than Head-to-Toe Inspections." In this case, the approach is a simple matter of asking permission to sell to them. This approach does two things: It defuses the caller, and it sets up your presentation. You would say to the caller, "That's a good point; we are more expensive than Head-to-Toe. May I tell you why?" We will look at this strategy more carefully in Study Session 8.

Presenting to the Homebuyer

After dealing with real estate agents, brokers, and office managers, the presentation to a homebuyer is simple. You will be answering questions, drawing out information by asking questions, and presenting the benefits of your inspection service.

Closing the Homebuyer

The close for the homebuyer is often done for you. The homebuyer will be satisfied with the information that you have provided and may book an inspection on the spot. If they don't, you can do a few things to close the deal. If the homebuyer asks you for information but appears ready to move on to call someone else, you should initiate a close. Say, "Can we set up an inspection time that is convenient for you?" If yes—book it. If no, say, "What additional information do you need before you go ahead and set up the inspection?" Try to draw out the objections so you can overcome them. Very often, even if they were not planning to book an inspection immediately, if you suggest it they will just go ahead and book it. It's a simple technique, but it is amazing how often it works.

Remember, the person who goes to the effort of calling you wants to be convinced you are the right company. People want to get the decision made and move on to other things, especially when buying a home. Make it easy for them. Assume they want to hire you. End the search for them. Make the decision for them. Relieve them of the chore of selecting a home inspector. If you let them call someone else, chances are they won't be calling you back.

KEY TERMS

approach	customer management	presentation
ask for the order	offering a trade	prospecting
close		

STUDY SESSION 7 QUICK QUIZ

You should finish Study Session 7 before doing this Quiz. Write your answers in the spaces provided. Then, check your answers in Appendix A.

1. List the five parts of the sales process.

    1. _____
    2. _____
    3. _____
    4. _____
    5. _____

2. List the three targets to whom you sell.

    1. _____
    2. _____
    3. _____

3. Explain the concept behind "offering a trade."

    _____
    _____
    _____

4. What is the best approach if you are having a really difficult time getting into a particular real estate office?

    _____
    _____
    _____

5. Which is the best way to close with an agent? Circle one.

    a. "If you need someone for your next inspection, give me a call."

    b. "Can I count on you to refer your next inspection to me?"

6. When approaching an office manager or broker on the phone, a good technique is to let them know you will need only five minutes of their time to show them what you have to offer. Circle one.

    a. True

    b. False

7. Using props in a sales presentation can be effective in arousing interest and creating desire. Circle one.

    a. True

    b. False

8. A homebuyer looking for an inspection is a highly qualified lead. Circle one.

    a. True

    b. False

9. Because there's no way to tell what kind of personality your customers will have, don't bother thinking about personality types. Treat everyone the same way. Circle one.

  a. True

  b. False

If you had trouble with the Quiz, reread Study Session 7 and try the Quiz again. If you did well, it's time for Study Session 8.

S T U D Y   S E S S I O N   8

MOVING FROM OBJECTIONS TO CLOSING

Study Session 8 helps you anticipate and deal with the various objections that customers are likely to have. It also looks in more depth at the closing step in the sales process.

LEARNING OBJECTIVES

At the end of Study Session 8 you should be able to

- list three different sentences that can help you close a deal;

- write a sentence using the feel, felt, found technique;

- apply the law of six to your home inspection business;

- describe the hot button technique, give an example of a hot button issue, and explain how you might address it;

- list the three steps to turning objections to your advantage;

- state an acceptable response to unreasonable objections; and

- develop closing statements that feel natural and comfortable to you.

Study Session 8 may take you roughly 60 minutes to complete.

In Study Session 8 we will look at some typical customer objections you can expect to encounter and strategize about ways to overcome them. We also will take a closer look at the most critical step in the sales process: closing. You will want to develop a natural flow from handling objections to asking the prospect for his or her business.

THE IMPORTANCE OF OBJECTIONS

Assume Prospects Have Objections

So far we have presented sales as a simple matter of finding out the customer's needs and explaining how the benefits of your services satisfy those needs. Once you have made your case, it's a simple matter of bringing the transaction to a close and waiting to hear "yes" or "no." In reality, the sales process involves your prospect expressing concerns about your service offering. In many cases, if your prospect is not expressing any objections, you are losing the battle. Customers today are overwhelmed by sales offerings and there is more competition than ever. As a result, most people are very careful about how they spend their money. It is natural for people to have questions and concerns about your offerings.

Another way to look at it is, if the prospect has heard what you have to say, and they are not booking an inspection, or booking an office presentation, or agreeing to refer business to you, they must have some reason for it. This reason is their objection. The easiest thing for a prospect to do is just say, "Thank you very much, I will get back to you." and then never get back to you. It is more difficult for them to tell you the truth, that they have objections. If you could see into the prospect's mind, you might find that 75 percent of the time, the objection is something that should not be a problem to overcome, if only they gave you the opportunity to explain. The other 25 percent of the time, the objection is intangible and there is no way you can overcome this anyway—maybe they think you don't fit the picture of what they imagined a home inspector to be. You can't win them all, but it would be nice to win 75 percent of them.

THE LAW OF SIX

The whole job of sales is to draw out objections and explain how you can satisfy your prospect. This seems like a daunting task because you are probably imagining many, many objections. How could you possibly deal with them all? The **law of six** states that for any service offering, it's unlikely that anyone can think of more than six objections to your service. If you sit down and look at anything you are offering, you will be hard pressed to come up with more than six possible objections. The trick is to figure out what the six objections are and to come up with compelling answers to the objections.

Let's consider homebuyers and assume that every prospect that calls us is speaking to several home inspection companies and comparing them before making a decision. We must first determine what the most common objections are so that we can develop concrete answers to all of them. Following is a list of common objections:

- It's too expensive.
- You don't have enough experience or qualifications.

- You don't have enough insurance.
- You don't offer any extra services.
- You don't offer any guarantees.
- You are not available on short notice.
- It's too expensive.

We have inserted "It's too expensive" twice because it's the most common objection. You might come up with another one or two. If you do, then feel free to call it the "law of seven or eight."

After listing the objections, come up with compelling answers to the objections. For example, let's examine the most common objection with all products and services—price. Several different strategies can be used to deal with price objections.

One of the best ways to answer the "it's too expensive" objection, regardless of the product or service, is to do the following:

- Agree that it is more expensive than others (not that it's too expensive). By agreeing, you make the prospect more comfortable.
- Then ask, "May I tell you why?"
- You then tell them about the great value the benefits of using the product or service provides.

Another strategy in overcoming price objection is to uncover the reason they feel you are expensive in the first place:

- "I know price is very important to you. May I ask why you feel we are too expensive?" or "Is price your only concern?"
- Once you know the reason for the objection, you can then focus on the reasons why your service satisfies their need.

No matter what approach you use, remember that the value of your service must exceed the price from your customer's perspective. It won't do you any good to be defensive about trying to justify your price. You should be proud of what you charge; in fact, most home inspectors don't charge enough for the value of the service they provide.

Most purchases of services are not made based on price. Did you choose your doctor or dentist by price? We are not selling a commodity; we are offering a professional service that can easily be differentiated from your competitors' services.

Other Common Objections

Here are some other common objections:

- "You're not a professional engineer or architect," or some other preconceived idea of what a home inspector should be.
- The prospect doesn't like you (which they will not likely say to your face). Maybe you look too young or too old, or they don't like your manner. Don't forget, an objection could be something that the client is thinking but does not say.
- You are a little company, and the prospect thinks they would be better off with a big, national company just in case there is a problem down the road.
- The prospect's agent prefers XYZ company.

Think about how would you respond to each of these objections based on your unique business.

MORE TECHNIQUES FOR HANDLING OBJECTIONS

Feel, Felt, Found Technique

Following are a few other approaches to handling objections:

One technique for handling virtually any objection is called the **feel, felt, found** technique. It goes like this. Your prospect (agent, manager, homebuyer, lawyer) indicates that they don't want to use you because of objection "X." You answer is, "I understand why you *feel* that way. Many of my happy clients *felt* that way initially, too, but they *found* that . . ." And here's where you explain some of the benefits that might convince the prospect to proceed.

This technique validates the objection rather than dismisses it. It also makes the client feel smart because others felt the same way. After you have told them that their concern is valid and shared by others, they relax a little. They will then be more receptive to the solution, especially since it is presented as an indirect testimonial: "It's not me saying this; it's what other clients have found."

This technique has the benefit of being simple, and you can use it for any objection. If you have it at your fingertips, you can pull it out when you hear an objection you were not prepared for. At least you will have ten seconds to think of an answer.

Hot Button Technique

A **hot button** is the one thing that is most important to your prospect. If you can identify your prospect's hot button, you're as good as there. For example, a real estate agent may lament to you that all she wants is for home inspectors to be "even-keeled." She doesn't care what problems are identified during the inspection, as long as the inspector keeps them in perspective. You now have your hot button. During your presentation, you come up with half a dozen different ways that you "keep an even keel." For example, you present instances of your good bedside manner, how you help clients keep things in perspective, your down to earth style, your balanced approach, and your non-alarmist presentation of house conditions. Forget about all of the other benefits of your service and work the hot button.

Timing is Everything

We said that the sales process involves discovering people's objections and addressing them. Until these have been dealt with, you cannot assume the prospect is ready to be asked to make a buying decision. There are, however, different times in which you can choose to deal with objections, which can create some challenges:

- You can answer objections as they are presented to you.

- You can figure out what the objections are when the prospect is not entirely forthcoming about them during the course of the presentation and then bring them up yourself.

- You can address objections later when you feel the time is right. This is especially important when discussing price, particularly if it comes up early in the conversation. You are better off acknowledging that you understand that price is an important issue and asking the customer if you can come back to it.

Offer Proof

Offering proof is a good way to diminish someone's objection. Here's an example. If you are on the phone with a client who thinks your fee is too high, as we noted earlier, you should agree with the prospect that you are more expensive and ask if you can explain why. Once you have elaborated on the benefits of your service, you can add, "You can see that while we are more expensive than some other inspection companies, we offer more value. Furthermore, we are only $25 more expensive than other professional home inspection companies. My three main competitors charge X, Y, and Z." This last piece of information is the proof. You are offering specific data. Even better, you could fax your competitor's price schedule. Some people respond well to concrete information like this.

Provide Testimonials

Another example of concrete proof is the testimonial. This works for both prospective clients and real estate agents. If you can get an agent to write you a testimonial about how great your inspections are, you can pull out the letter as an answer to an objection. For example, say the agent you want to work with expresses concern about you because their current inspector is very good with the agent's clients; the agent doesn't want to lose that.

Feel, Felt, Found Revisited

You can use the "feel, felt, found" technique in conjunction with a testimonial letter. "I understand how you *feel*. Most of the agents that are referring business to me *felt* that way, too, but they *found* that my client-handling skills were better than they'd ever seen. In fact, they are so happy with my skills that I get letters like this." Then you pull out a testimonial letter that articulates how well you handled a difficult situation. This is a lot more powerful that simply saying, "Relax, I know how to handle my clients."

A Web site is a great tool for presenting testimonials. The more credible the testimonial, the more valuable. If possible, get permission to use the person's name, rather than initials. To add another dimension and make the testimonial even more credible, include a photo of the person offering the testimonial. You will have to ask permission, of course.

Think of the objection simply as a request for clarification or more information about your service. If the prospect is objecting to something, it means they are interested in your service. It sounds strange, but you have managed to strike a chord and now have the opportunity to respond. Until the benefits of your service are clear to the prospect, there will always be doubt. There can't be any obstacles in your prospect's mind before you can proceed with closing the sale.

Turn the Objection into a Question

An objection can leave you searching for a way to flip the conversation into a discussion of the benefits of your service, or to simply answer the objection. Let's say a real estate agent says you are too inexperienced. There are two techniques you can use to move the conversation along. The first is to turn the objection into a question. If a real estate agent says, "You are too inexperienced," just pretend they said, "Show me how experienced you are." Your response might then be, "Good point, experience is key, may I tell you why I have more experience than most of the home inspectors out there, even though my company is only six months old?"

Ask the Prospect To Elaborate

If the prospect is objecting in some way, it is often appropriate to ask them to explain what they mean in more detail. This approach usually breaks down one big objection into smaller objections that you can deal with. This approach works well when the objection seems insurmountable because it's so broad, such as a real estate agent saying something like, "Hiring you is just too risky for me." Your answer might be, "Can you do me a favor? Explain to me how it's too risky." The agent will then break it down into particular objections that you can handle. You need to come up with a line that does not sound defensive. You can't, for example, say, "What do you mean by that?" Even in your nicest voice, it sounds defensive. An experienced salesperson will say something like, "Please explain that for me," or, "Risky in what way?"

Artificial Objections

What's more difficult than handling an objection? Handling a bogus objection. Sometimes the objection a real estate agent, or potential client, will throw up is not the real objection. The real objection is something that the prospect feels they cannot say. For example, I'm sure you have had people solicit you for one charity or another. They come to the door and say, "We are selling these plastic pins for five dollars, and all the money is going to feed starving children." Your answer might be, "I just can't afford it right now, things are very tight." The fact is you probably *can* afford five dollars, but you are tired of the daily knocks at the door by every charity in town. You can't look this person in the eye and say, "I don't want to feed starving children," so you say something more palatable.

Get to the Real Objection

The way to get the real objection to the surface is to ask, "What would it take to get you to refer me?" or "What would it take to get you to hire me for your inspection?" This will sometimes evoke a very direct response; the real estate agent may say, "You have to guarantee you won't screw up my deal." This request does not mean you have to do what they ask, it just brings up the real objection—fear. You then go to work addressing the fear.

The Unreasonable Objection

Some people will raise an objection they know you cannot overcome. "I need an inspector whose fees are under $150," or "I need you to guarantee to be available to be at any house on one hour's notice." A good strategy for these objections is to point out that no competent professional will be able to reasonably commit to this requirement. Don't hold yourself up to an impossible standard. Measure yourself against your peers.

Look Forward to Receiving the Objection

Life would be much simpler if we didn't get any objections, but because we know objections are a given, react positively. You should never be defensive in your response. Always compliment the objection by telling the customer that you are glad they brought that up. Be patient and hear the person out before responding. (This is good advice for every conversation you'll ever have!)

Speak at Your Prospect's Pace

Pacing is a concept you can apply when you make a sales presentation, speak to a client, do a home inspection, or in any one-on-one communication. The logic for this concept goes like this: You can win people's trust if you speak in a manner similar to theirs. We are talking specifically about pacing here, not copying people's mannerisms or accents. If the person you are speaking with is a quick, get-to-the-point type, then speak that way and get to the point. If the person is a slow, meticulous speaker, then take your time. Because you will have a much better chance of succeeding in the close if your prospect likes you, it makes sense to stack everything you can in your favor.

Some salespeople will even match tone, rhythm, and volume in addition to the rate of speech. Our suggestion is to stick with pace because if people feel you're mimicking them, you will lose the trust you were hoping to gain.

MORE ON CLOSING

Once you have addressed all of the prospect's objections, you must move to what is probably the most difficult part of the sales process: asking for the order. Many of us are comfortable taking real estate professionals out for lunch, or maybe even speaking at a first-time buyers' seminar. But when it comes to looking an agent in the face and asking for the order, we may fall apart. If you cave at this point, your efforts will have been for nothing.

The fear of rejection is the biggest reason salespeople don't ask for the close. But, you are not alone. The customer is also afraid that they will make a bad decision. That makes this part of the sales process the most stressful for both parties.

The "close" is so important that many experts believe you should write your close first and then build a sales process around the close. In other words, everything you say to the prospect is designed to enable you to use a specific close.

You will have to decide if you like this highly scripted approach, or if you would prefer to have a handful of possible options that you can use as needed.

Earn Their Trust

If your presentation is successful in showing the prospect how you can meet their needs, they want and can afford your service, and they feel comfortable with you, then you have earned the right to ask for a commitment. By earning the trust of your prospects and customers, you will be more confident in your approach and your prospect will be less concerned about making a bad decision. If you focus only on the sale, rather than building trust and clarifying your prospects' needs, you will likely end up with nothing.

Before you ask for the close, make sure the prospect doesn't have any other questions or concerns. There should be no doubt in their mind about what you are offering. If they are not ready, it is because there is something you must address before asking them to make a decision. The easiest way to confirm that the timing is right is to ask, "Do you have any other questions or concerns about the home inspection process that I have not covered yet?"

Choose Comfortable Closing Method

There are a number of approaches to bring the conversation to a successful close. Let's examine some of them so you can choose a method that suits you.

One method is simply to invite the prospect to make a decision. This is a less direct approach and feels comfortable for most people. Here is an example: "Why don't we go ahead and arrange a time that is convenient for you?" or "When would you like to arrange for this inspection to be done?"

Here is another good example that works well with a real estate professional: "Why don't you give me a try?" This simple line will often have the desired effect. You are inviting the real estate agent to make a decision about you. If you say, "Will you refer me?" you have created a yes or no question that leaves no room for a third option. Furthermore, it sounds too committal. The line, "Why don't you give me a try?" is great because it allows a third option other than yes or no, the third option being some objection that you can then work on. Also, the line has a noncommittal feel to it. The real estate agent does not feel like they are making a commitment, they are just giving you a try.

A more direct approach that works well with a prospect over the phone is to assume they are ready to take the next step. "If you have no further questions, the next step is to get some information about the property you are interested in, and we will take care of the rest." Or "Alright then, I just need to ask you a few questions about the property, and I'll take care of all the details for you."

Another strategy is to focus on a secondary issue by making the assumption that if they accept the secondary issue, then they have already made the decision to use your service. For example, let's assume your client has several questions about ancillary services and most of your conversation involves how you can satisfy a need for them in one particular area. You can structure your closing statements around that need with the assumption that they will also be using you for other services: "If I could just ask you a few questions, we can go ahead and schedule your termite inspection along with your home inspection."

Other Sample Closing Lines

Here are specific examples that can be used for real estate agents:

- "I understand you have a relationship you are happy with. Does it make sense for me to be your second choice if your usual inspector is booked, on vacation, or sick?"

- "Would you allow me to perform an inspection for one of your clients so you can say with confidence that you have checked others and your regular inspector is the best?

■ "I believe I can provide a level of service for you and your clients that you have not seen before. "

Here are specific examples that can be used for homebuyers:

■ "I have the experience and skill to provide a great service for you. I'm so confident about it I will commit that if you do not find the inspection exceeds your expectation, the inspection will be free. Why don't you give it a try?"

■ "The decision to buy a home is huge. It is too important to trust to just any home inspector. I will do the best possible inspection for you. I just need to ask you a couple of questions about the home, and we can go ahead and arrange something for you."

One of the weaknesses with all of the closes above is that they use the word "I" a great deal. This is a clue that it is about the inspector, not the buyer or agent. The best closes continue in the problem-solving mode and are directed to the buyer's or agent's benefit:

■ To a homebuyer. "You are making a big decision in buying this home, and we need to make sure you have all of the possible information to make the right decision for you. Can we go ahead and set up the inspection for 9:00 A.M. Thursday?"

■ To an agent. "From our discussion, it's clear that your success comes from taking great care of your clients. For all the reasons we've talked about, our service seems like a good fit and an excellent way to show your clients that you care. Should we try working together and see if we're right?"

Be Yourself, with Conviction

Your close has to be rehearsed, and it should fit your own style and character. The goal is to get a commitment from the customer. They will not usually commit unless you ask them to. Your close has a specific request, and just like the rest of the discussion, you have to know what the possible responses are, and how your will handle each. The prospect or real estate agent will say "yes" or "no" or express more objections. Let's look at each possibility.

The Prospect Says, "Yes"

If the prospect says, "yes" when you ask for a commitment, say, "thank you" and cement the commitment with an action. If it is a prospective home inspection client, schedule the inspection. If it is a real estate agent, ask if they are working with any clients who will need an inspection in the next few days.

The Customer Says, "I Will Think It Over"

If your customer wants to think it over, then this means they want to say goodbye even if they are close to saying "Yes." If your customer responds this way, agree with them by saying, "I understand, I realize this is in an important decision." Then ask them what it is they need to think over. "I am sure you have a very good reason for wanting to take the time to think about this, may I ask what it is? Is it the price you are concerned about?" You won't uncover the real reason they aren't ready unless you ask. This may also give you an opportunity to ask for the close again if there was an underlying objection that didn't surface earlier in the conversation.

The Customer Says, "No"

If you cannot get a commitment, ask what would have to change for them to commit to working with you. They have an objection that you need to extract.

Address Additional Objections

If you get another objection, address it. Sometimes you will not be able to address the objection to their satisfaction. You won't convert everyone, but when you fail, study the reasons and prepare a better response to the objections. If you know that they are simply not interested, it is a great opportunity to practice your closing techniques knowing you have nothing to lose. And if you know you have not converted them, there are two things you can say:

1. "Please do me a favor and visit our Web site, *www.abcinspections.com* before deciding on an inspection company." Your Web site may get across the message that you could not.

2. "Please do me a favor. If you don't choose us to perform your inspection, choose another ASHI member (or whatever designation)." This will show the prospect you care about their interests.

Say Something

Don't use our words. Create a close that you are comfortable saying and that works with your presentation of your services. If this seems difficult, then you are in good company. Most home inspectors fall short in this area. If you don't ask for commitment, you have wasted your time and theirs. Whatever approach you decide to take, remember that you must give people a reason to try your service. It's unfair to ask them to give you something if there is nothing in it for them. If the behavior doesn't change as a result of the discussion, it's as if the discussion never took place. It's all about risk and reward. The potential reward for working with you must outweigh the risk in trying it.

KEY TERMS

feel, felt, found technique	hot button pacing	the law of six

STUDY SESSION 8 QUICK QUIZ

You should finish Study Session 8 before doing this Quiz. Write your answers in the spaces provided. Then, check your answers in Appendix A.

1. What does the "law of six" refer to? Circle one.

    a. Calling six agents in six days

    b. Expecting six objections to your sales pitch

    c. Offering six benefits of your service to a client

    d. Calling six previous clients for ancillary services

2. During the sales process, why should you expect that the prospect will have objections?

_____

_____

3. Why is it important to agree with the prospect when they object to the price?

_____

_____

4. How can you go about uncovering the reason why they feel you are too expensive? What would you say?

_____

_____

_____

5. Explain how you can use a testimonial to answer an objection.

_____

_____

6. What is an "artificial objection" and when are they used?

_____

_____

7. List three conditions that must exist before you have earned the right to ask for a commitment?

    1. _____

    2. _____

    3. _____

8. Why is it important to make sure the prospect doesn't have any other questions before asking for a commitment?

_____

_____

9. If a prospect says "yes" when you ask for a commitment, what should the next step be?

_____

_____

10. How would you handle a customer that says, "I will have to think it over," when asking for a commitment?

_____

_____

_____

If you had trouble with the Quiz, reread Study Session 8 and try the Quiz again. If you did well, it's time for Study Session 9.

MANAGING CUSTOMERS AND BUILDING RELATIONSHIPS

Study Session 9 focuses on relationship aspects of the home inspection business. We will look more closely at the customer management part of the sales process and at strategies for building and maintaining customer relationships.

LEARNING OBJECTIVES

At the end of Study Session 9 you should be able to

- explain four reasons for a gap between what customers expect and what they perceive they received;

- list four purposes for lunch meetings with real estate agents you already know;

- list at least five questions you can ask a caller in order to get a booking;

- develop a list of discussion topics for a focus group;

- list seven tactics for evaluating and improving telephone sales and answering service; and

- develop approaches for closing customers who call to inquire only about price.

Study Session 9 may take you roughly 60 minutes to complete.

In Study Session 9 on sales topics, we will focus on the relationship aspects of home inspection. Your success depends in part on your ability to build and maintain customer relationships.

CUSTOMER MANAGEMENT

We said earlier that maintaining a customer is cheaper than finding a new one. Between prospecting, approaching, presenting, and closing, the cost to acquire the customer is tremendous. Fortunately, it is much easier to maintain the relationship once you have earned their trust. You will achieve success faster and easier by developing long-term relationships.

Personality Is Critical

The most critical factor in building and maintaining relationships is to make sure the customer likes you and believes in you. Because of the breadth of knowledge required to do an inspection, it is very difficult for customers to really understand or appreciate what home inspectors do. As a result, the relationship you develop with a real estate agent for example, becomes more important than the inspection itself. As long as the agent likes you and believes that you are delivering on your promises, he or she will continue to trust you with his or her clients. The easiest way to build this kind of relationship is to treat your customers the same way you would treat your friends or family. Because home inspection is an interpersonal process, we must be able to get along with all sorts of people. This includes clients, sellers, and agents who have relatively high levels of stress because of the nature of the real estate transaction. You will become more respected and liked in your personal life and your profession by being courteous, caring, appreciative, complimentary, and attentive towards others.

Loyalty Critical to Long-Term Success

The most effective way to maintain customer loyalty is to treat your customers as if you were on the verge of losing them. Customers today are more demanding than ever. They expect the world when it comes to service, quality, and value. They have more choices and they want everything done yesterday. Have you ever had a real estate agent call you and say, "I need you to come out today to do an inspection?" It doesn't matter if you already have three inspections scheduled that day; they expect you to deliver. If they are a good customer, you will do everything you can to accommodate them without compromising your professional integrity. Your success relies on your ability to find and keep customers. You should concentrate on the second, third, and fourth sale. Referrals from successful real estate agents and satisfied clients are a very effective way to grow your business. Technical Assistance Research Program's (TARP) research found that the cost to get a new customer is 2 to 20 times higher than retaining a customer. Customers want assurance, attention, reliability, and responsiveness. If you build a reputation for delivering these, you will develop customers for life.

Let Your Customers Sell for You

Word of mouth is an important influence on customer behavior. If you consistently provide outstanding customer service, your customers will sell for you. There is a good chance your client knows someone who is also thinking about buying or selling a home. According to TARP, an organization specializing in customer satisfaction and loyalty, the average satisfied customer will tell five others about their experience. The average unsatisfied customer will tell ten others. Word of mouth can work for or against you, depending on the quality of your service.

Why Customers Defect

Much research has been done on customer defection. Defection results from a discrepancy between what a customer expects to get and what they perceive they got. In other words, we have the perception that we are delivering good service but in the customer's mind, we may not be meeting expectations. The reasons for this gap include the following:

- We don't know our customers well enough. We assume we know them, but we don't ask the right questions. Interviews, focus groups, surveys/questionnaires, and handling complaints are all great ways to solicit feedback from your customers. By understanding what your customers need and want, you will better serve them and keep them happier. Just ask; they will tell you what they want.

- We don't listen to our customers. We must give our customers our full attention. This makes them feel important. Listen actively and acknowledge them by smiling and agreeing with them. If you don't understand what the customer is saying or need further clarification, ask questions.

- We over-promise and under-deliver. If the customer has certain expectations, and you value offering promises to fulfill those expectations, then you better deliver. Sometimes the customer's expectations are unrealistic.

- We are not sufficiently responsive to customers. When the client has a question about your service or a complaint, a fast response will build trust and loyalty. Nine out of ten customers will come back if their complaint is resolved quickly and to their satisfaction. TARP's research indicates that customers who have a complaint resolved to their satisfaction are up to 8 percent more loyal than customers who have no complaint.

Strive for Service Excellence

Customer satisfaction is considered to be the minimum benchmark when it comes to serving your customers. As long as your customers are satisfied, your business should be able to sustain itself. Unfortunately, with more and more competition, customer satisfaction is not always good enough if you want to grow your business. Your competitors should largely determine the quality of your service. Whatever they are doing, you must be doing it better if you want customer loyalty. You should strive to exceed expectations. Everything you do beyond what was expected will be recognized and remembered. Great service means you enjoy giving people a little more than they expect.

STRATEGIES FOR BUILDING RELATIONSHIPS

The importance of building and maintaining high-quality relationships cannot be overstated. In this section we will look at two strategies to build and maintain relationships with real estate agents and allow you to get feedback about your service:

1. The real estate agent lunch
2. The real estate agent focus group

The Real Estate Agent Lunch—Building a Relationship

Offer an Even Trade

Buying lunch for a real estate agent is a great way to interact, build, and maintain a relationship. It's great because it's an even trade. You ask a real estate agent to give you some of their time in return for you buying them lunch.

Set the Stage

We have found that asking a real estate agent to lunch works better if you have set the stage first. The real estate agent has to know you. Giving an office talk is a great way to become known. It positions you as the local expert. At the very least, the real estate agents who attended the talks will know who you are. Besides, very few people will have lunch with someone they have never met. Would you?

One note of caution is needed here: The top agents do not always attend the office meetings, and you may not become known to them through meetings. You may have to approach them individually. The broker or office manager can tell you which agents do not attend the meetings.

Start with Those You Know

Start with real estate agents you already know. You might think it's a waste of time and money preaching to the converted, but we'll give you the following reasons it is not a waste:

Increase Referrals

- Get more of their business. Not only will you reinforce an already good relationship, you may even get more business. Some real estate agents give several names when referring home inspectors, some don't. If the agent does not refer all of their business to you, there is room to get more referrals. If the agent strongly believes they should give several names, you should not try to change their mind. But, if the real estate agent likes you, your business card may go on the top of the stack. The real estate agent may give their client three names but add a few words about you: "Here are three good inspectors. John Smith is interesting because he specializes in old homes like the one you are buying."

Solidify Relationship

Educate Them

- Cement the relationship. The lunch date is an opportunity to periodically strengthen the relationship and remind the real estate agent about the benefits of your service. The agent, in turn, can explain your service benefits to their clients. If the agent tells prospects how good you are, not only is it easier to turn prospects into clients, but it may also set the stage for raising your prices.

Get Some Feedback

- Ask them how you are doing. Is there anything they particularly like about your service? Anything they dislike? Anything you might do differently? Positive feedback can become a testimonial. Negative feedback can be used to improve your service. Both kinds are great. Either way, your agent will see that you are being sensitive to their needs.

Get Referred to Another Agent

- Ask for an introduction to another agent. One of the best ways to meet a real estate agent is to get their name from an agent you already do business with. You could say, "I am growing my business and would like meet more top real estate agents like you. Do you know someone I should speak to?"

Remove the Fear

If you call a real estate agent that you know well, it's easy to say, "Let's do lunch, I have something I want to run by you." If you are calling an agent that has only met you at an office talk, and has never referred business to you, you should take more care. When you offer to take someone out for lunch, they respond with the fear that we all have, "There is no such thing as a free lunch." You have to remove the skepticism from the start. We have found that giving something concrete up front is better than having the agent wonder what they will have to give in exchange. For example, you can do the following:

Offer Something Up Front

- Gather information. You are meeting with top agents to find out what ancillary services homeowners would be most interested in.

■ Introduce something new. You would like to show them how prelisting inspections can be a great tool for them.

■ Tell them you want their business. You tell them you want half an hour of their time to explain how they will benefit by referring you, in exchange for your buying them lunch.

Expect a "No"

Don't expect that every real estate agent will say, "Yes." The best you can hope for is that some of the agents will agree to meet. In our experience, those that don't want to have lunch with you don't turn you down completely. The more likely scenario is that they say they are too busy to have lunch with you, but that you could drop something in at their office. You should use this response to your advantage. If the agent seems to be looking for an out, ask the agent if he or she would be willing to give you five minutes of their time in their office instead.

Send the Material

An invitation to send material may not be what you had in mind, but this can be a good opportunity. Material that combines a compelling message with a call to action can be powerful, and it is likely to be well received if accompanied with a handwritten note and a useful token of appreciation. Follow-up is a key to success here. People may appreciate the material and the gesture, but few will change their behavior based on this alone.

Be Flexible and Persistent

In our experience agents are hard to nail down for a particular date. They are not like office workers who go to the same place every day and eat lunch at noon. Their schedules are always changing. If you call an agent and book lunch for next Wednesday at 12:15, they will often cancel. By Wednesday, they may have booked a meeting with a client. This is understandable because agents survive by being flexible, moving quickly, and meeting the needs of their clients. If a client calls their real estate agent on Tuesday night to see a house on Wednesday at 12:15, the agent will not say to the client, "That doesn't work for me because I am have having lunch with someone who is not going to make me any money."

Be aware that if you call to confirm on Wednesday morning, you may have a hard time reaching the agent. He or she may be in the middle of a meeting or presenting an offer on a house.

The answer is to respect the way agents work and work with it. Here are three approaches you can take:

Roll with the Punches

1. Call at the last minute. You could call real estate agents and ask if they are available that same day, or the next day, for lunch. For example, always carry a contact list of agents. That way, when an inspection unexpectedly cancels and you have three hours on your hands, you can call an agent and arrange to meet.

2. Use the **tentative-booking technique,** that is, call to book a tentative time. Get the agent to commit to a date and time and offer to call them in the morning to verify that it still works for them.

3. Ask an agent at an inspection. Let's say you do an inspection for a client, and you have not met the agent before. Offer to take them out for lunch to explain how your system can work for them. The secret is to offer a benefit for the agent. It's not about you. It's about them. The only caution is not to ask the agent in front of the client.

Another option is to offer to drop in at an open house they are hosting, and make the presentation when there is no one else in the home. This requires flexibility and patience on your part, but it is often a rewarding approach.

Make the Close

Do not be timid when it comes to sales. If you have lunch with an agent to explain how your service will help them, you can't drop the ball there. You have to then "ask for the order." If you have addressed all of their questions and concerns try the following tactics:

- Ask if the real estate agent will add you to their list of inspectors.
- Ask if the real estate agent will refer business to you.
- Ask if the real estate agent will refer their next inspection to you.
- Ask "What would it take?" This does not ask the agent to commit, yet it obliges them to try you out if you satisfy the following conditions:
  - "What it would take to get you to refer a client to me?"
  - "What would it take to get you to refer your next client to me?"
  - "What would it take to get all of your business?"
    Variations:
  - "What would it take to make you comfortable referring clients to me?"
  - "What would it take for it to be in your best interest to refer clients to me?"

Extend Yourself

You will have to decide how aggressive to be, but in general, remember that most of us have a tendency to be too timid when it comes to asking for business. Try extending yourself a bit. You don't have anything to lose. All they can say is "No."

The Real Estate Agent Focus Group—Finding Out What They Need

Invite a Group of Agents

A **focus group** is several people brought together to offer their views on an issue, idea, or product. It is an information gathering session. We have experimented with focus groups in which we assemble a group of agents over lunch to discuss our home inspection service. A formal focus group is a complicated process that requires a great deal of experience to run. Many marketing experts question the validity of information gathered at a focus group. Our suggestion is don't take yourself too seriously. This is just a lunch with some real estate professionals where you will be soliciting some input and creating relationships.

We have found that a focus group of eight people is ideal. Any more and the group breaks down into two subgroups; many fewer and you are not making effective use of your time. And remember what we said about their schedules. Assume one or more will cancel at the last minute.

Take Control

To maintain some sense of order and control, we create an agenda that is mailed to the attendees prior to the lunch. Don't try to cover too much. Here is an example of an agenda we would send:

Dear _____,

Thank you for agreeing to attend the lunch at Bar Italia. To confirm, the date is Wednesday, April 23 at 12:30 P.M. I will ask your comments on the following two issues:

1. What is the difference between a good home inspector and a great home inspector?

2. What is the responsibility of the home inspector when something goes wrong?

Thanks again and I look forward to seeing you Wednesday!

J. Smith.

The advantages of a group lunch include the following:

Make More Connections

- It allows you to include some agents you know well, and some you don't. You may also include a real estate lawyer and/or a mortgage lender.

- It's not threatening to the agent because you've removed the pressure of the one-on-one meeting. You can list the people that have already agreed to participate. They may know each other.

- You can outline a specific agenda. This reduces the agent's anxiety. If you are getting resistance, ask if you can send them the agenda before they answer.

- You can reach several agents and other real estate professionals at the same time.

The disadvantages of a group lunch are as follows:

It Takes Time and Money

- You will have to run this at a nice restaurant and, with perhaps eight people, it will be expensive.

- It takes time to organize the schedules of several real estate professionals.

- It's hard to control a group. You may just end up having a lunch or dinner without ever getting to the agenda. But because you are seeking relationships, you shouldn't worry too much about the agenda.

Topics Are Important

You can pick a topic that leads into a discussion: "Is there any value in doing first-time buyers' seminars—what's your experience?" Not only will you get a few opinions, but later you can also approach any agents or mortgage lenders that showed some interest in doing a first-time buyers' seminar.

Ask only questions that matter. Will you change what you do based on the response you get? Curiosity is not a valid reason to ask a question. One good strategy is to say that you are planning on doing something differently, and want their advice. For example, "We are thinking about adding termite inspections to our list of services. Would this be useful to you?"

Go Around the Table

It is often tough to control the conversation. Suggest that everyone speak in turn around the table. This helps prevent the most vocal person from dominating the conversation, and it ensures that the quietest person is heard from.

TELEPHONE SALES TECHNIQUES

Refine Your Telephone Sales Techniques

The telephone is a relationship tool worthy of special mention because it is such a common point of communication between you and your customers. One of the best and cheapest ways to increase your inspection volume is to refine your telephone sales techniques. These will help you with prospecting and getting appointments, dealing with customer complaints, and converting more prospects to customers.

Increase Your Conversion Rate

If you get ten calls from prospective clients, how many of those calls can you convert to deals? You may be one of the lucky ones with a high conversion rate because your referral sources sing your praises. But if you are like most people, you have to work for your deals. Of the people who call, 50 percent may just want to book the inspection. This is an order-taking function, not a sales function. So, effectively, 50 percent of your callers are already converted. Let's ignore these.

What about the other 50 percent? They are the ones we need to work on. These people have questions. If you convert 50 percent of these into clients, you are doing something right. But many inspection firms convert 70 percent to 80 percent of inquiries into customers. The goal is 100 percent, of course. If a few simple techniques can help you increase your conversion rate to 90 percent, that would be a good investment—zero cost, resulting in an increase in business. Some simple sales techniques could double or triple the sales of a new inspection business overnight.

Marketing Is Not Sales

Let's review the difference between marketing and sales. When someone calls to inquire about your service, your marketing has done its job. Whether through a Yellow Pages advertisement, a referral, a Web site, or a newspaper or magazine article, the prospect found you and was intrigued enough to call. This is a tremendous commitment! You overcame their lack of knowledge about you and their natural inertia. They are calling because they have a need, and they hope you can satisfy it.

Think of it this way: Someone who calls want to be sold. No one likes shopping on the telephone for a service. No one likes the time spent, the uncertainty about whether they are asking the right questions, the doubt about some of the information they get back, or the process of making the decision. When someone calls you about your service, they want to feel that they have called the right place; a place where people understand them and can meet their needs. They want to feel assured that calling you was the best thing they could have done.

Knowing all this, it is easy to convert an inquiry into a sale! All you have to do is reinforce the hunch that made them call. How do you do that? Eight ways follow:

1. Thank them for calling.

2. Show them you care about what they need.

3. Ask questions that show you understand what they are going through.

4. Give them some tips that reduce their anxiety. They won't know how long to allow for the inspection, whether they should attend, when they will get their report, whether they have to take notes, when they pay you, what your scope of work is, and so on.

5. Show them that many people have found your service to be exactly what they needed.

6. Ask them if they have any questions, and keep asking until they say, "No." Then they will be ready to book the inspection.

7. Assume they want to book the inspection. Ask for the address and suggest a date and time. Don't ask, "What would be convenient for you?" This is courteous, but it forces them to make another decision. They may also choose a date or time that does not work for you, which may feel like poor service to them.

8. Thank them again for calling and reinforce the fact they have made a very good decision. "We look forward to doing a great job for you, Ms. Smith!"

Do It Better than Your Competition

The fact is, as more people get into the inspection business, you will face more competition. When a real estate agent gives a homebuyer a list of three home inspectors to call, you should be ready to sell over the phone.

Close the Sale on the First Call

Your goal is to book the inspection on the first call. If you don't, the caller may book with someone else. The agent may give their client three names to call, and you are the first call. If the caller has not seen a difference among the inspectors, he or she will book with the last call. Why? Because the last call is on the line already. It's more work to end the call and contact someone else. In fact, it's worse than that because with each successive call, the caller will describe to the next inspector what the one before said, and the next inspector will find a way to trump the previous call. Finally, the most recent call is always the most vivid for the caller. If you are the first call, it's unlikely you'll get called back. That is why you want to *close the sale on the first call.* The rest of this section gives you tips on how to make this happen.

Who Is Answering the Phone?

You may think you are the best one to answer your phone. That may be true some of the time, but not all of the time. If you are answering the phone during a home inspection, it's difficult to sell the prospect on the phone with your client standing next to you. Not only is it inconsiderate to your client, but when you are pressed for time, it's hard to do justice to the process. One of the challenges facing a small home inspection company is figuring out how to answer the phone while you are inspecting.

If nobody answers your phone, you are losing deals. Some inspectors use voice mail and call the prospects back between inspections. Others have someone else answer the phone for them. It may be an answering service or a spouse. If you have a spouse who is willing and available to answer the phone, you may have an ideal situation.

Remember, Your Answering Service Represents You

If you have someone else answering the phone, they should know as much as you do about your business and the sales process. Here are seven things you can do that will pay off in short order:

1. Have the person who answers your phone accompany you on a few inspections. This will give them a much better idea what you do and the dynamics involved when dealing with the real estate agent, the seller, and the homebuyer.

2. Get sales training for the person answering the phone. This is a valuable investment. Pay for a night course, or have them study the relevant portions of this section. This person is your front line. Your business depends on them; they should have every possible tool at their disposal. You don't want your business underperforming by 20 percent based solely on the way your people answer the phone.

3. Give them a script and answers to all of the tough questions they will get. Have them document any new questions and their answers. Review the script and the list of frequently asked questions regularly and polish it continually.

4. Sit down with this person initially, and periodically, to discuss how to handle the objections they are hearing, how to explain the benefits of your service, and how to convince a caller to book the inspection rather than letting the caller promise to call back. Make sure he or she is representing you the way you would represent yourself.

5. Teach your telephone person or people how to close the sale. This is the easiest part of the script for them to skip because it is the hardest part to do.

6. Track the conversion rate. Ask your phone staff to track how many inquiries they get in a day and how many of these book inspections. This will help you measure the effectiveness of your system.

7. Phone your office to see if you would hire your own company. Or have someone you trust do it. Pay particular attention to the close.

Don't Be a Commodity

Many callers just want to know your fee and get off the phone. This is logical because until you tell them differently, they will think all home inspectors are the same. This is especially true if someone has given them three names. The prospect assumes that all three have been screened for quality and are equivalent. Money is a language that everyone can relate to. Price shoppers are simply trying to put your service into this common language so that they can compare apples to apples. There are good apples and bad ones, and it's up to you to show callers the difference. A good approach is to say to them, "I know price is important to you, but may I please come back to that in a moment?" You then need to explain why you are different than the rest. Guaranteeing your service is also a good way to help deal with price shoppers. Not only does it differentiate you from others, but you will get their attention if you tell them that "I am glad you asked about price because if my service doesn't meet your needs, then there is no charge." Remember our discussion of risk reversal?

Easy Comparisons

People also like to shop by price because it is easy to measure. It doesn't require a lot of intellectual effort to compare price. Measuring other benefits is more difficult. What is the dollar value of the following:

- Receiving the report on site
- Having an experienced inspector
- Having a well-qualified inspector
- Having an engineer do the inspection
- Having access to free telephone technical support for as long as you own your home
- Receiving estimated costs for the improvements recommended during the inspection
- Receiving a home maintenance program as part of the service
- A money back guarantee

Slow Down the Price Shopper

A script such as the following may be useful:

"It sounds like you are going to choose your home inspector based on the inspection fee. It's logical for you to *feel* this is the best approach. Many of our clients *felt* that way, but they *found* that price is only one aspect of choosing an inspector. To make sure you get the best *value,* you need to know that all home inspectors are not the same. For example, not everyone

1. invites you to attend the inspection,
2. provides a 400-page report outlining every aspect of caring for your home,
3. has 25 years of home building experience,
4. offers a money back guarantee, and add

5. whatever your unique selling proposition is.

As you speak to prospects, you may want to use this tool. "Please visit our Web site *www.abcinspections.com* and read *Fifteen Questions You Should Ask Your Home Inspector.* A copy of the text of this tool is included on the Resources CD that accompanies this book.

The rationale here is to draw the caller to your Web site, where they can become more comfortable with you and your firm. Your 15 questions should be written to help clients understand your unique selling proposition.

Engage the Caller in Conversation

One of the best sales techniques for the phone, and in person, is to draw out information from the caller, to engage them in conversation, for the following reasons:

- The more time someone spends talking with you, the more likely they are to book with you rather than calling another inspector.

- Because you will be providing information as you answer the questions, the caller will start to connect with your company. They are already relying on you in the sense that you are equipping them with information they need.

- Help them out by answering questions they didn't ask but should have asked. This is probably their first time. You are the expert who knows what they need. Clients will appreciate that you offered to help, rather than just did the minimum.

- Once you have invested time in them and shown interest in them and the property they are buying, a caller will start feeling somewhat indebted to you and will be more likely to book an inspection rather than call around.

- Demonstrate knowledge of the area or house type. In many cases, you will be familiar with the house and/or the area. You can ask questions that demonstrate your knowledge of local conditions or house issues. You may be able to say, "Are you on the part of Elm Street with the underground stream?" Or, "Is it one of the houses with the sag in the master bedroom floor?"

Ask Questions

Often, you get a caller that is planning to quickly call three home inspection companies to compare their fees. It seems ridiculous to a home inspector that the only thing the caller wants to know is how much you charge. But, they logically assume that all home inspections are created equal. A good way to turn this kind of call into a booked inspection is to ask the caller some questions. This is not as difficult as it seems because there are usually a few questions you need to ask just to give them a price anyway.

Here are a few tips to get them talking: Ask where the home is located, how many levels it has, its square footage, whether it has a basement or crawlspace, and how old it is. As you get this information, you can throw in the odd comment to make things more personal. For example, if they tell you the home is over 100 years old, you can comment that old homes happen to be your specialty, or that you love older homes, or that you love the old homes in that area. Sometimes these comments will lead people into conversation mode rather than information gathering mode. Maybe the caller says, "I like older homes, too, but we are worried that we are getting into something that's going to cost us money." This statement gives you a perfect opportunity to tell the caller what you can do for them.

Questions Lead to Booking

Other questions you may be able to ask in the context of gathering information for the quote include the following:

- "Have you used our services before?"
- "How did you hear about us?"
- "Have you made an offer on a home already?"
- "How long do you have to get the inspection done?"

You have led the caller down the path of booking the inspection. You know they need an inspection, and the next logical step is to suggest a date and a time for the inspection.

If you sense that your questions are not leading to conversation, or that your caller would get annoyed if you don't tell them your fee, try the following: say, "The inspection fee for your home will be $425. May I tell you what that includes?" Most people will respond to this in a positive way. This is an opportunity to discuss the seven biggest benefits of your service:

1. A two-and-a-half hour examination of all the major systems of the home performed by an experienced member of the American Society of Home Inspectors
2. A written report delivered to you at the end of the inspection that includes a description of every recommended improvement with a time frame for completion and ballpark cost for completion
3. Our 400-page *Home Reference Book,* a $95 value
4. Free consulting service for as long as your own the home
5. Access to a low cost group insurance program for your home and car
6. A one-year subscription to Manage My Home, our Web-based home maintenance program
7. A money back guarantee, good for as long as you own the home

And so on, being sure to feature your unique selling proposition (USP).

Book the Inspection

If the caller is just looking for prices, you might say, "Let me give you our prices, but before I do that, we should find out whether we can work within your time frame." The availability discussion can be easily turned into an inspection booking using the following techniques:

- Suggest a date and time and ask if that is convenient.
- Explain that weekend dates are popular and should be booked early.
- Offer to book a tentative inspection slot just to reserve a time. (There is no obligation; they can cancel with 24 hours' notice.)

We have found that engaging the caller in conversation often leads to a booking. You can ask whether they have a conditional offer, how long the condition is, whether they are available to accompany the inspector, and so on.

Create Scarcity

Tell your prospect that you are very busy, but do have an opening for Thursday at 9:00 A.M. Homebuyers do not stop to think about how much lead-time inspectors need or know and that good inspectors are always busy, whether it's doing inspections or marketing.

Reserve an Inspection Time

Use the Tentative-Booking Technique

The tentative-booking technique is a great way to remove the pressure for the caller, and it often leads to an inspection. You will have to make a business decision about offering the option to cancel with 24 hours' notice. We have found that the benefit of being able to offer tentative bookings outweighs the downsides of cancellations.

The tentative booking draws people in. Once they have booked an inspection, they often drop their plans to call three inspection companies. With these calls, you wrap up the conversation by stating that you've made a booking and an inspector will be at the home at 9:00 A.M. on Friday. We recommend you call back to confirm the appointment the next day rather than assume you are doing the inspection unless you hear from them; you may end up arriving at the home and finding no client there.

If you have a Web site, invite them to visit the site to learn more about you and the home inspection process.

Know How To Answer All of the Common Objections

Make sure you can answer any objection your prospects raise. The most common objection you may get is the inspection fee. We have discovered that the following three-step process is the best way to answer the "too expensive" objection over the phone:

- **De-crystallize.** This word comes from a negotiating vocabulary. Crystal is a hard substance that doesn't generally move. You may get a customer whose views have crystallized.
- Ask **permission to sell.**
- Move the discussion from the inspection fee to the benefits of your inspection.

In the first step, de-crystallizing, you break the stalemate created by their price objection. You can't argue with your caller about the fee, or whether you are expensive or reasonable. If a caller says you are expensive, the only way to de-crystallize the situation is to agree with them. Agree that you are more expensive than some, but not too expensive.

For the second step, you should ask permission to explain why your fee is higher than some other inspectors. If you don't ask permission, you risk turning the discussion back into an adversarial one. You need to get them to say "yes" or agree with you on something before moving on.

Finally, in step three, you **convert** the discussion. The goal here is to explain the benefits of your service. This is the only way you can create a sense of value relative to your inspection fee. Whether people realize it or not at first, everyone wants value. Very few people buy the least expensive house, car, or clothes on the market. They buy the one that best meets their needs and represents great value. Great value means they would rather have the product or service than the money because the product or service means more to them than the money.

The three-step process should flow seamlessly. You should practice it until you have wording that you are comfortable with, for example: "Yes, that's a good point, we are more expensive than some of our competitors. May I take a moment to explain why?" Usually the caller will say, "sure." You then can explain the benefits of your service. You can also say something like this, "Home inspection is like many service businesses. The businesses that cannot compete on quality, value, or experience tend to compete on price. While there are some very good home inspectors around, I would advise you to think carefully about selecting your inspector based on price."

It's a great idea to practice in front of a mirror and smile while you talk.

Be Positive

As much as possible, you should use positive statements. It takes a little scripting, but after some time, you will find a way to answer positively to the most negative things. Here is a good example of turning a negative into a positive: A prospect might ask for an inspection Monday morning at 9:00 A.M. You are booked at 9:00 A.M. but you have an opening at noon. Your response might be, "We can't do the inspection at 9:00. Is 12:00 noon alright?" Or "Unfortunately, we are booked for 9:00 A.M. but we would be more than happy to do the inspection at noon." A much better approach is to get rid of the negative words and the word "unfortunately" and put a positive spin on it. Say, "You're in luck, we have an opening at noon." This changes the perspective from letting your client down, but finding a second rate alternative, to a positive experience.

Summary

We have shared several sales ideas with you. As you explore and grow, you will find some of these concepts work for you and others do not. You will also discover your own methods and tools. We hope that we have stimulated your interest in sales and encouraged you to make a difference in the market with your great customer focus, professionalism, and high-quality service.

KEY TERMS

convert	permission to sell	tentative-booking
de-crystallize	real estate agent lunch	technique
focus group		

STUDY SESSION 9 QUICK QUIZ

You should finish Study Session 9 before doing this Quiz. Write your answers in the spaces provided. Then, check your answers in Appendix A.

1. What critical factor must exist in order to successfully build and maintain a relationship with an agent?

   _____

   _____

2. Treating your customers as if you are on the verge of losing them is an effective way to maintain customer loyalty. Circle one.
   a. True
   b. False

3. Explain how your customers can actually sell for you.

   _____

   _____

4. List two reasons why customers defect.
   1. _____
   2. _____

5. There are a number of things you can offer to entice an agent out for lunch, besides picking up the tab. Which of the following is a good offer for *both* of you? Circle one.
   a. Tell the agent they will get a free lunch while you introduce your service.
   b. Tell the agent you'll sponsor their business card.
   c. Tell the agent you know their brother.
   d. Tell the agent you want to give them the *Home Reference Book* and to explain its benefits.

6. The main goal of a focus group for real estate agents is to interact with the attendees, not to extract valuable information. Circle one.
   a. True
   b. False

7. List one advantage and one disadvantage of a focus group.

   _____

   _____

8. Why is it important to close the sale on the first call?

   _____

   _____

9. It is better to have someone other than yourself answer the phone. Circle one.
   a. True
   b. False

10. A prospect shopping for price has likely made the assumption that all home inspectors are the same. Circle one.

    a. True

    b. False

11. If a prospect calls and asks for your fee, it is better to give it to them and then explain why not all inspectors are created equal. Circle one.

    a. True

    b. False

If you had trouble with the Quiz, reread Study Session 9 and try the Quiz again. If you did well, it's time for the final test.

APPENDIX A

ANSWERS TO QUICK QUIZ QUESTIONS

Section I: Marketing Concepts and Practice

Study Session 1 Quick Quiz

1. a. F
   b. B
   c. B
   d. F
   e. B
2. a. True
3. b. No
4. d. Real estate agents
5. 1. The inspection report
   2. The first five minutes in which the client meets you at the property
   3. The telephone call with the client or the referral
   4. The inspection
   5. The referral from someone the client knows
   6. A good business card
   7. A good brochure
6. c. Clean button-down shirt, blazer, and slacks
7. c. "There's a gap between the stairs and the wall. Without removing the drywall beside the stairs, I simply cannot tell what's going on."
8. A value proposition is a combination of your unique selling proposition (USP) and the benefits someone gets when they hire you.

Study Session 2 Quick Quiz

1. b. False
2. b. False
3. A domain name is a name you reserve (preferably your company name) for the World Wide Web such as *www.inspectionarian.com.*
4. b. False. Using your name may only be a detriment if you want to sell your company down the road. Then again, it could be an asset for the buyer if the name has become recognized in your industry.
5. b. Marketing to a single market segment
6. b. False. It's better to stand for one thing. You have a better chance of getting positioned as the expert in that thing in the mind of your customers and clients.
7. a. True. Positioning is how the customers see you. You can try to help create that image, but you cannot force it.

Study Session 3 Quick Quiz

1. a. A service opportunity.
2. b. False. Think like your client. You want to see things from his and her perspective.
3. 2. Don't use a scale of 1 to 10.
   3. Don't survey agents at the inspection site.
4. a. True

5. 1. Offer the client a free disposable camera for the inspection.

2. Provide the client the free use of a digital camera for the inspection. E-mail the client the pictures.

3. Send cookies to a real estate office once a month.

4. Send a welcome letter to the client for the day they move in, inviting them to call you with any house questions.

Study Session 4 Quick Quiz

1. b. False. It's a waste of your time to write a narrative. Your client will be more impressed with a ready-made reporting system with your customized notes inserted.

2. b. False. This method of risk reversal puts too much risk on you because the commission is several times larger than the inspection fee.

3. You could offer to give the client the inspection for free if the client was not happy with it.

4. *Sympathizing* occurs when you share the client's feelings and opinions of the problem. "I agree that the leak is a big problem." *Empathizing* occurs when you understand how the client feels without agreeing with the diagnosis. "I understand how discouraged you must feel."

Study Session 5 Quick Quiz

1. b. False. Competing on price does not guarantee you will get the work, unless people think all home inspectors are the same.

2. a. True. Set your prices to reflect what values you add, not what it costs to do the work. Get paid for what you know, rather than what you do.

3. The ratcheting technique suggests that when you raise your prices, your business volume might fall by 20 percent. That extra time you now have can be devoted to marketing. When you get that business volume back up, you can ratchet up your prices again and repeat the process.

4. Home inspection pricing is inelastic. Sales will not dramatically decrease with higher pricing.

5. a. Suggests your product or service is high quality.

6. b. False. Always keep your agents in the loop so that they don't misquote your fee to a client. They don't want to look sloppy, and you want to help the agent look good.

7. b. Your referring agent.

Study Session 6 Quick Quiz

1. 1. Increase number of customer transactions
2. Increase your fee
3. Sell more services to each client

2. Net worth or marginal net worth refer to a calculation that demonstrates how much a customer is worth to you in business transactions over a business lifetime.

3. Opportunity cost is the cost of your time. The time you spend chasing an opportunity is time you are not doing inspections. So, the opportunity should have good potential for a high rate of return.

4. b. False. You should always see why because you could be jumping to the wrong conclusion.

5. 1. Indoor air-quality testing
2. Pest and insect testing
3. Carbon-monoxide testing
4. Lead-paint testing
5. A general improvement check up

6. A "back-end" refers to the kinds of follow-up services have to offer. It's the part of your business where you offer an ancillary service. The front end is the inspection, because it's the main part of your business.

Study Session 7 Quick Quiz

1. 1. See if the agent has taken out an ad in the paper.
2. See if the real estate office publishes a list of their top producers.
3. Ask another top producer.

2. A mortgage specialist works for the bank and deals only with mortgages. A mortgage broker works independently from the bank.

3. A *joint venture* is something you do with someone with whom you do not directly compete for business. You share resources and you both benefit. For instance, if you pay for postage to mail a newsletter to a real estate lawyer's contacts, the lawyer can include a message in the newsletter. The lawyer gets a free mailer and you get contacts. A *strategic alliance* means your services are so compatible with another company's that you can sell each other's services, as long as you have an exclusive deal with each other.

4. Companies or individuals that you might form a strategic alliance with include the following:

1. Real estate lawyer
2. Bank financing

3. Insurance company
4. Moving company
5. Carpet cleaning
6. Painting
7. Locksmith
8. Deck building
9. Basement finishing

5. Companies or individuals that would not be good candidates for a strategic alliance with a home inspection company include the following:

1. Roofer
2. Contractor
3. Basement waterproofing
4. Electrician
5. Plumber
6. Heating contractor
7. Renovator

6. If you contact someone higher on the chain, you become the hunted rather than the hunter. For instance, an agent might use you to cover some of his and her costs and you may benefit very little from the advertising.

Study Session 8 Quick Quiz

1. Strengths, weaknesses, opportunities, threats

2. b. Pick the best marketing strategy and reject the rest.

3. b. False. You should know your market segment and you should never position yourself as something generic, such as a home inspector. You want to be an expert in some part of home inspecting.

4. Questions to investigate if you want to know about your competition include the following:

1. What is their service area?
2. How long have they been in business?
3. From whom do they get referrals?
4. What are the features and benefits of their business?
5. How does their service compare to yours?

5. a. True. Marketing opportunities are not "once in a lifetime." Because they are plentiful, the challenge is to pick the optimal ones for your business.

6. *Tracking* refers to determining how much profit you gained from a particular strategy. *Testing* refers to refining your strategy—adjusting it to see whether you can make it work even better.

7. The four parts of the marketing cycle are the following:

1. Build—create a strategy or tactic or program.
2. Implement—try it out.
3. Measure—track and test to see how successful it is.
4. Refine—based on your measurement, consider some changes.

Study Session 9 Quick Quiz

1. b. False. One approach does not work equally well with all clients.

2. b. To maximize your client's understanding of what you can and can't do in the inspection.

3. b. False. Disclosing your errors and omissions insurance up front may increase the likelihood of client complaints. Clients may find it easier to blame you for a mishap because they can justify that it's "just business."

4. d. What you write in your report should be a reflection of what you tell your client in person.

5. c. Validater

6. To resolve complaints effectively, remember the following:

1. It's just business—don't take it personally or it will consume you.
2. A complaint is an opportunity.

7. The three reasons are as follows:

1. An opportunity to satisfy your client
2. An opportunity to generate good will
3. An opportunity to avoid bad publicity

8. a. True

9. a. "Our loyalty is to the house. Our goal is to represent the condition of the house as accurately as possible."

10. b. False. The best approach is to phone the client directly, even if the letter came from a lawyer.

Study Session 10 Quick Quiz

1. The responsibility yardstick components are the following:

1. Is there a problem?
2. Is the problem in the report?
3. Is the problem within the scope?
4. Would a competent inspector have found the problem under the same circumstances?

2. b. False. You need to adjust the information and decide on the best course of action. You may need to do some research. A decision made on-the-spot may be made more with emotion than reason.

3. You don't want your client coming back for more compensation for every little detail they find wrong with their house.

4. b. False. It is not necessarily true that once a client signs this, he or she is stuck with it. This clause may be ignored by courts in some areas, for example. It may also be shown that the agreement was signed under duress.

5. *Betterment* refers to a situation in which your client asks for compensation that results in bettering the client's original component.

6. Filling out a tracking form and attaching it to the report is important in case you ever get another complaint for the same property; you can review the discussion(s) you had at the time.

Study Session 11 Quick Quiz

1. The Internet makes it easier for customers to find out about us, but it also means consumers can more easily challenge our position as experts because they can research a topic quickly and easily.

2. Consumers are better informed because access to information is easy, quick, and cheap, thus raising expectations.

3. Big business is interested in the leverage that the home inspection gives them. Big business would consider the home inspection a loss leader for their other products and services.

Section II: Advertising, Public Relations, and Sales

Study Session 1 Quick Quiz

1. Attention, interest, desire, action

2. b. Include the word "free" somewhere in your ad if possible.

3. Approaches to business cards include the following:
   1. The simple approach—keep the card simple but elegant.
   2. The useful approach—put valuable information on the card, such as a maintenance calendar for the furnace.

3. The tell-your-whole-story approach—put all your credentials, licenses, and the benefits of your service on the card.

4. b. False

5. a. True

6. Register your domain name.

7. a. True. The key is giving key information and limiting the bells and whistles.

8. d. Information on how to advertise in your information package

Study Session 2 Quick Quiz

1. b. False. You have to pay for each listing.

2. b. False. This advertising is not targeted.

3. a. Single-line entry

4. 1. An easily-identifiable market
   2. Highly focused marketing material
   3. No time critical component
   4. A simple delivery mechanism
   5. Easy-to-explain product or service

5. a. True. You can always find another agent.

6. If you are solicited for an ad you can request the following:
   1. A list of all of the real estate agents in the office
   2. A meeting with the real estate broker
   3. Help to set up an office presentation
   4. Ten copies of the folder with your ad in it

7. b. False. The printing company is acting on its own, and the real estate office has no intention of offering you referrals because you advertise in the presentation folder.

8. Ask each customer how he or she heard about you.

9. The *three-hit rule* refers to connecting with your prospect three different times in relatively close succession. For instance, if you deliver a real estate agent talk, you should then call back with follow-up information and then a thank you letter.

Study Session 3 Quick Quiz

1. b. False. PR puts you on the map, but it does not change agent behavior dramatically.

2. The main purpose of participating in a first-time buyers' seminar is to network with agents, bankers, real estate lawyers, and first-time buyers.

3. Sponsors of buyer seminars are typically bankers and real estate agents

4. 1. Agents
   2. Bankers
   3. Real estate lawyers
   4. Home inspectors

5. Don't split costs because you are the least likely to get clients at this seminar.

6. b. False. People lose interest at longer seminars. Keep it short and to the point.

7. A real estate agent *office talk* is a presentation to agents in a broker's office. Real estate agents help get you known in that community.

8. b. False. The broker gets calls all day long from people hoping to get a meeting with agents. You'd better be offering something of use to the agents.

9. 1. Solving insurance hassles
   2. Putting structural issues into context

10. a. True. If you omit information, you have a reason to call back

Study Session 4 Quick Quiz

1. b. False. You could send a newsletter to past clients to acquaint them with your ancillary services.

2. d. I want to help you; I provide useful information.

3. The editor

4. b. False. Weekly columns will eat into too much of your time. Make it a monthly or quarterly column.

5. Put all important information in the first paragraph because many people won't read much more than that.

6. b. False. It's better to target industry publications.

7. 1. Press release
   2. Your bio
   3. An interesting fact sheet about your company

8. a. True. Writing pieces is about exposure, not referrals.

9. Three topics you could present in a newsletter, column or on a radio show or TV spot include the following:
   1. Urea Formaldehyde Foam Insulation—Much Ado About Nothing. Discusses how the "problem" with UFFI may not actually be much of a problem.
   2. Home Improvement Costs
   3. In Search of the Perfect House

Study Session 5 Quick Quiz

1. b. False. You may not be good at circulating in a large group. Your sponsorship may be buried in a list. The event may not be well attended.

2. In addition to a listing in the banquet program for a golf tournament, consider the following in return for your sponsorship:
   1. Ask for a list of attendees, prize or award winners.
   2. Ask for help getting an office presentation.
   3. Ask if you can attend the banquet, if there is one.

3. A high visibility prize is one that is less expensive than sponsorship but gets noticed by participants, attracting attention to your company. Examples include the following:
   1. A color television
   2. A fun item on which you could advertise your company

4. At a banquet, the best time to network is before the meal, when people are milling around.

5. b. False. You should have a single goal because people only have a minute or two to absorb your message at a booth.

6. Your promotion effort should be to get leads.

7. b. False. Home inspections depend on time-sensitive bookings. You will not likely find people who are about to buy a home at the home show.

8. Thank them for coming to your booth and wish them well for the rest of the show.

9. Prize draws at home shows have become a matter of course, so everyone will put their business card in your bowl. You will be overwhelmed by unqualified prospects.

10. An open-ended question draws out information; a closed-end question does not.

Study Session 6 Quick Quiz

1. A good salesperson is an educator who helps people make good decisions, rather than someone who convinces people to buy something they don't need.

2. Fear

3. 1. Get your name front and center.
   2. Build a relationship.

4. 1. Answer a problem or satisfy a need.
   2. Answer a key question.

5. Aim for a soft rejection by improving your sales technique. Develop a script that solves a problem or satisfies a need.

6. a. Call one real estate agent per day.

7. b. Educational sales

8. Ask the person what they want and listen carefully to the answer.

9. a. Open-ended question

Study Session 7 Quick Quiz

1. 1. Prospecting
   2. The approach
   3. The presentation
   4. The close
   5. Customer management

2. 1. The broker
   2. The agent
   3. The homebuyer

3. *Offering a trade* involves giving them something in return for their time.

4. The best approach is to have an agent with whom you have a good working relationship refer you to the broker or person responsible for scheduling meetings.

5. b. "Can I count on you to refer your next inspection to me?"

6. b. False. You aren't offering a fair trade in return for their time.

7. a. True. Most adults are visual learners. Your message is more likely to be understood with visuals.

8. a. True. Because most of the work is already done, you just need to close the sale.

9. b. False. If you aren't sensitive to certain kinds of personalities and the approach they would best respond to, you are cutting yourself off from potential deals.

Study Session 8 Quick Quiz

1. b. Expecting six objections to your sales pitch

2. If they don't have any objections, chances are they are not interested in your service.

3. By agreeing, you are making the prospect feel more comfortable.

4. By asking them. A good approach might be to say, "I know price is very important to you. May I ask why you feel we are too expensive?" or "Is price your only concern?"

5. A *testimonial* provides concrete proof that you overcame a similar objection with someone that you now have a good working relationship with.

6. An *artificial objection* is one that is not really true. Artificial objections are used when the real objection is something that the prospect feels they cannot say.

7. 1. You have meet their needs.
   2. The prospect wants and can afford your service.
   3. The prospect feels comfortable with you.

8. There should be no doubt in their mind about what you are offering. You must address all of their concerns by asking questions before you can ask them to make a commitment.

9. You must cement the commitment with an action.

10. By agreeing with them and asking them what it is they need to think about. You won't uncover the real reason they aren't ready unless you ask.

Study Session 9 Quick Quiz

1. The agent must like you and believe in you.

2. a. True. It is cheaper to maintain a customer than to find a new one. Work hard to keep customers.

3. A satisfied customer will tell others about the positive experience they had.

4. Reasons for customer defection include the following:
   1. We don't solicit their feedback.
   2. We don't listen actively and acknowledge our customers.
   3. We over-promise and under-deliver.
   4. We are not responsive enough to their concerns.

5. d. Tell the agent you want to give them the *Home Reference Book* and to explain its benefits.

6. a. True. It's much more important to build relationships than to focus on gathering information.

7. The advantages of a group lunch include the following:
   1. It allows you to include some agents you know well, and some you don't.
   2. It's not threatening to the agent because you've removed the pressure of the one-on-one meeting.
   3. You can outline a specific agenda. This reduces the agent's anxiety.
   4. You can reach several agents and other real estate professionals at the same time.

The disadvantages of a focus group include these:
1. They are expensive.
2. It takes time to organize the schedules of several real estate professionals.
3. It's hard to control a group.

8. It's important because it is unlikely they will call back if you don't close the sale on the first call.

9. a. True. While you may feel you are the best qualified, it is not good to answer the phone while doing an inspection. Also, your business cannot grow if you have to answer every phone call.

10. a. True. Unless people are told there is a difference, they will reasonably conclude that home inspection is a commodity.

11. b. False. It is better to explain to a client that all inspectors are not the same, and then explain your unique selling proposition. It is also helpful to offer risk reversal before quoting your fee.

APPENDIX B

BIBLIOGRAPHY

Abraham, Jay. *How to Get From Where You Are to Where You Want to Be.* Vols. 1–12, Illinois: Nightingale-Conant Corporation, 1997.

Abraham, Jay. *Stealth Marketing: An Abridged Version.* California: Abraham Publishing Group, Inc., 1995.

Beckwith, Harry. *Selling the Invisible: A Field Guide to Modern Marketing.* New York: Warner Books, 1997.

Beckwith, Harry. *The Invisible Touch: The Four Keys to Modern Marketing.* New York: Warner Books, 2000.

Beckwith, Harry. *What Clients Love: A Field Guide to Growing Your Business.* New York: Warner Books, 2003.

Hiam, Alexander Wateson, and Schewe, Charles D. *The Portable MBA in Marketing.* New York: John Wiley & Sons, Inc., 1998.

Kennedy, Dan. *Magnetic Marketing.* Illinois: Nightingale-Conant Corporation, 1997. (This is a binder product that you can order from Nightingale-Conant Corporation, 7300 N. Lehigh Avenue, Niles, IL 60714. Tel 1-800-525-9000).

Kennedy, Dan. *The Psychology of Selling: The Art of Closing Sales.* (This is a collection of cassette tapes. You can order from Nightingale-Conant Corporation, 7300 N. Lehigh Avenue, Niles, IL 60714. 1-800-525-9000).

Livingstone, John L. *The Portable MBA in Finance and Accounting.* New York: John Wiley & Sons, Inc., 1997.

Misner, Ivan R. *The World's Best Known Marketing Secret: Building Your Business with Word-of-Mouth Marketing.* Texas: Bard & Stephen, 1994.

Neilsen, Jakob. *Designing Web Usability, The Practice of Simplicity.* Indianapolis, Indiana: New Riders Publishing, 2000.

Seybold, Patricia B. *Customers.com: How to Create a Profitable Business Strategy for the Internet and Beyond.* New York: Random House, 1998.

Siskind, Barry. *The Power of Exhibit Marketing.* USA: Self-Counsel Press, 1990.

Weinman, Lynda. *Designing Web Graphics 4.* Indianapolis, Indiana: New Riders Publishing, 2003.

Zemke, Ron. *The Service Edge.* New York: New American Library, 1989.

INDEX

Notes

Notes

Notes

Notes

Notes

Notes

Notes

Notes